HULK

SMASHTRONAUT!

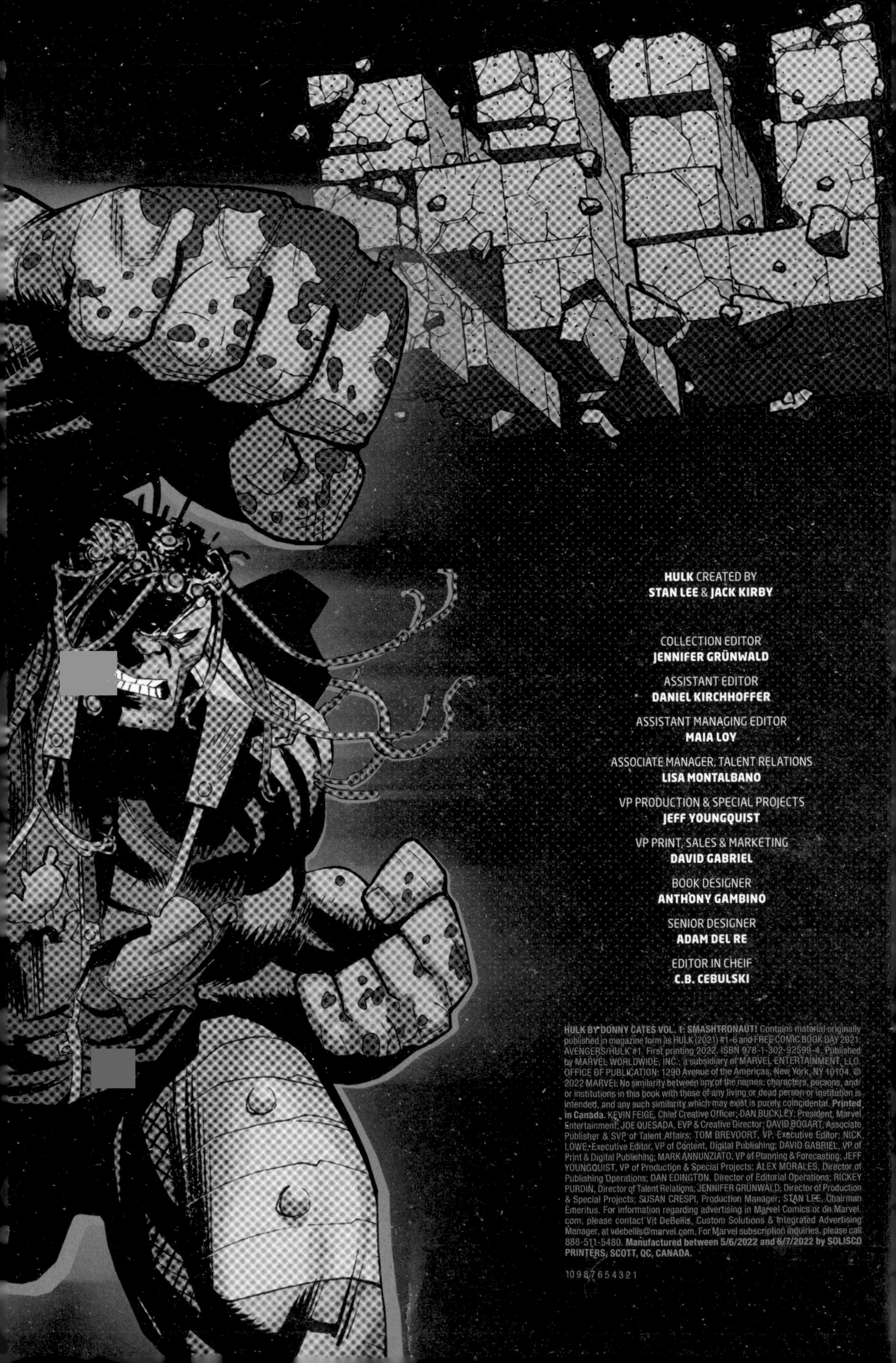

HULK CREATED BY
STAN LEE & **JACK KIRBY**

COLLECTION EDITOR
JENNIFER GRÜNWALD

ASSISTANT EDITOR
DANIEL KIRCHHOFFER

ASSISTANT MANAGING EDITOR
MAIA LOY

ASSOCIATE MANAGER, TALENT RELATIONS
LISA MONTALBANO

VP PRODUCTION & SPECIAL PROJECTS
JEFF YOUNGQUIST

VP PRINT, SALES & MARKETING
DAVID GABRIEL

BOOK DESIGNER
ANTHONY GAMBINO

SENIOR DESIGNER
ADAM DEL RE

EDITOR IN CHEIF
C.B. CEBULSKI

HULK BY DONNY CATES VOL. 1: SMASHTRONAUT! Contains material originally published in magazine form as HULK (2021) #1-6 and FREE COMIC BOOK DAY 2021: AVENGERS/HULK #1. First printing 2022. ISBN 978-1-302-92599-4. Published by MARVEL WORLDWIDE, INC., a subsidiary of MARVEL ENTERTAINMENT, LLC. OFFICE OF PUBLICATION: 1290 Avenue of the Americas, New York, NY 10104. **Printed in Canada.** KEVIN FEIGE, Chief Creative Officer; DAN BUCKLEY, President, Marvel Entertainment; JOE QUESADA, EVP & Creative Director; DAVID BOGART, Associate Publisher & SVP of Talent Affairs; TOM BREVOORT, VP, Executive Editor; NICK LOWE, Executive Editor, VP of Content, Digital Publishing; DAVID GABRIEL, VP of Print & Digital Publishing; MARK ANNUNZIATO, VP of Planning & Forecasting; JEFF YOUNGQUIST, VP of Production & Special Projects; ALEX MORALES, Director of Publishing Operations; DAN EDINGTON, Director of Editorial Operations; RICKEY PURDIN, Director of Talent Relations; JENNIFER GRÜNWALD, Director of Production & Special Projects; SUSAN CRESPI, Production Manager; STAN LEE, Chairman Emeritus. For information regarding advertising in Marvel Comics or on Marvel.com, please contact Vit DeBellis, Custom Solutions & Integrated Advertising Manager, at vdebellis@marvel.com. For Marvel subscription inquiries, please call 888-511-5480. **Manufactured between 5/6/2022 and 6/7/2022 by SOLISCO PRINTERS, SCOTT, QC, CANADA.**

10 9 8 7 6 5 4 3 2 1

BRUCE BANNER HAS SOMEHOW MANAGED TO SPLIT THE HULK INTO THREE DISTINCT PARTS: THE HULK'S BODY HAS BEEN TURNED INTO A STARSHIP. BANNER'S PSYCHE PILOTS IT FROM WITHIN THE HULK'S MIND. AND THE HULK'S PSYCHE FUELS THE STARSHIP WITH HIS ANGER, WHICH BANNER HARNESSES BY LOCKING THE HULK IN THE "ENGINE ROOM" AND SENDING ESCALATING LEVELS OF OPPONENTS FOR HIM TO FIGHT.

WITH THE WORLD BLAMING THE HULK FOR A MYSTERIOUS, DEADLY INCIDENT IN EL PASO, BANNER PILOTS THE STARSHIP HULK THROUGH A PORTAL TO AN UNSTABLE POCKET DIMENSION, WARNING THE HEROES OF EARTH THAT HE IS LEAVING BECAUSE NONE OF THEM WILL KNOW HOW TO DEAL WITH WHAT HE IS GOING TO BECOME...

SMASHTRONAUT!

DONNY CATES *writer*

RYAN OTTLEY *artist*

RYAN OTTLEY (#1, *FREE COMIC BOOK DAY*) &
CLIFF RATHBURN (#2-6) *inkers*

FRANK MARTIN WITH **FEDERICO BLEE** (#3) *colorists*

VC's **CORY PETIT** *letterer*

RYAN OTTLEY WITH
FRANK MARTIN (#1-3, *FREE COMIC BOOK DAY*) &
ROMULO FAJARDO JR. (#4-6) *cover art*

KAT GREGOROWICZ & KAITLYN LINDTVEDT *assistant editors*
WIL MOSS WITH ALANNA SMITH *editors*

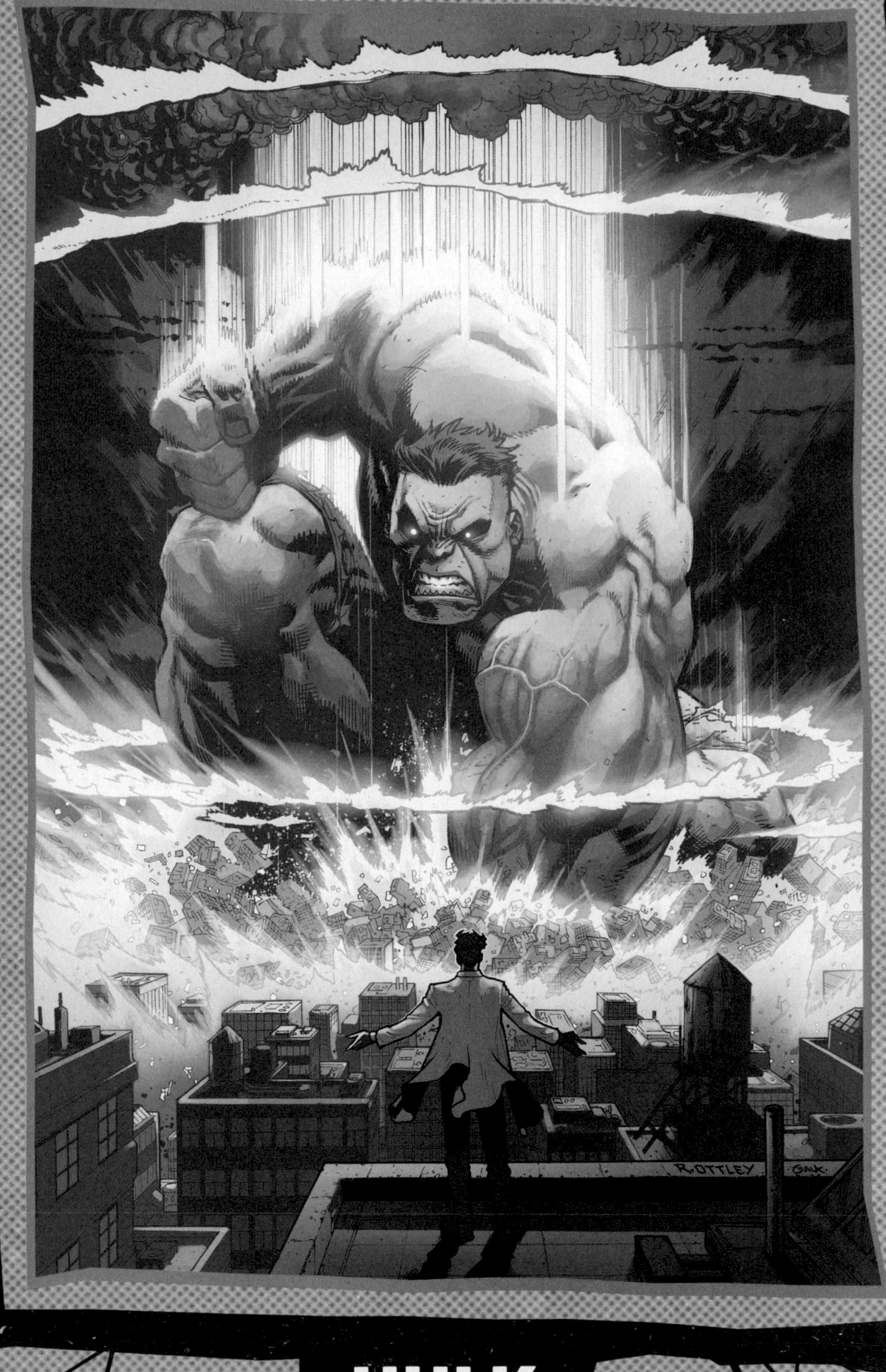
R. OTTLEY
GMK.

HULK
NUMBER 1

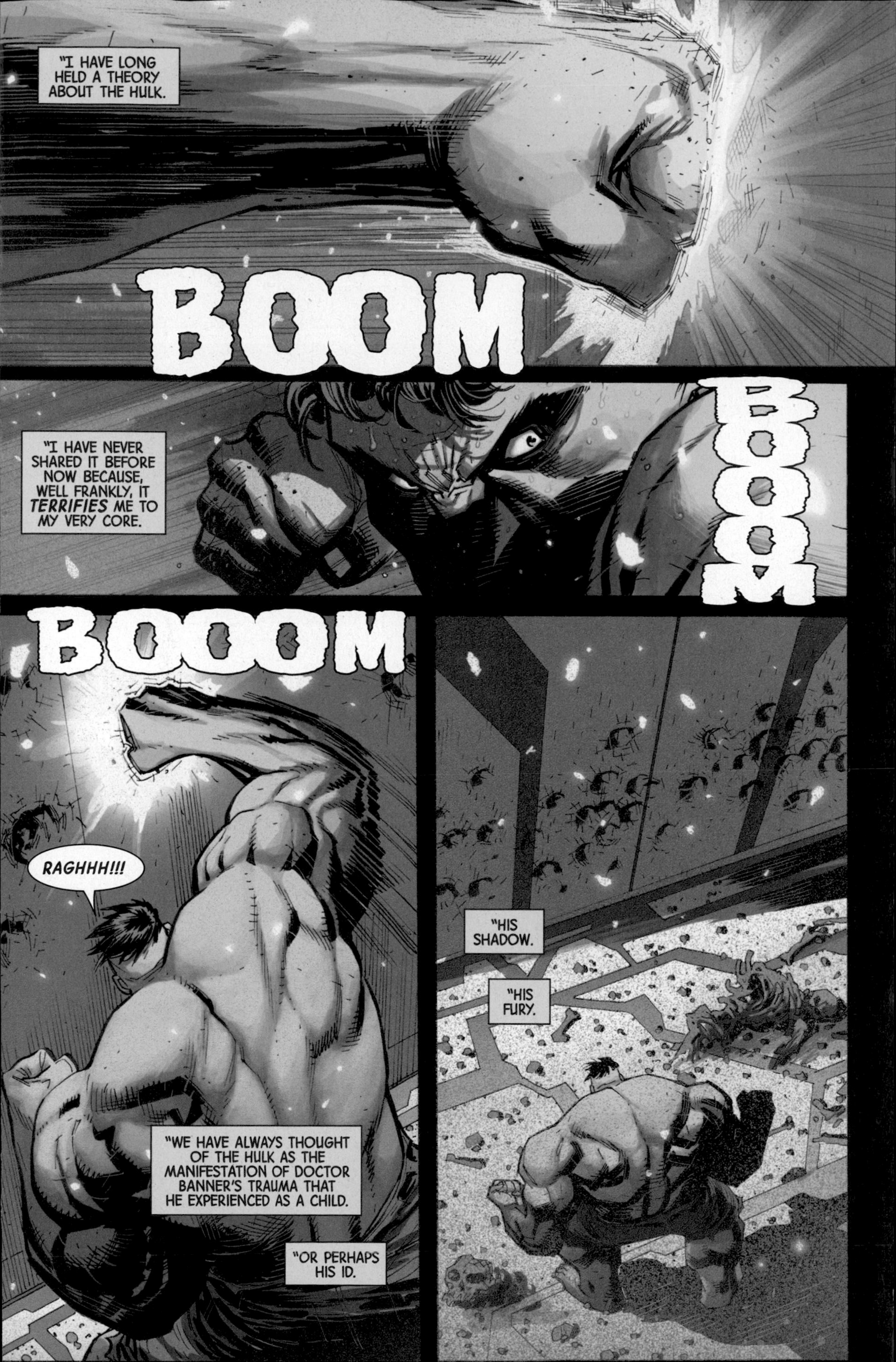
"I HAVE LONG HELD A THEORY ABOUT THE HULK.
BOOM
"I HAVE NEVER SHARED IT BEFORE NOW BECAUSE, WELL FRANKLY, IT *TERRIFIES* ME TO MY VERY CORE.
BOOOM
BOOOM
RAGHHH!!!
"WE HAVE ALWAYS THOUGHT OF THE HULK AS THE MANIFESTATION OF DOCTOR BANNER'S TRAUMA THAT HE EXPERIENCED AS A CHILD.
"OR PERHAPS HIS ID.
"HIS SHADOW.
"HIS FURY.

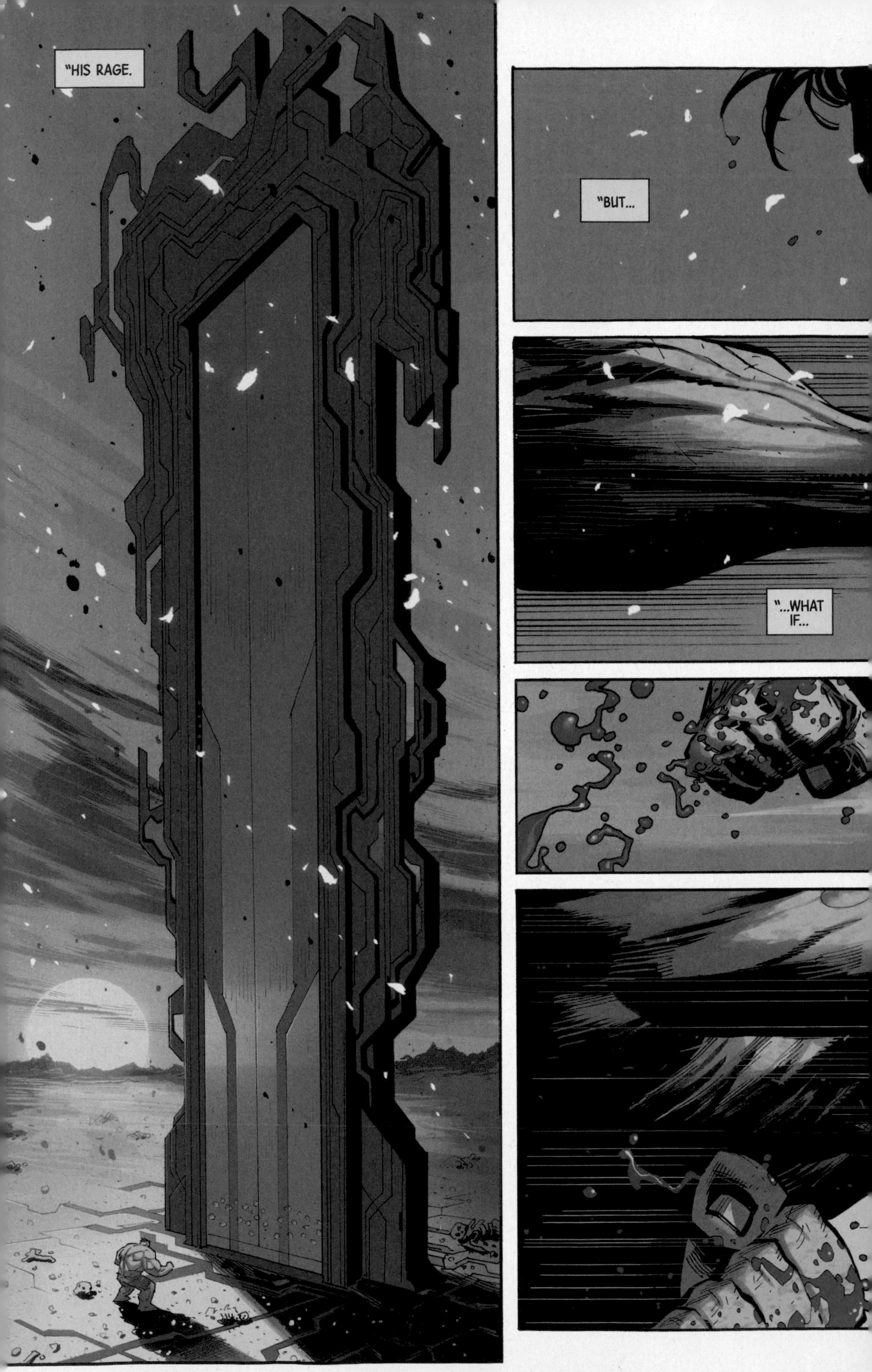
"HIS RAGE.
"BUT...
"...WHAT IF...

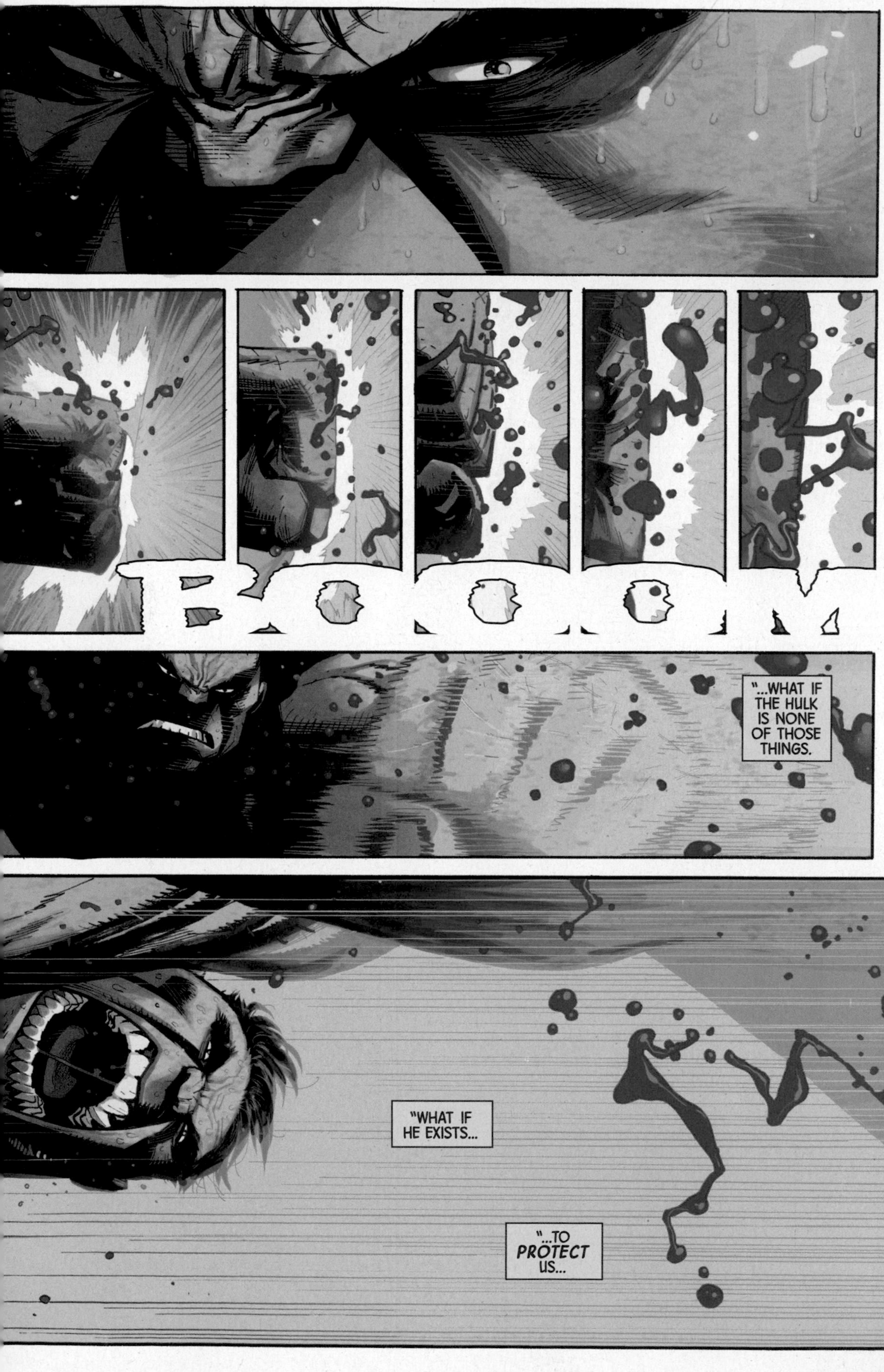
BOOOOM
"...WHAT IF THE HULK IS NONE OF THOSE THINGS.
"WHAT IF HE EXISTS...
"...TO PROTECT US...

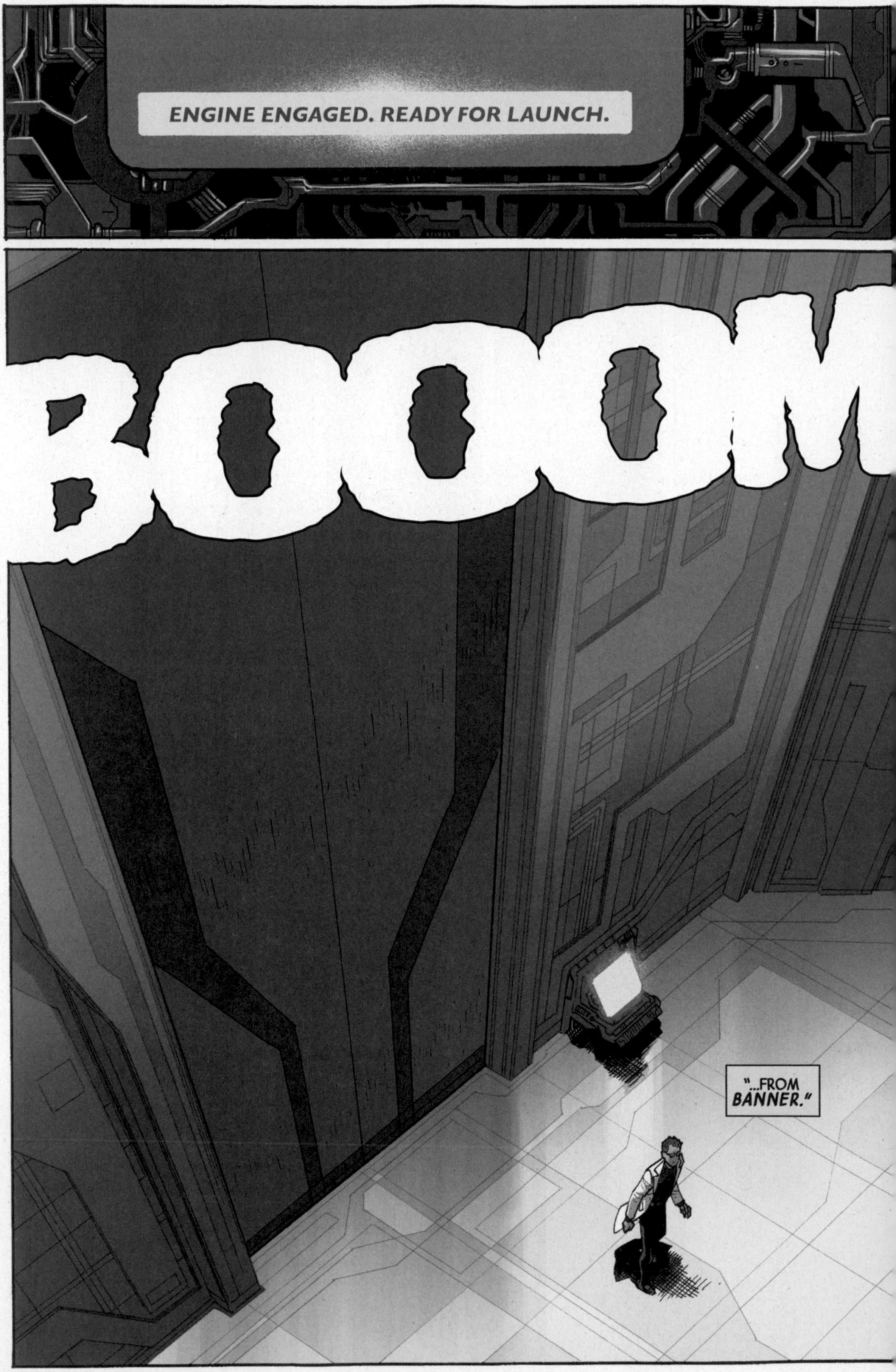
ENGINE ENGAGED. READY FOR LAUNCH.
BOOOM
"...FROM BANNER."

YOU CAN'T BLAME YOURSELF FOR WHAT HAPPENED IN EL PASO.

BRUCE, HE'S JUST A CHILD....

YOU EVER SEEN THE OMEN?

I'M WORRIED ABOUT YOU. YOU'RE HURTING YOURSELF, HURTING HIM.

...YOU.

IT WOULD APPEAR I VERY MUCH CAN.

YOU KNOW YOU CAN'T KEEP HIM LOCKED IN THERE....

YOU... SHOULDN'T BE HERE.

BETTY.

WHAT ARE YOU DOING?

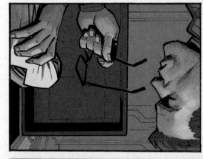

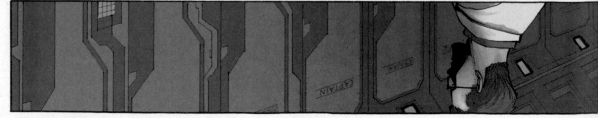

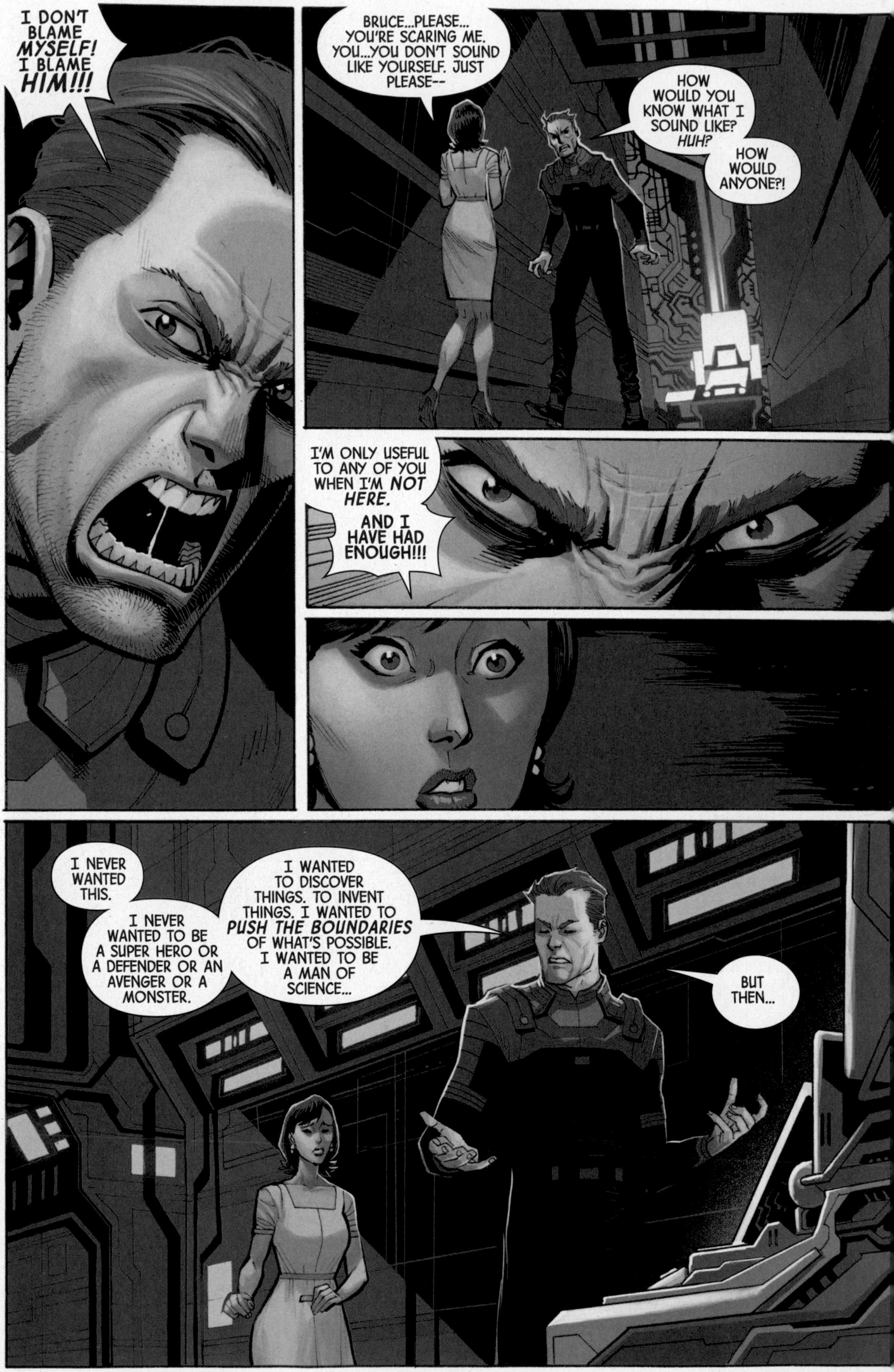
I DON'T BLAME *MYSELF!* I BLAME *HIM!!!*
BRUCE...PLEASE... YOU'RE SCARING ME. YOU...YOU DON'T SOUND LIKE YOURSELF. JUST PLEASE--
HOW WOULD YOU KNOW WHAT I SOUND LIKE? *HUH?*
HOW WOULD ANYONE?!
I'M ONLY USEFUL TO ANY OF YOU WHEN I'M *NOT HERE.*
AND I HAVE HAD ENOUGH!!!
I NEVER WANTED THIS.
I NEVER WANTED TO BE A SUPER HERO OR A DEFENDER OR AN AVENGER OR A MONSTER.
I WANTED TO DISCOVER THINGS. TO INVENT THINGS. I WANTED TO *PUSH THE BOUNDARIES* OF WHAT'S POSSIBLE. I WANTED TO BE A MAN OF SCIENCE...
BUT THEN...

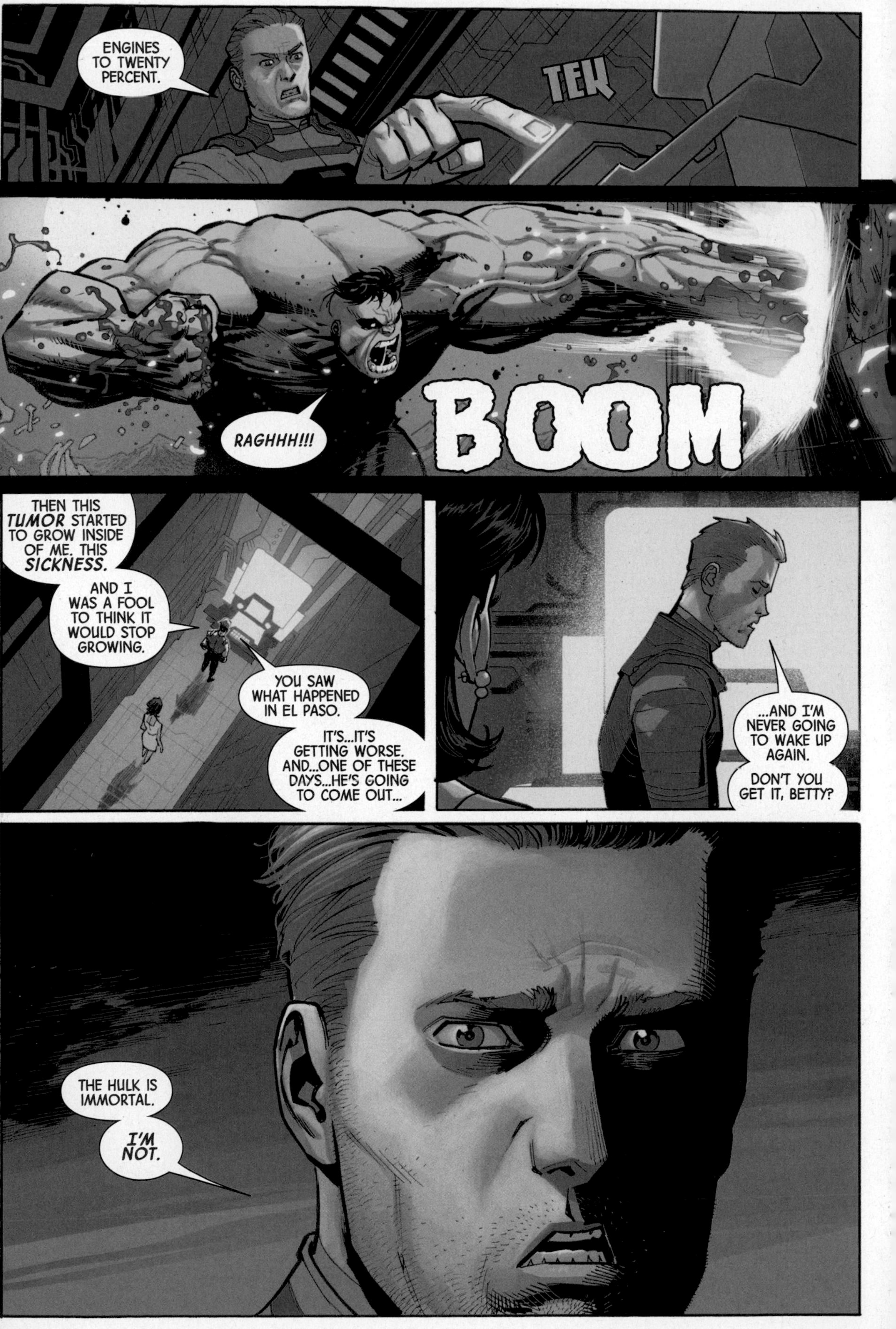
ENGINES TO TWENTY PERCENT.
TEK
RAGHHH!!!
BOOM
THEN THIS *TUMOR* STARTED TO GROW INSIDE OF ME. THIS *SICKNESS.*
AND I WAS A FOOL TO THINK IT WOULD STOP GROWING.
YOU SAW WHAT HAPPENED IN EL PASO.
IT'S...IT'S GETTING WORSE. AND...ONE OF THESE DAYS...HE'S GOING TO COME OUT...
...AND I'M NEVER GOING TO WAKE UP AGAIN.
DON'T YOU GET IT, BETTY?
THE HULK IS IMMORTAL.
I'M NOT.

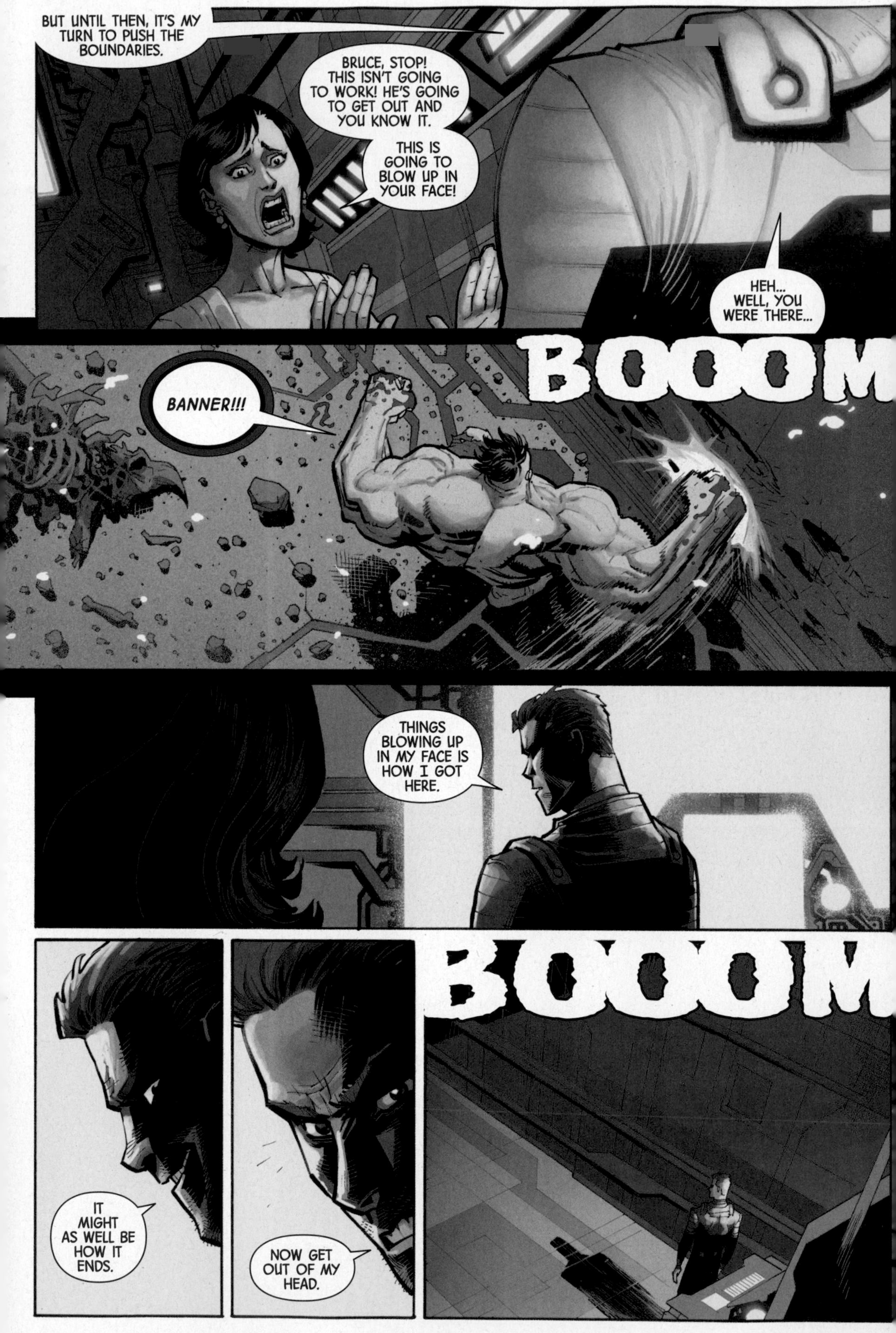
BUT UNTIL THEN, IT'S MY TURN TO PUSH THE BOUNDARIES.
BRUCE, STOP! THIS ISN'T GOING TO WORK! HE'S GOING TO GET OUT AND YOU KNOW IT.
THIS IS GOING TO BLOW UP IN YOUR FACE!
HEH... WELL, YOU WERE THERE...
BOOOM
BANNER!!!
THINGS BLOWING UP IN MY FACE IS HOW I GOT HERE.
BOOOM
IT MIGHT AS WELL BE HOW IT ENDS.
NOW GET OUT OF MY HEAD.

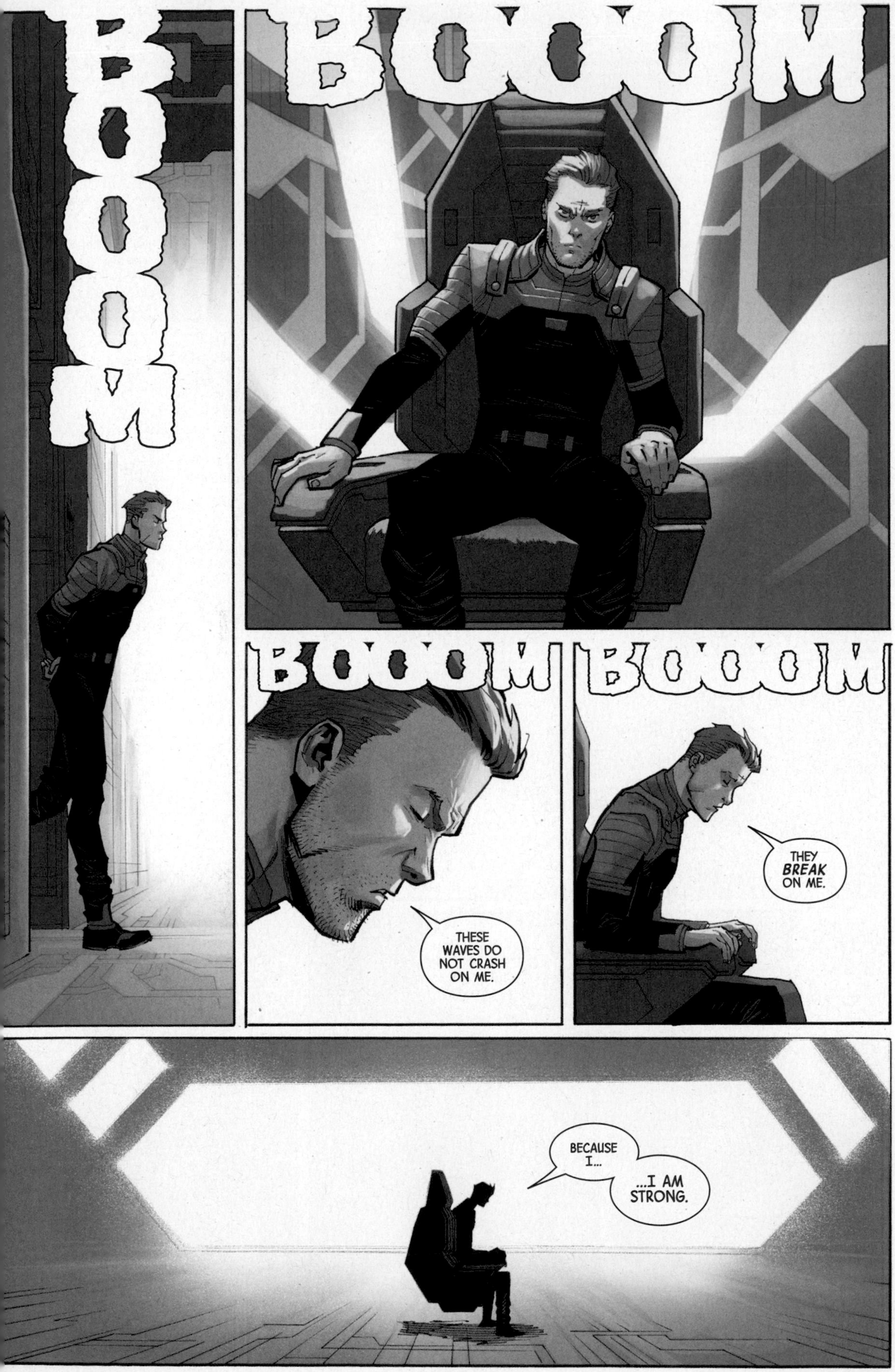
BOOOOM
BOOOM
BOOOM
THESE WAVES DO NOT CRASH ON ME.
BOOOM
THEY *BREAK* ON ME.
BECAUSE I...
...I AM STRONG.

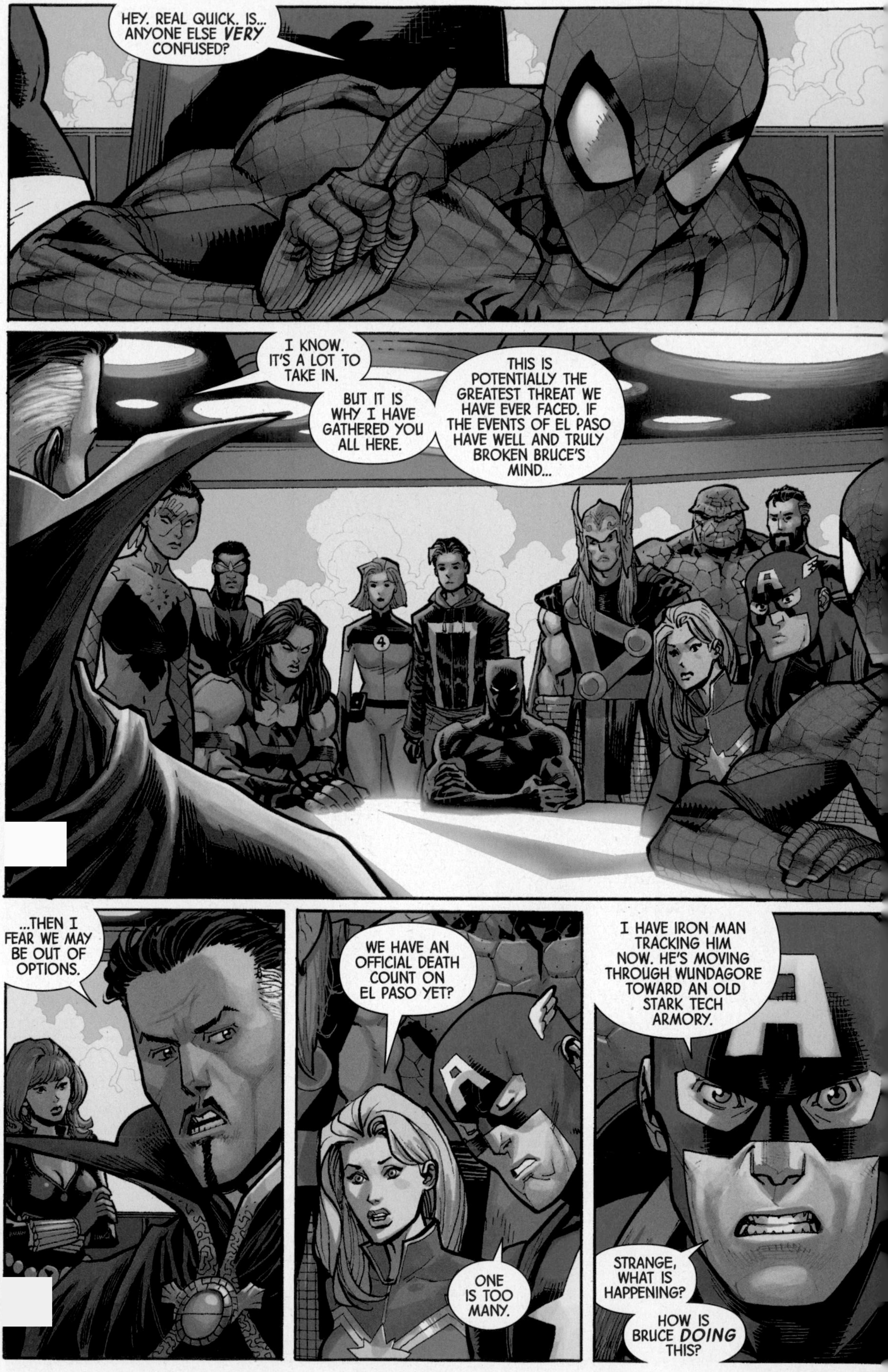
HEY. REAL QUICK. IS... ANYONE ELSE *VERY* CONFUSED?
I KNOW. IT'S A LOT TO TAKE IN.
BUT IT IS WHY I HAVE GATHERED YOU ALL HERE.
THIS IS POTENTIALLY THE GREATEST THREAT WE HAVE EVER FACED. IF THE EVENTS OF EL PASO HAVE WELL AND TRULY BROKEN BRUCE'S MIND...
...THEN I FEAR WE MAY BE OUT OF OPTIONS.
WE HAVE AN OFFICIAL DEATH COUNT ON EL PASO YET?
ONE IS TOO MANY.
I HAVE IRON MAN TRACKING HIM NOW. HE'S MOVING THROUGH WUNDAGORE TOWARD AN OLD STARK TECH ARMORY.
STRANGE, WHAT IS HAPPENING?
HOW IS BRUCE *DOING* THIS?

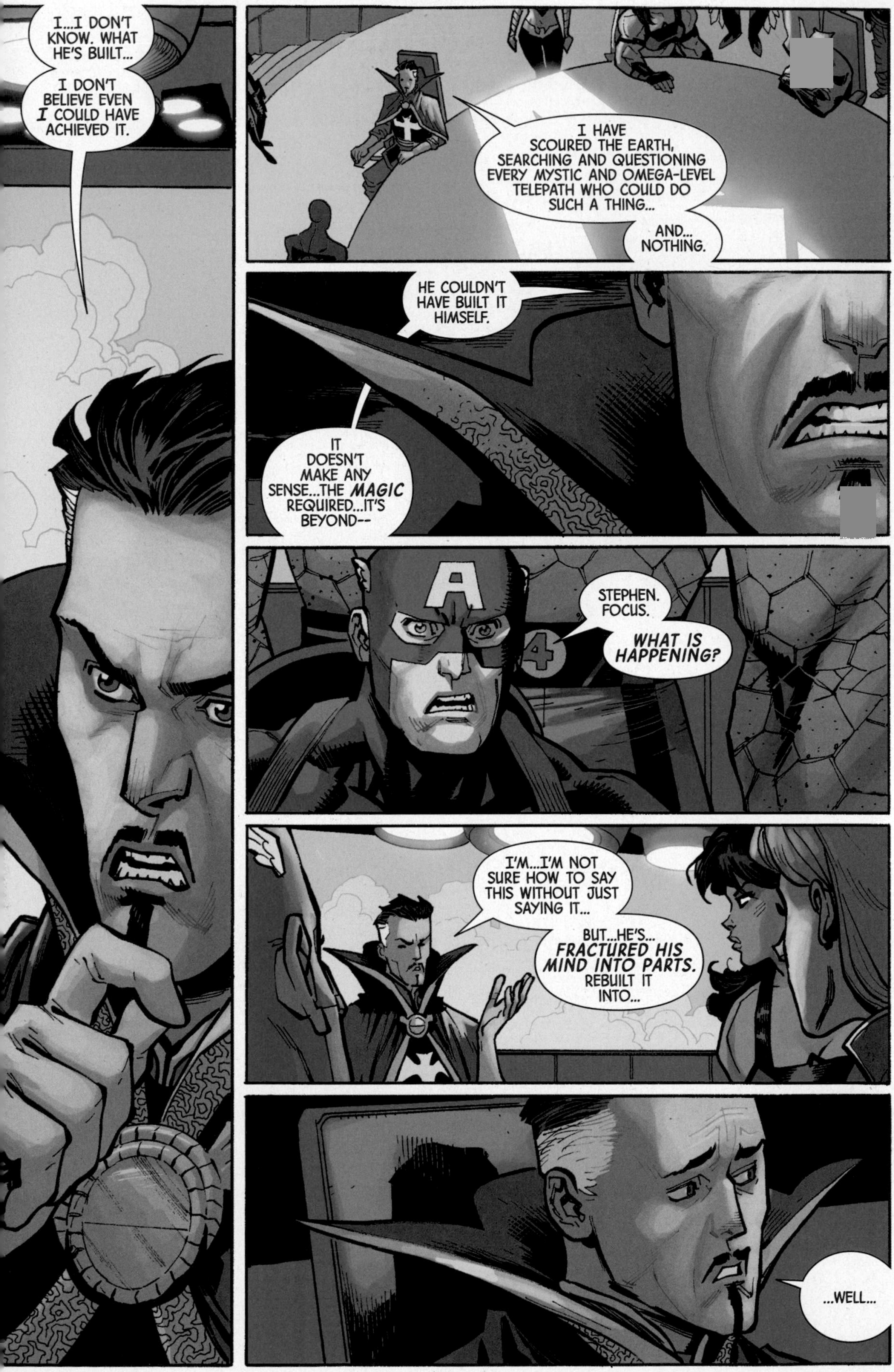
I...I DON'T KNOW. WHAT HE'S BUILT...
I DON'T BELIEVE EVEN *I* COULD HAVE ACHIEVED IT.
I HAVE SCOURED THE EARTH, SEARCHING AND QUESTIONING EVERY MYSTIC AND OMEGA-LEVEL TELEPATH WHO COULD DO SUCH A THING...
AND... NOTHING.
HE COULDN'T HAVE BUILT IT HIMSELF.
IT DOESN'T MAKE ANY SENSE...THE *MAGIC* REQUIRED...IT'S BEYOND--
STEPHEN. FOCUS.
WHAT IS HAPPENING?
I'M...I'M NOT SURE HOW TO SAY THIS WITHOUT JUST SAYING IT...
BUT...HE'S... *FRACTURED HIS MIND INTO PARTS.* REBUILT IT INTO...
...WELL...

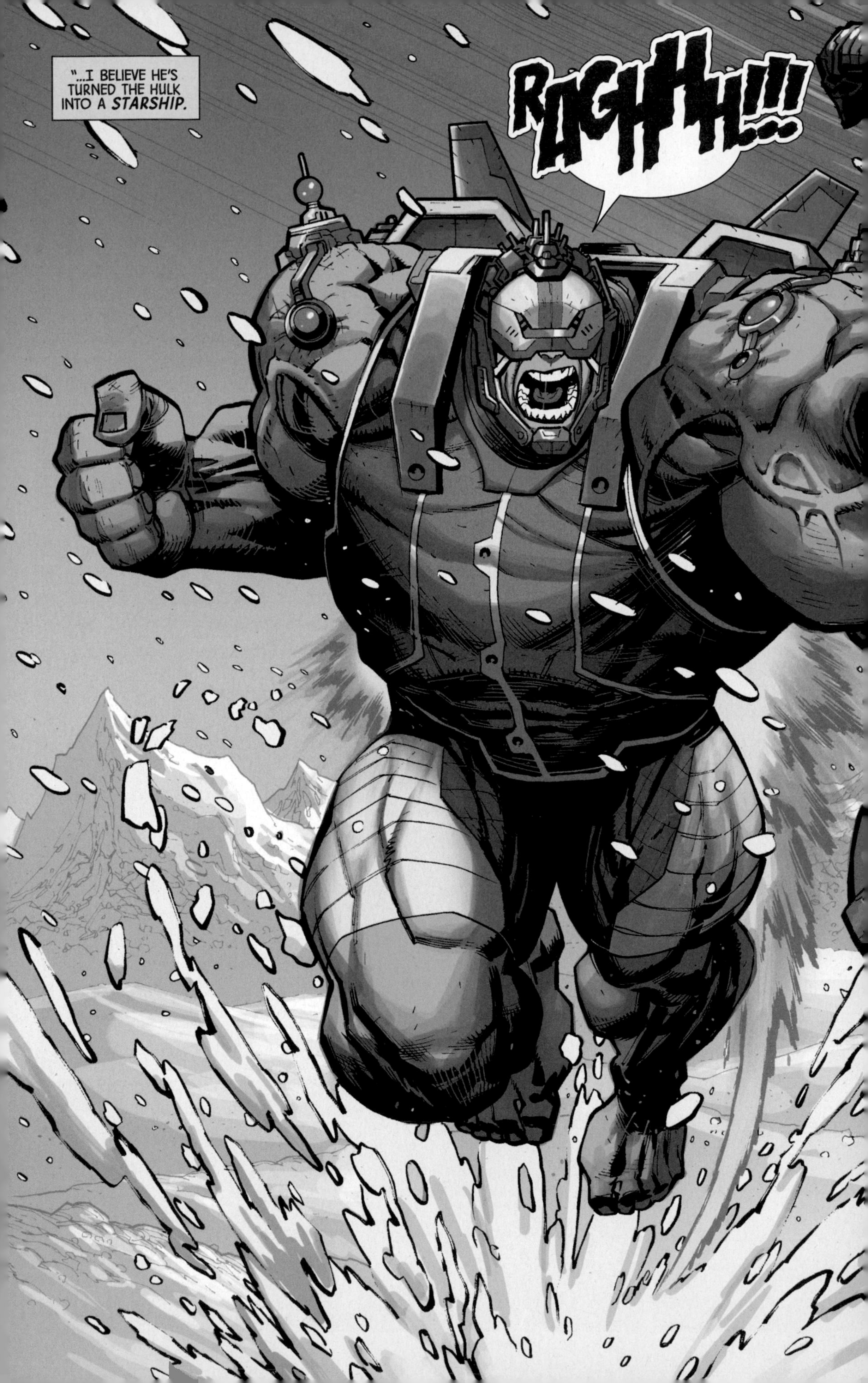
"...I BELIEVE HE'S TURNED THE HULK INTO A *STARSHIP*.
RAGHHH!!!...

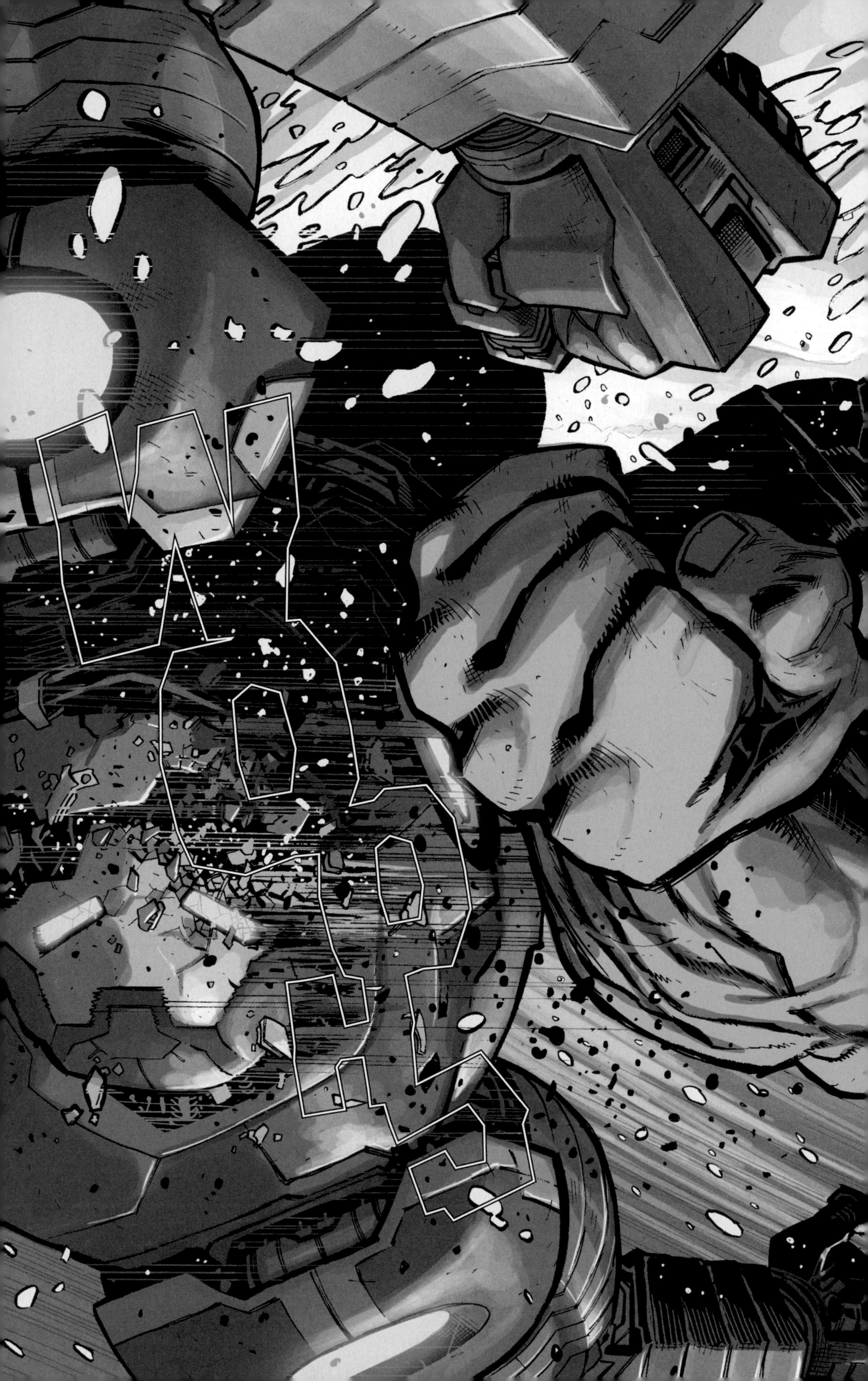

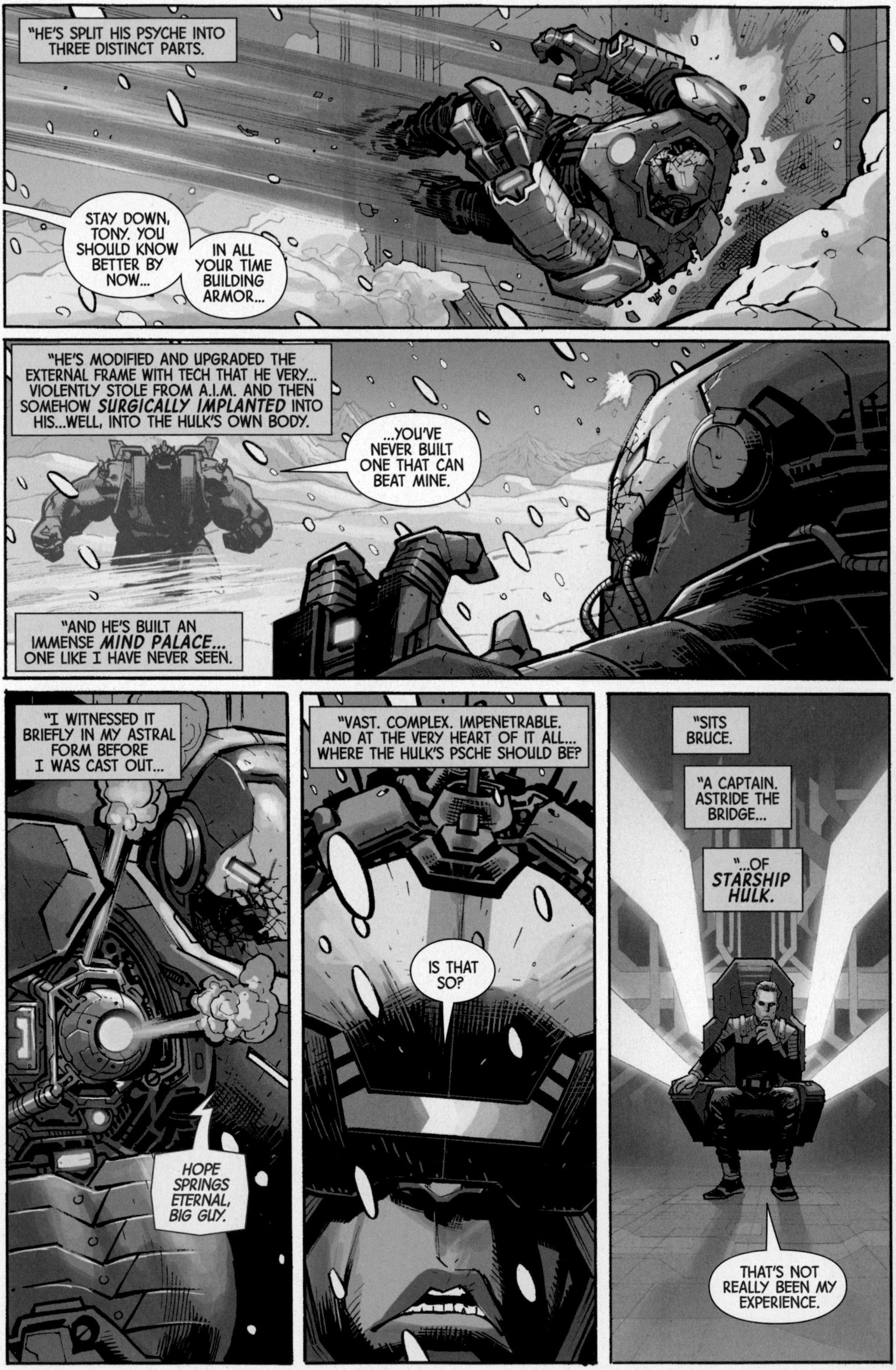
"HE'S SPLIT HIS PSYCHE INTO THREE DISTINCT PARTS.
STAY DOWN, TONY. YOU SHOULD KNOW BETTER BY NOW...
IN ALL YOUR TIME BUILDING ARMOR...
"HE'S MODIFIED AND UPGRADED THE EXTERNAL FRAME WITH TECH THAT HE VERY... VIOLENTLY STOLE FROM A.I.M. AND THEN SOMEHOW *SURGICALLY IMPLANTED* INTO HIS...WELL, INTO THE HULK'S OWN BODY.
...YOU'VE NEVER BUILT ONE THAT CAN BEAT MINE.
"AND HE'S BUILT AN IMMENSE *MIND PALACE*... ONE LIKE I HAVE NEVER SEEN.
"I WITNESSED IT BRIEFLY IN MY ASTRAL FORM BEFORE I WAS CAST OUT...
HOPE SPRINGS ETERNAL, BIG GUY.
"VAST. COMPLEX. IMPENETRABLE. AND AT THE VERY HEART OF IT ALL... WHERE THE HULK'S PSCHE SHOULD BE?
IS THAT SO?
"SITS BRUCE.
"A CAPTAIN. ASTRIDE THE BRIDGE...
"...OF *STARSHIP HULK.*
THAT'S NOT REALLY BEEN MY EXPERIENCE.

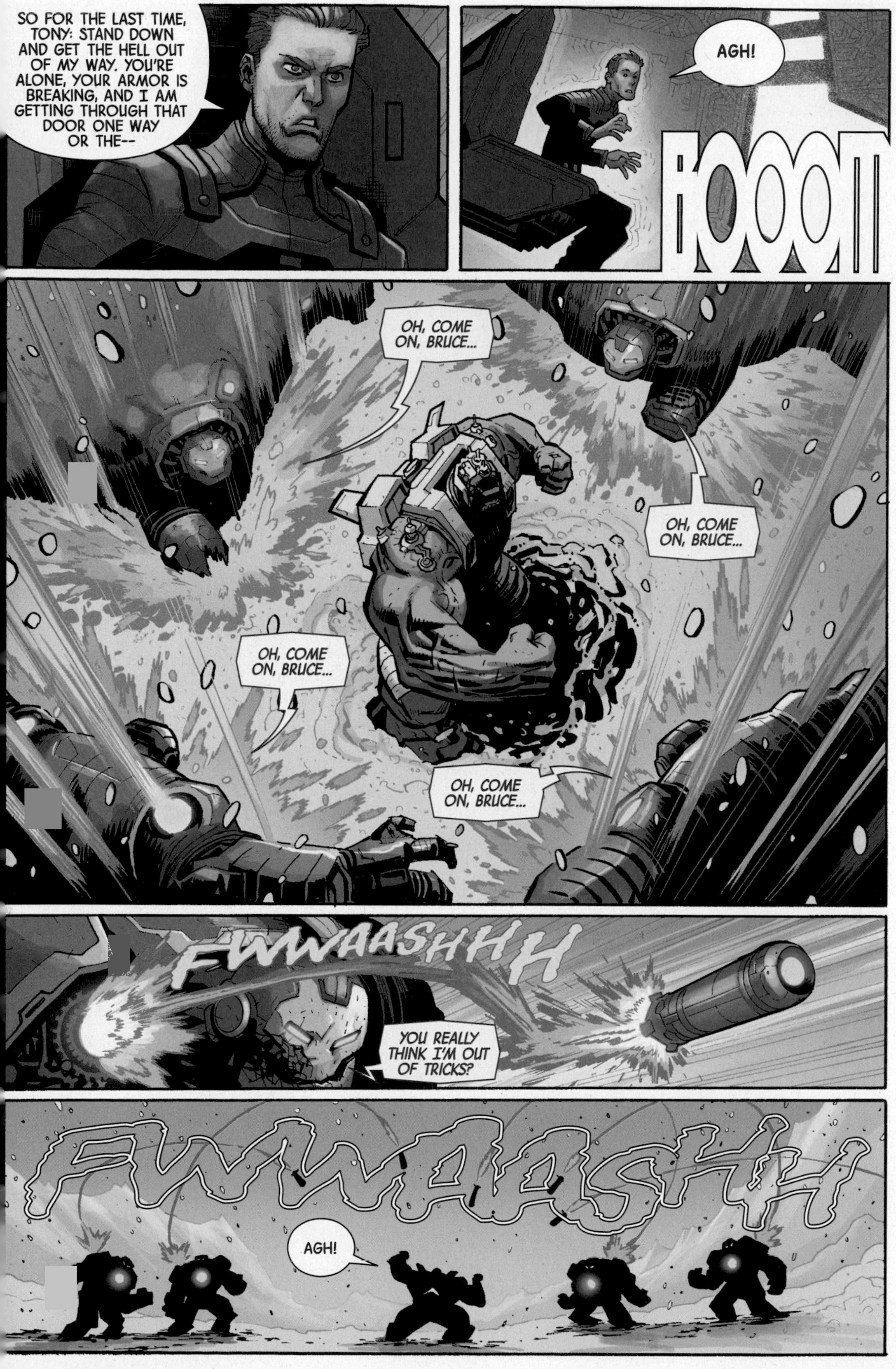
SO FOR THE LAST TIME, TONY: STAND DOWN AND GET THE HELL OUT OF MY WAY. YOU'RE ALONE, YOUR ARMOR IS BREAKING, AND I AM GETTING THROUGH THAT DOOR ONE WAY OR THE--
AGH!
BOOOM
OH, COME ON, BRUCE...
OH, COME ON, BRUCE...
OH, COME ON, BRUCE...
OH, COME ON, BRUCE...
FWWAASHHH
YOU REALLY THINK I'M OUT OF TRICKS?
FWWAASHH
AGH!

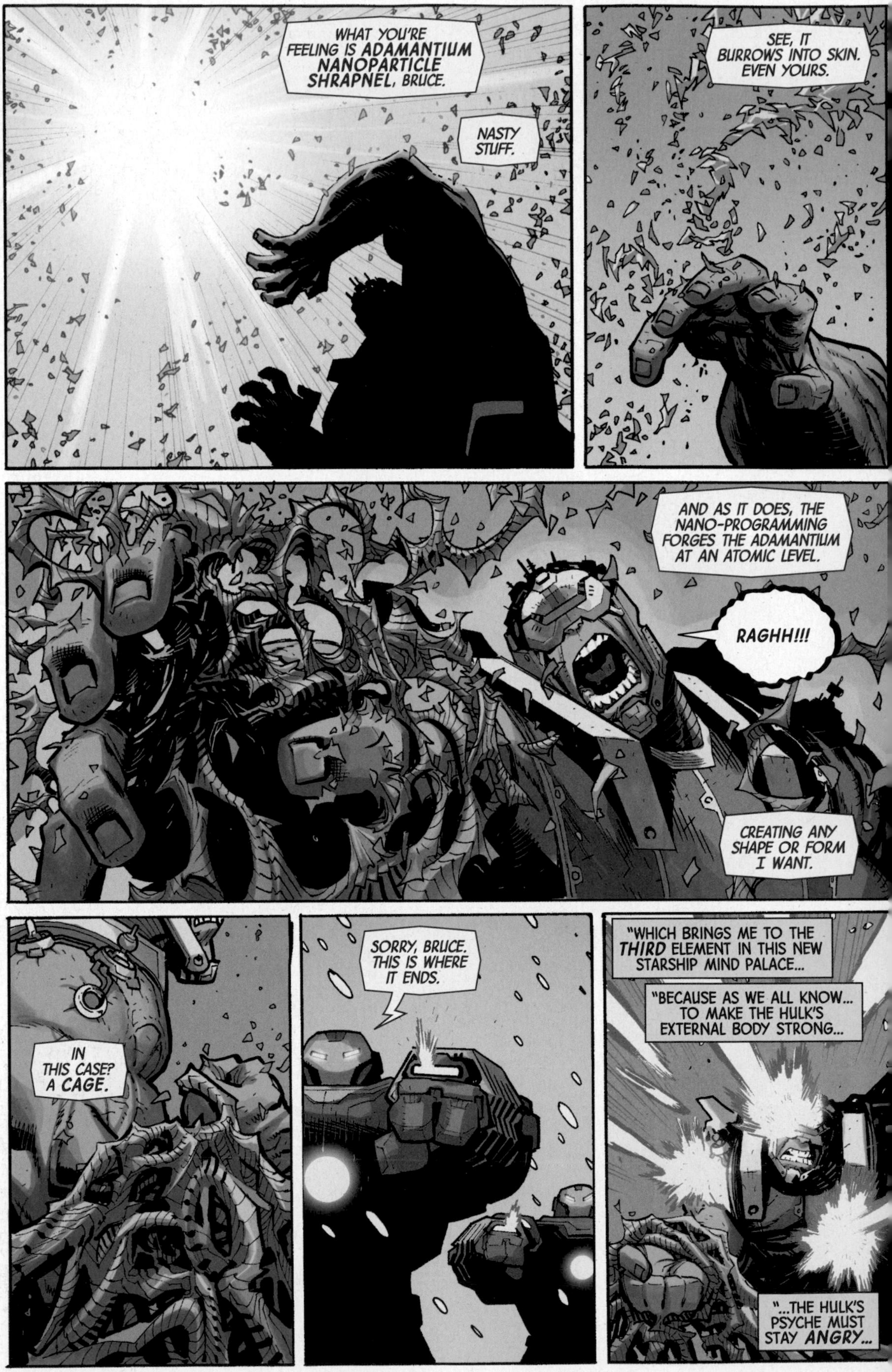
WHAT YOU'RE FEELING IS ADAMANTIUM NANOPARTICLE SHRAPNEL, BRUCE.
NASTY STUFF.
SEE, IT BURROWS INTO SKIN. EVEN YOURS.
AND AS IT DOES, THE NANO-PROGRAMMING FORGES THE ADAMANTIUM AT AN ATOMIC LEVEL.
RAGHH!!!
CREATING ANY SHAPE OR FORM I WANT.
IN THIS CASE? A CAGE.
SORRY, BRUCE. THIS IS WHERE IT ENDS.
"WHICH BRINGS ME TO THE THIRD ELEMENT IN THIS NEW STARSHIP MIND PALACE...
"BECAUSE AS WE ALL KNOW... TO MAKE THE HULK'S EXTERNAL BODY STRONG...
"...THE HULK'S PSYCHE MUST STAY ANGRY...

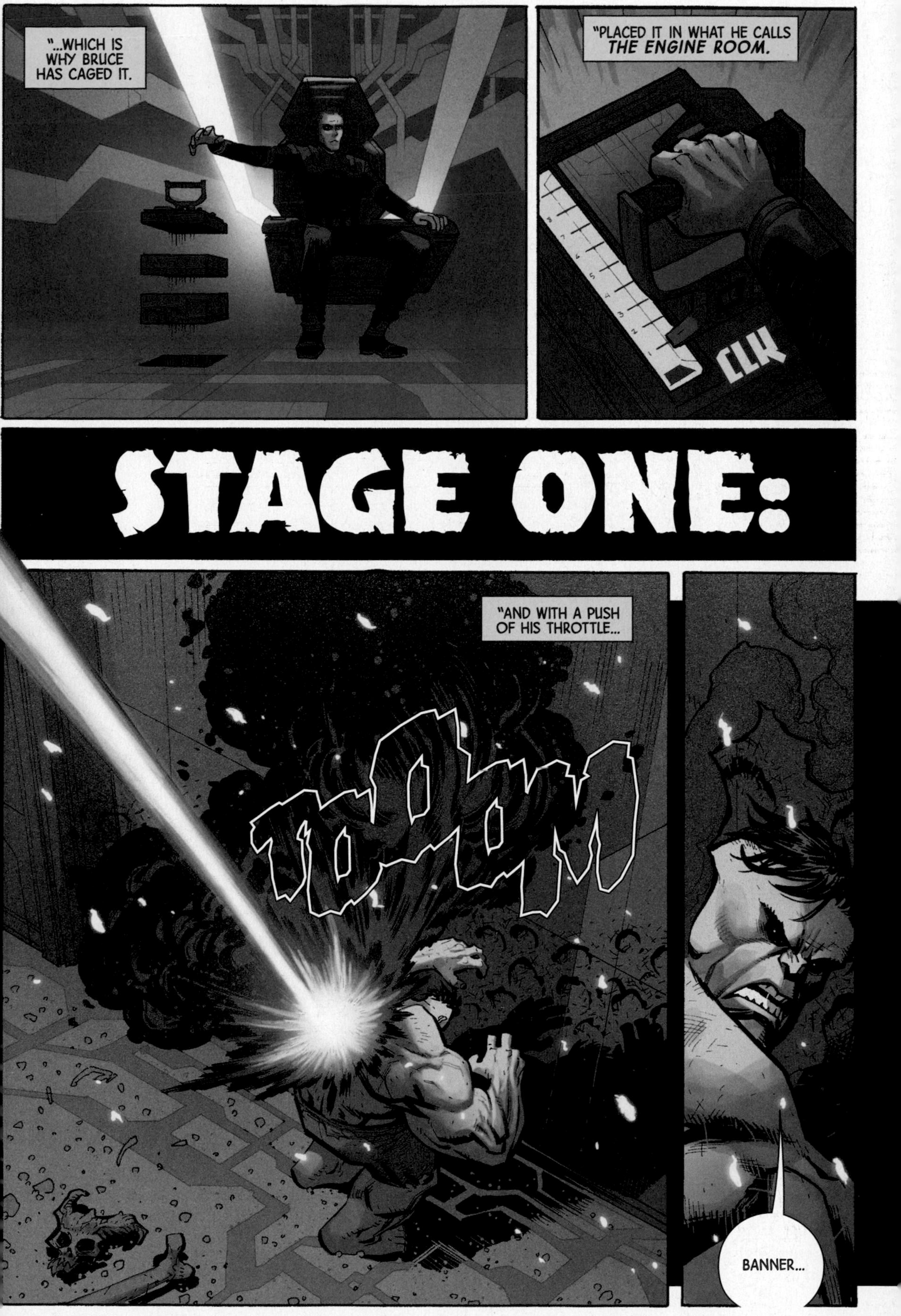
"...WHICH IS WHY BRUCE HAS CAGED IT.
"PLACED IT IN WHAT HE CALLS *THE ENGINE ROOM.*
CLK
STAGE ONE:
"AND WITH A PUSH OF HIS THROTTLE...
BANNER...

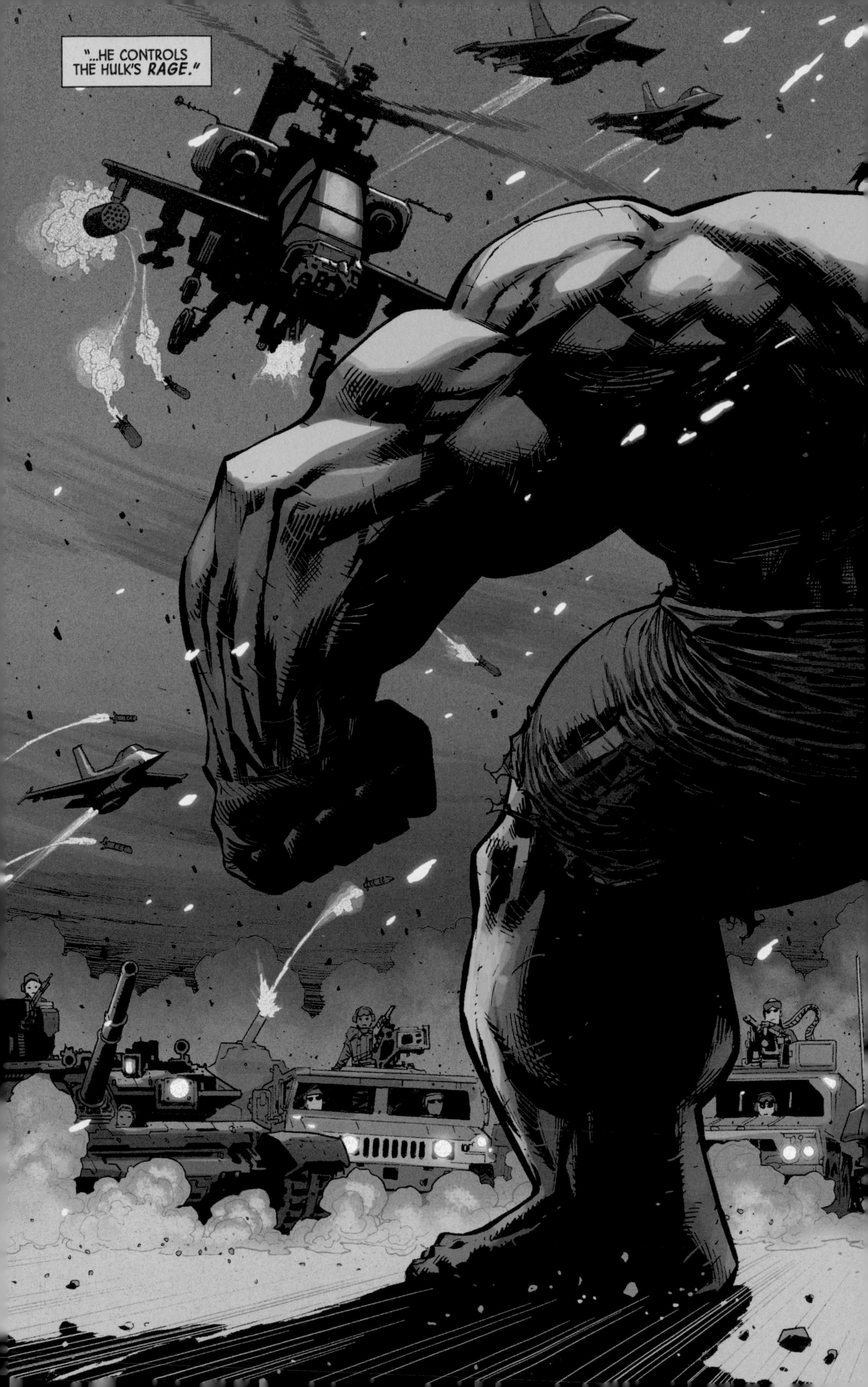
"...HE CONTROLS THE HULK'S *RAGE*."

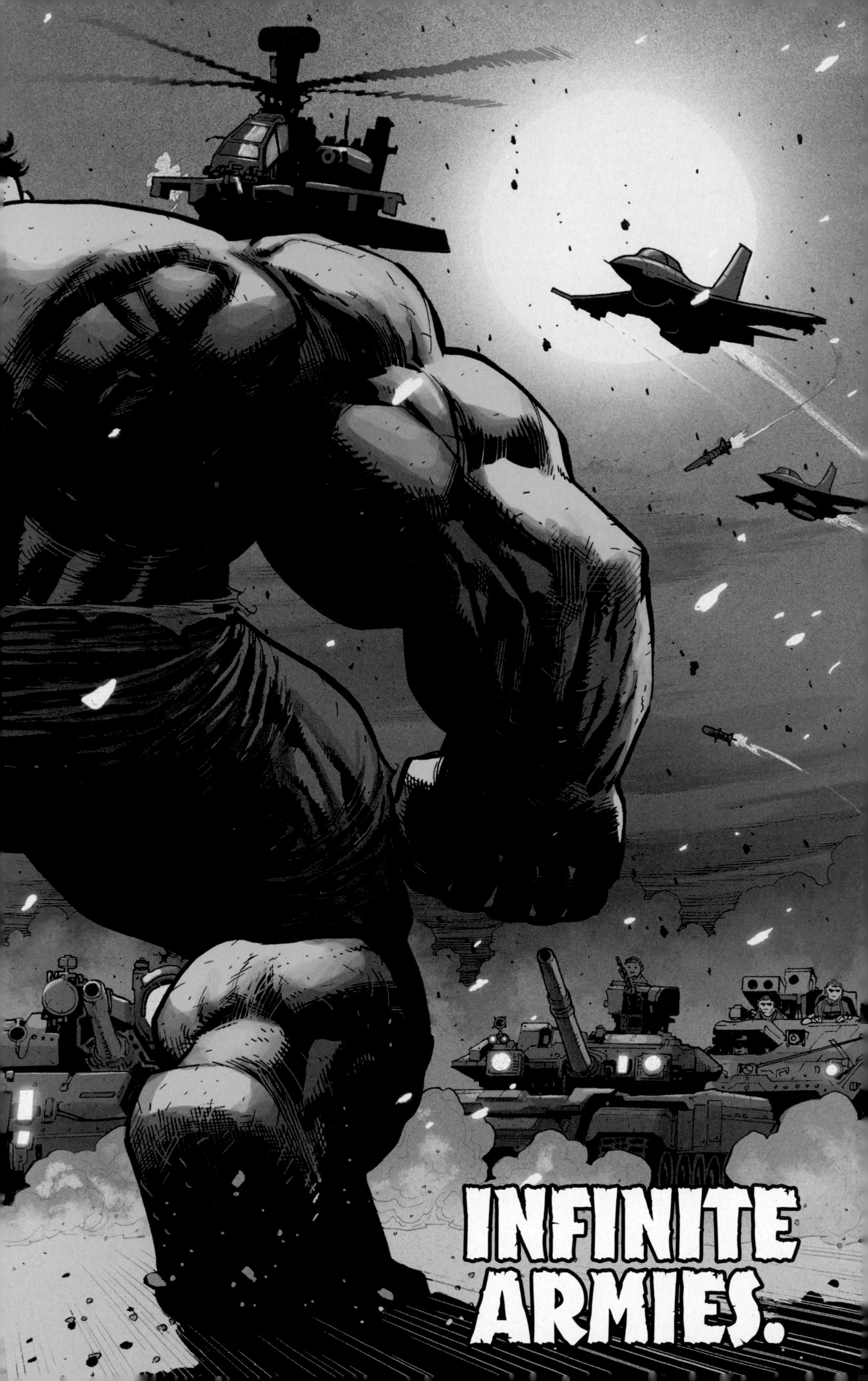
INFINITE ARMIES.

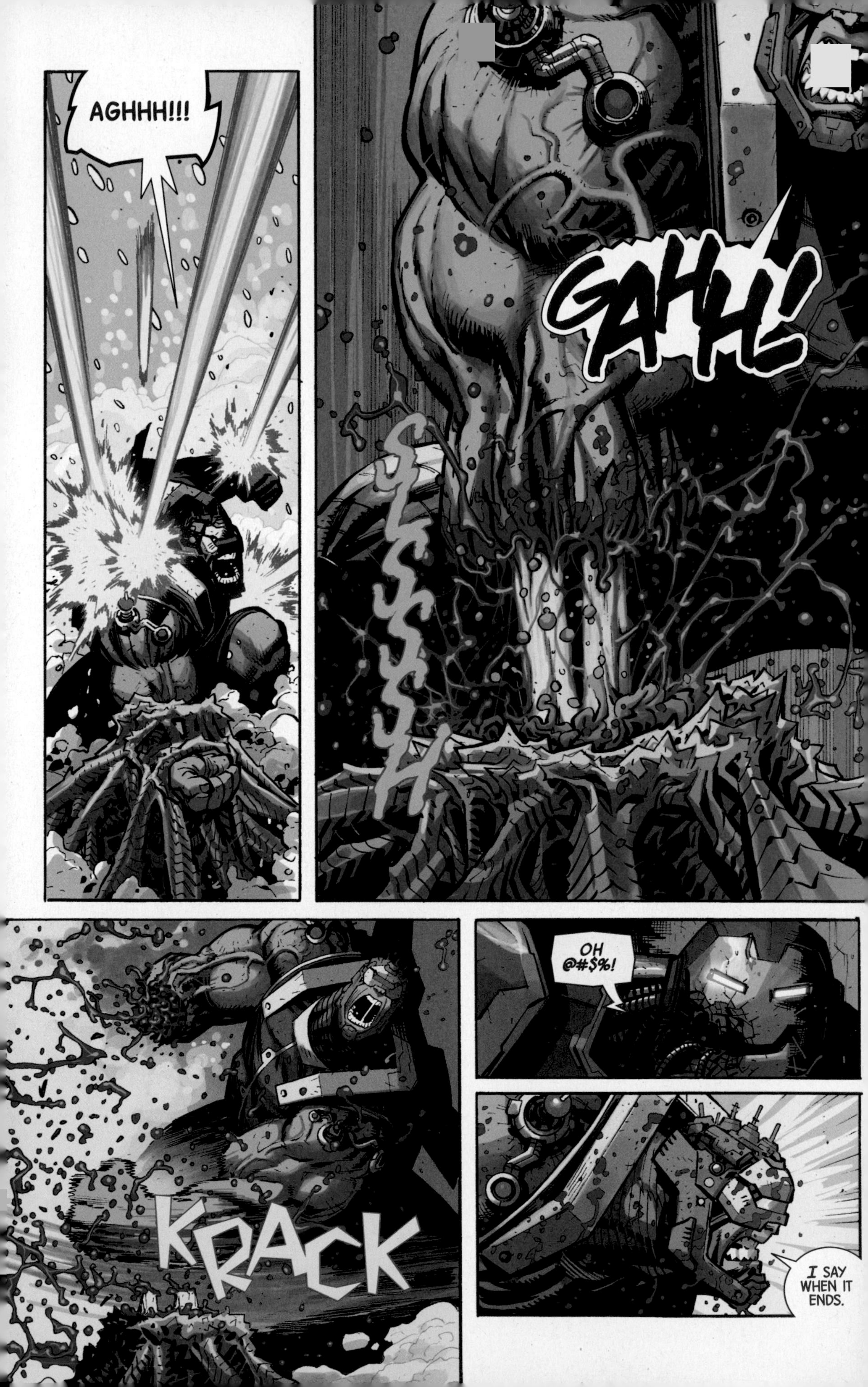
AGHHH!!!
GAHH!
SHHHH
OH @#$%!
KRACK
I SAY WHEN IT ENDS.

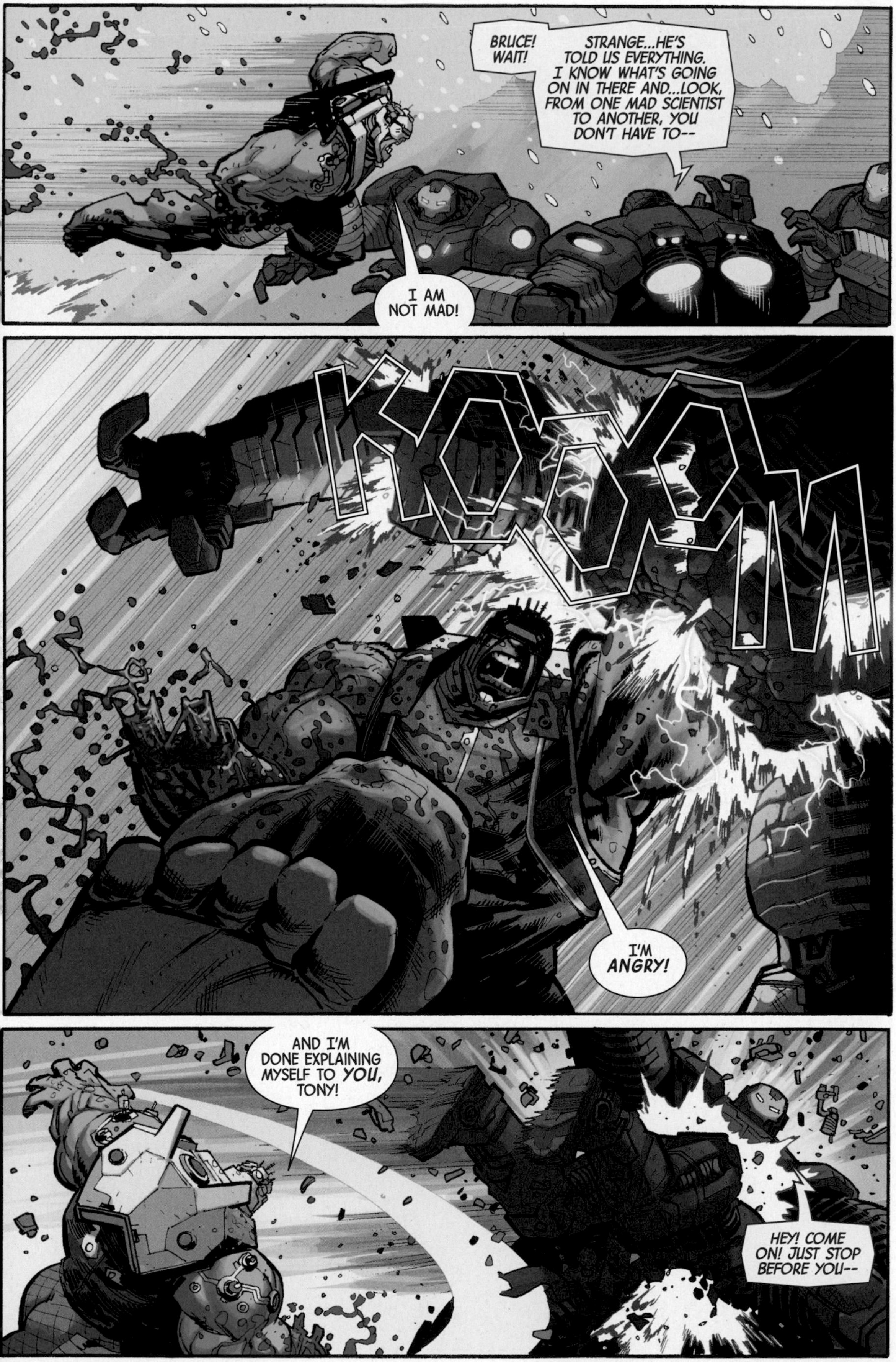
BRUCE! WAIT!
STRANGE...HE'S TOLD US EVERYTHING. I KNOW WHAT'S GOING ON IN THERE AND...LOOK, FROM ONE MAD SCIENTIST TO ANOTHER, YOU DON'T HAVE TO--
I AM NOT MAD!
KOOOOM
I'M ANGRY!
AND I'M DONE EXPLAINING MYSELF TO YOU, TONY!
HEY! COME ON! JUST STOP BEFORE YOU--

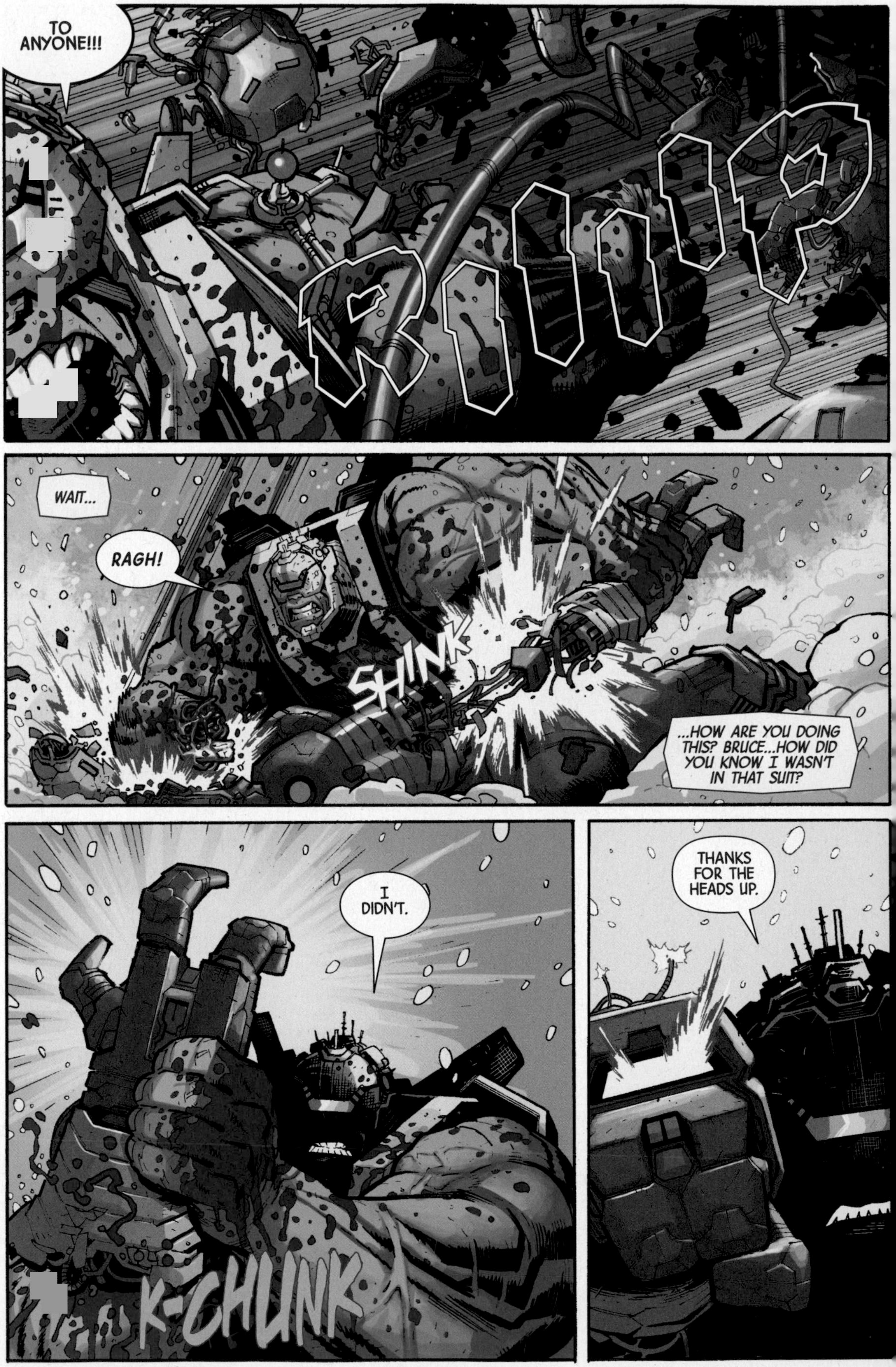
TO ANYONE!!!
ROOOP
WAIT...
RAGH!
SHINK
...HOW ARE YOU DOING THIS? BRUCE...HOW DID YOU KNOW I WASN'T IN THAT SUIT?
I DIDN'T.
K-CHUNK
THANKS FOR THE HEADS UP.

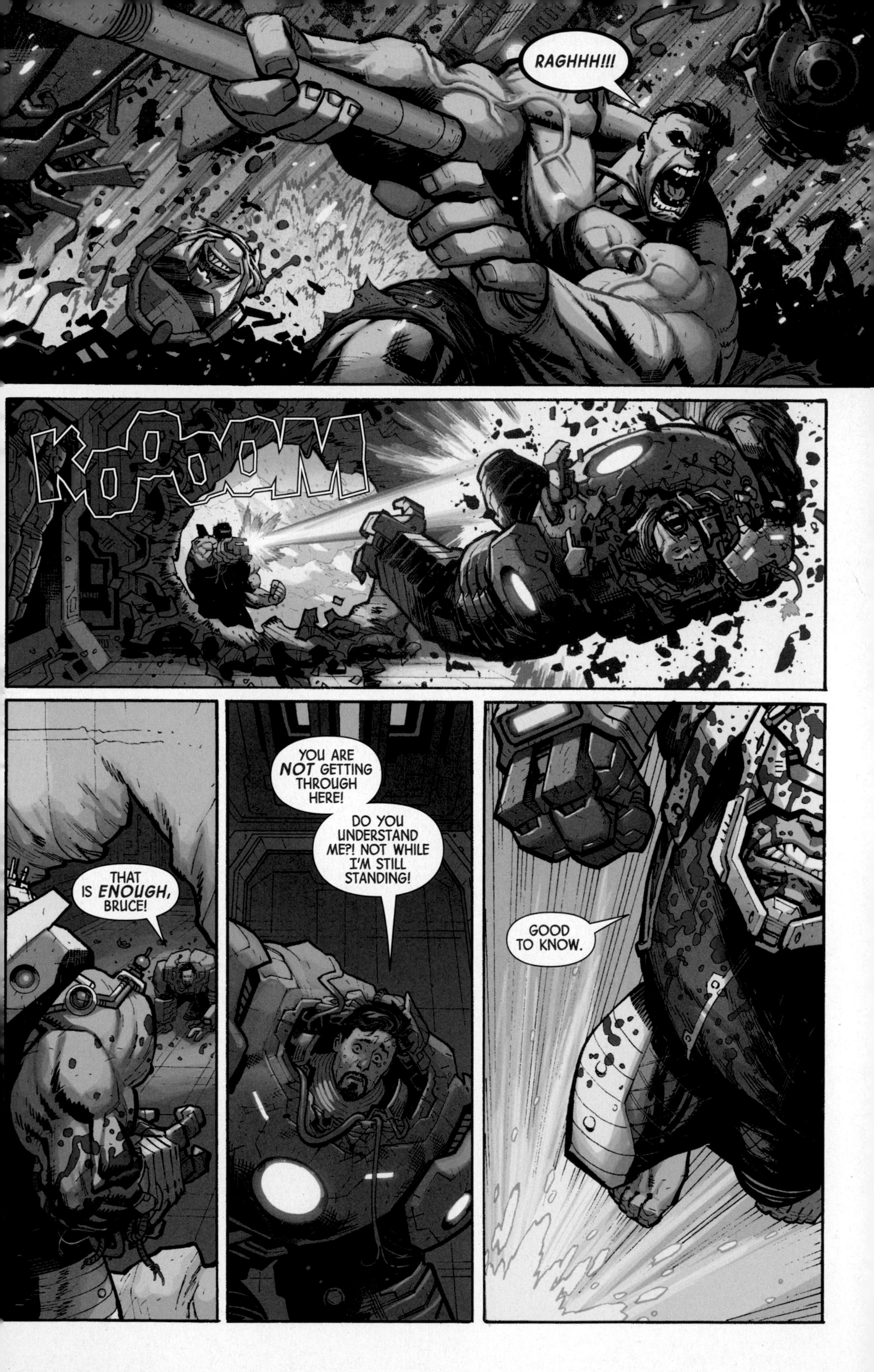
RAGHHH!!!
KOOOOOM
THAT IS ENOUGH, BRUCE!
YOU ARE NOT GETTING THROUGH HERE!
DO YOU UNDERSTAND ME?! NOT WHILE I'M STILL STANDING!
GOOD TO KNOW.

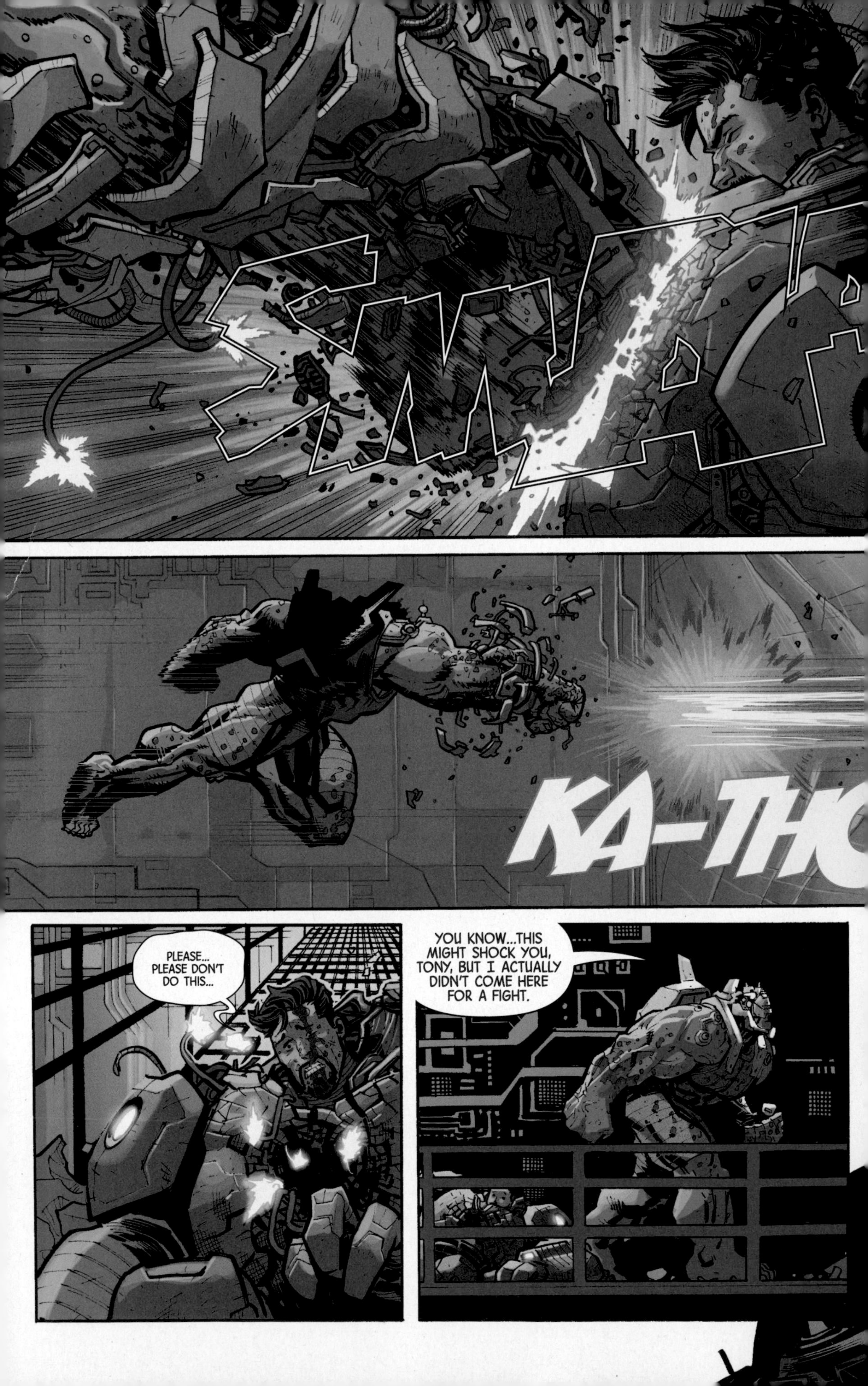
SMA
KA-THO
PLEASE... PLEASE DON'T DO THIS...
YOU KNOW...THIS MIGHT SHOCK YOU, TONY, BUT I ACTUALLY DIDN'T COME HERE FOR A FIGHT.

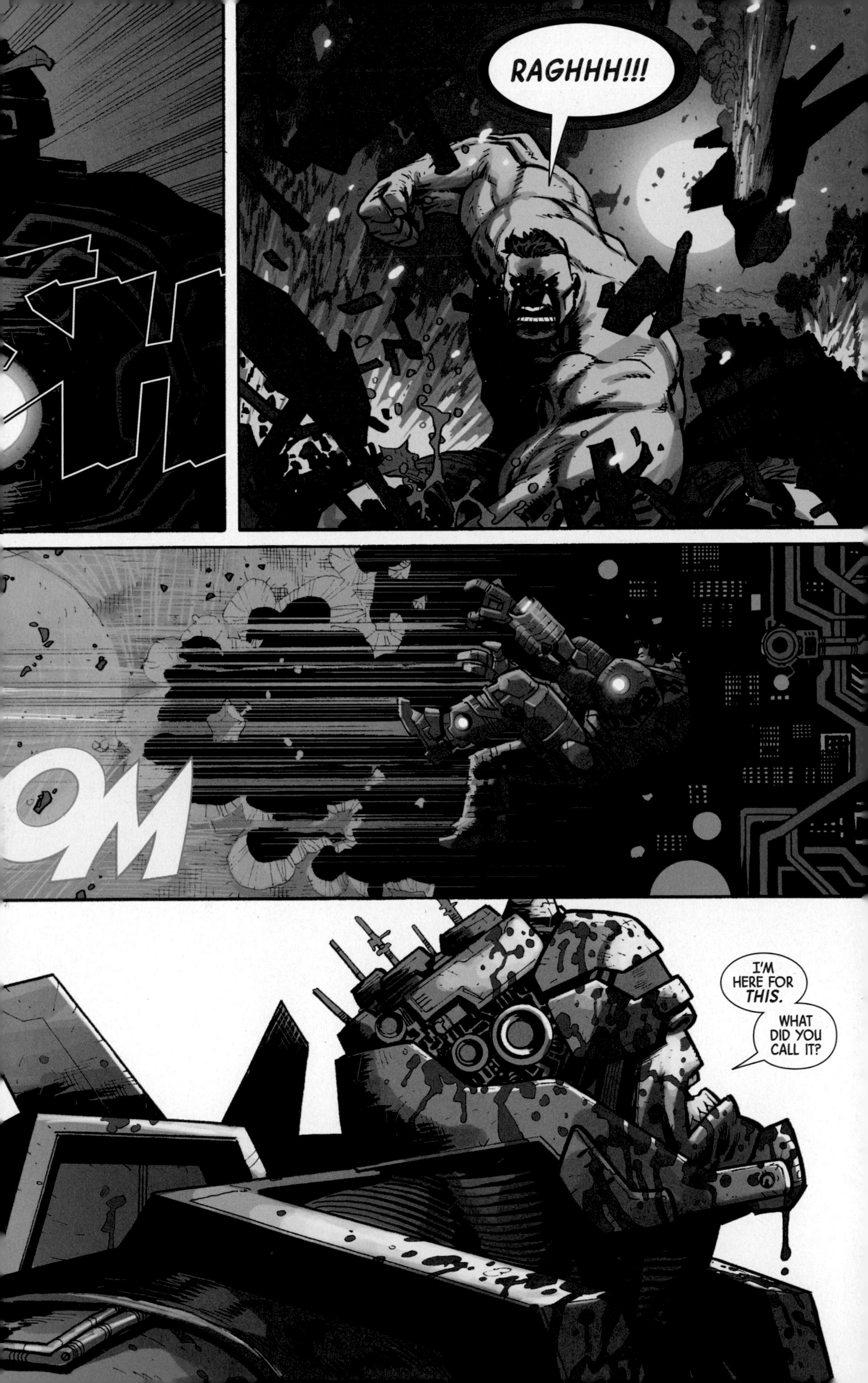
RAGHHH!!!
OM
I'M HERE FOR THIS.
WHAT DID YOU CALL IT?

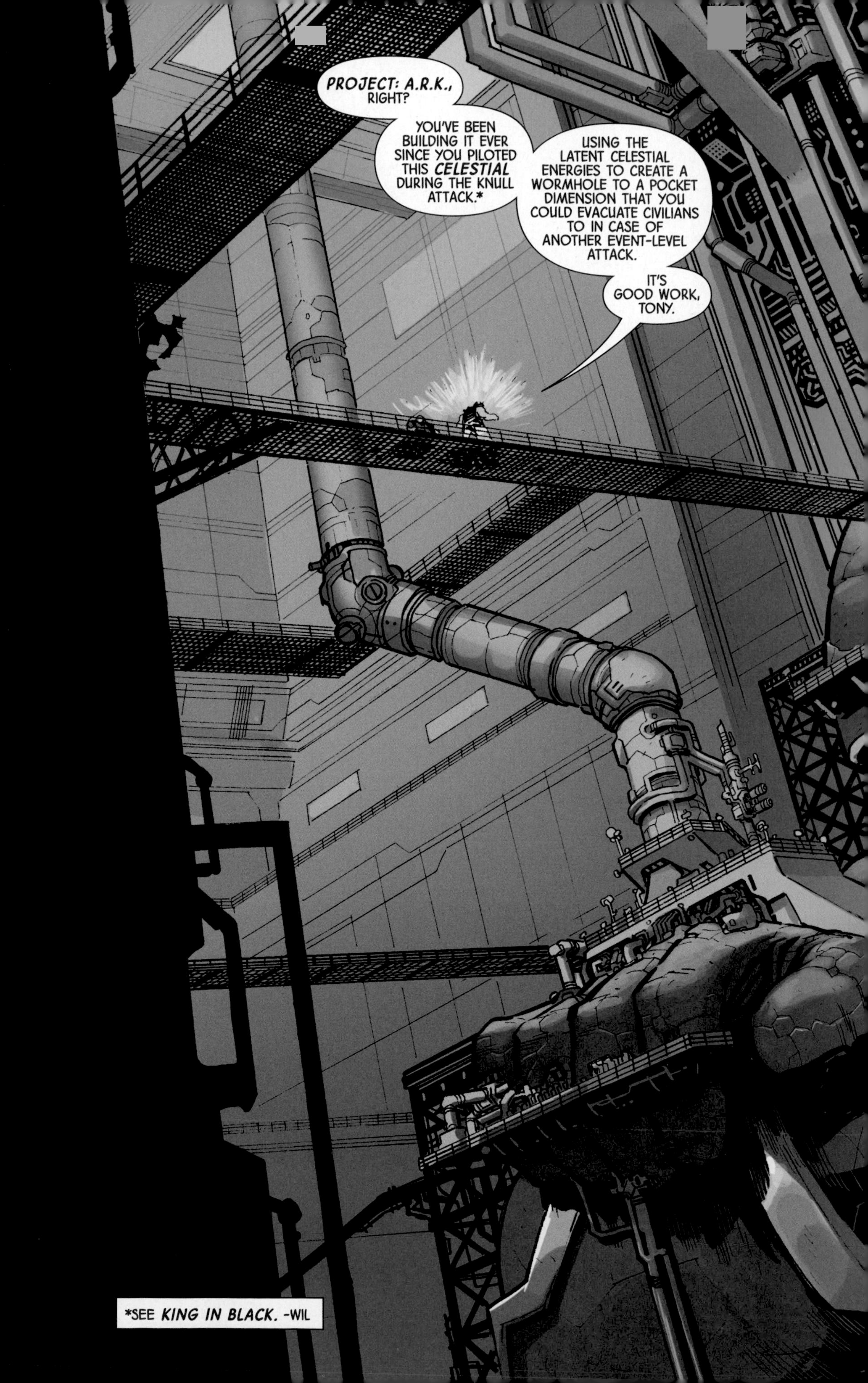
PROJECT: A.R.K., RIGHT?
YOU'VE BEEN BUILDING IT EVER SINCE YOU PILOTED THIS *CELESTIAL* DURING THE KNULL ATTACK.*
USING THE LATENT CELESTIAL ENERGIES TO CREATE A WORMHOLE TO A POCKET DIMENSION THAT YOU COULD EVACUATE CIVILIANS TO IN CASE OF ANOTHER EVENT-LEVEL ATTACK.
IT'S GOOD WORK, TONY.
*SEE *KING IN BLACK.* -WIL

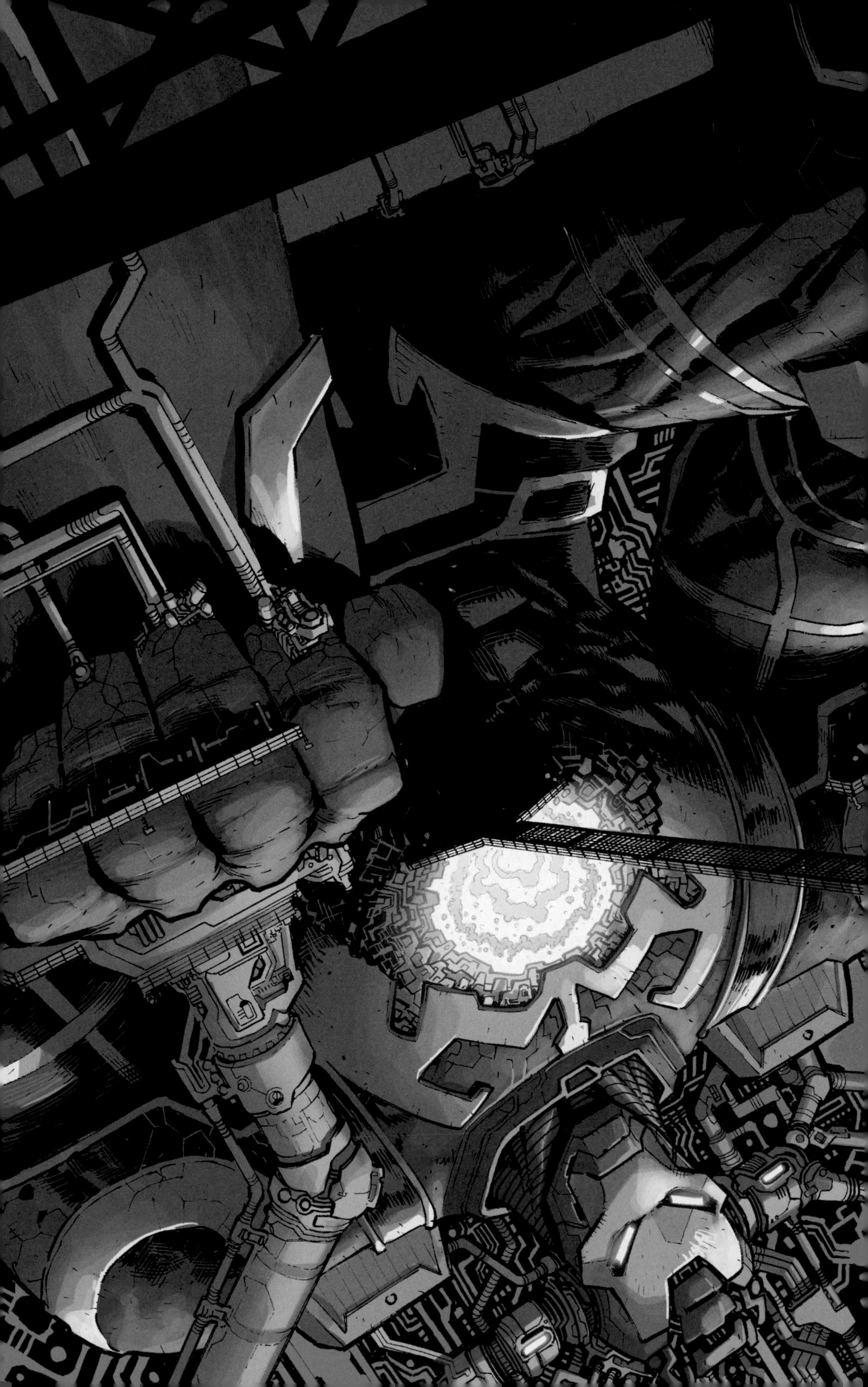

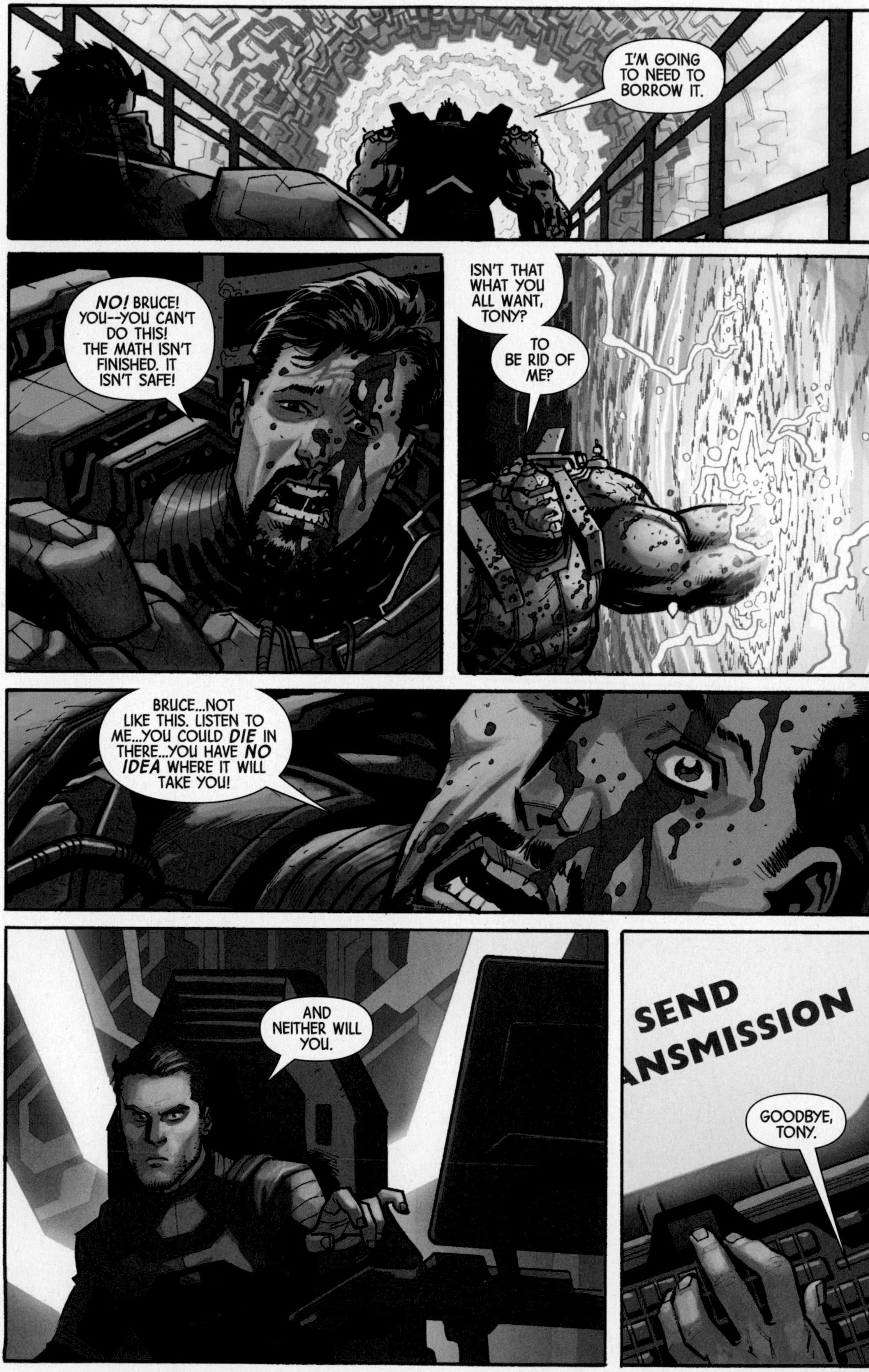
I'M GOING TO NEED TO BORROW IT.
NO! BRUCE! YOU--YOU CAN'T DO THIS! THE MATH ISN'T FINISHED. IT ISN'T SAFE!
ISN'T THAT WHAT YOU ALL WANT, TONY?
TO BE RID OF ME?
BRUCE...NOT LIKE THIS. LISTEN TO ME...YOU COULD DIE IN THERE...YOU HAVE NO IDEA WHERE IT WILL TAKE YOU!
AND NEITHER WILL YOU.
SEND
ANSMISSION
GOODBYE, TONY.

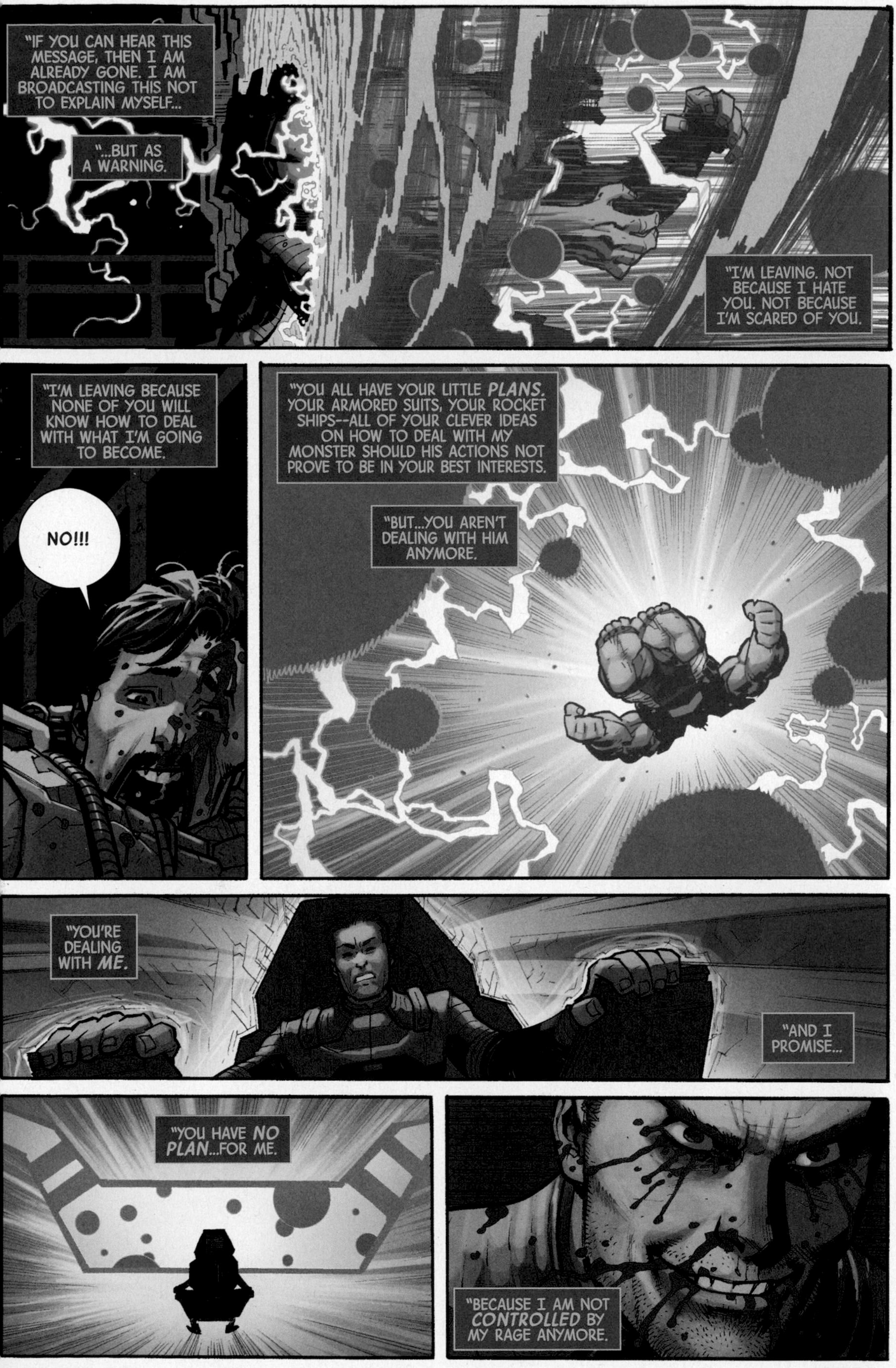
"IF YOU CAN HEAR THIS MESSAGE, THEN I AM ALREADY GONE. I AM BROADCASTING THIS NOT TO EXPLAIN MYSELF...
"...BUT AS A WARNING.
"I'M LEAVING. NOT BECAUSE I HATE YOU. NOT BECAUSE I'M SCARED OF YOU.
"I'M LEAVING BECAUSE NONE OF YOU WILL KNOW HOW TO DEAL WITH WHAT I'M GOING TO BECOME.
NO!!!
"YOU ALL HAVE YOUR LITTLE PLANS, YOUR ARMORED SUITS, YOUR ROCKET SHIPS--ALL OF YOUR CLEVER IDEAS ON HOW TO DEAL WITH MY MONSTER SHOULD HIS ACTIONS NOT PROVE TO BE IN YOUR BEST INTERESTS.
"BUT...YOU AREN'T DEALING WITH HIM ANYMORE.
"YOU'RE DEALING WITH ME.
"AND I PROMISE...
"YOU HAVE NO PLAN...FOR ME.
"BECAUSE I AM NOT CONTROLLED BY MY RAGE ANYMORE.

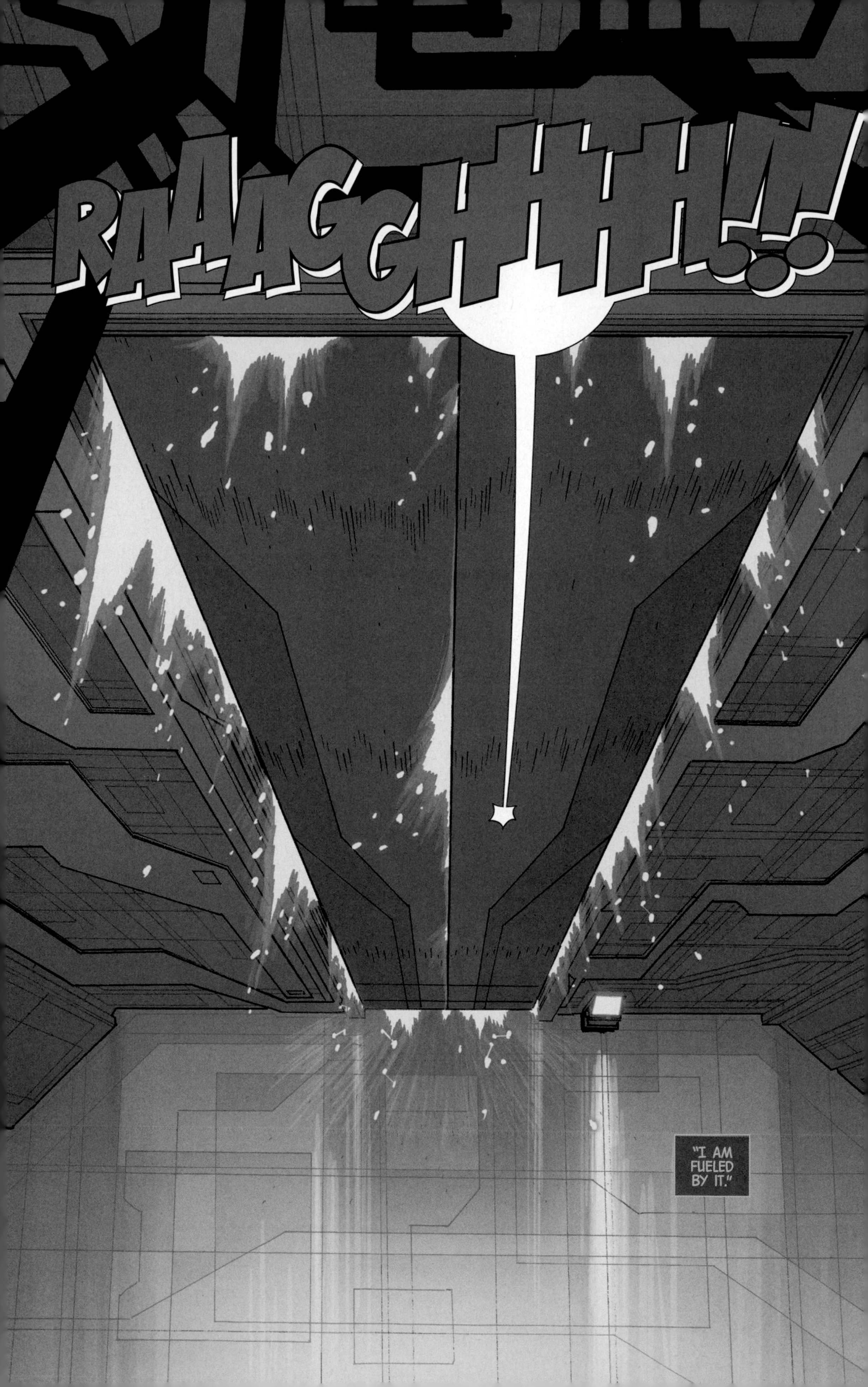
RAAAGGHHHH!!!
"I AM FUELED BY IT."

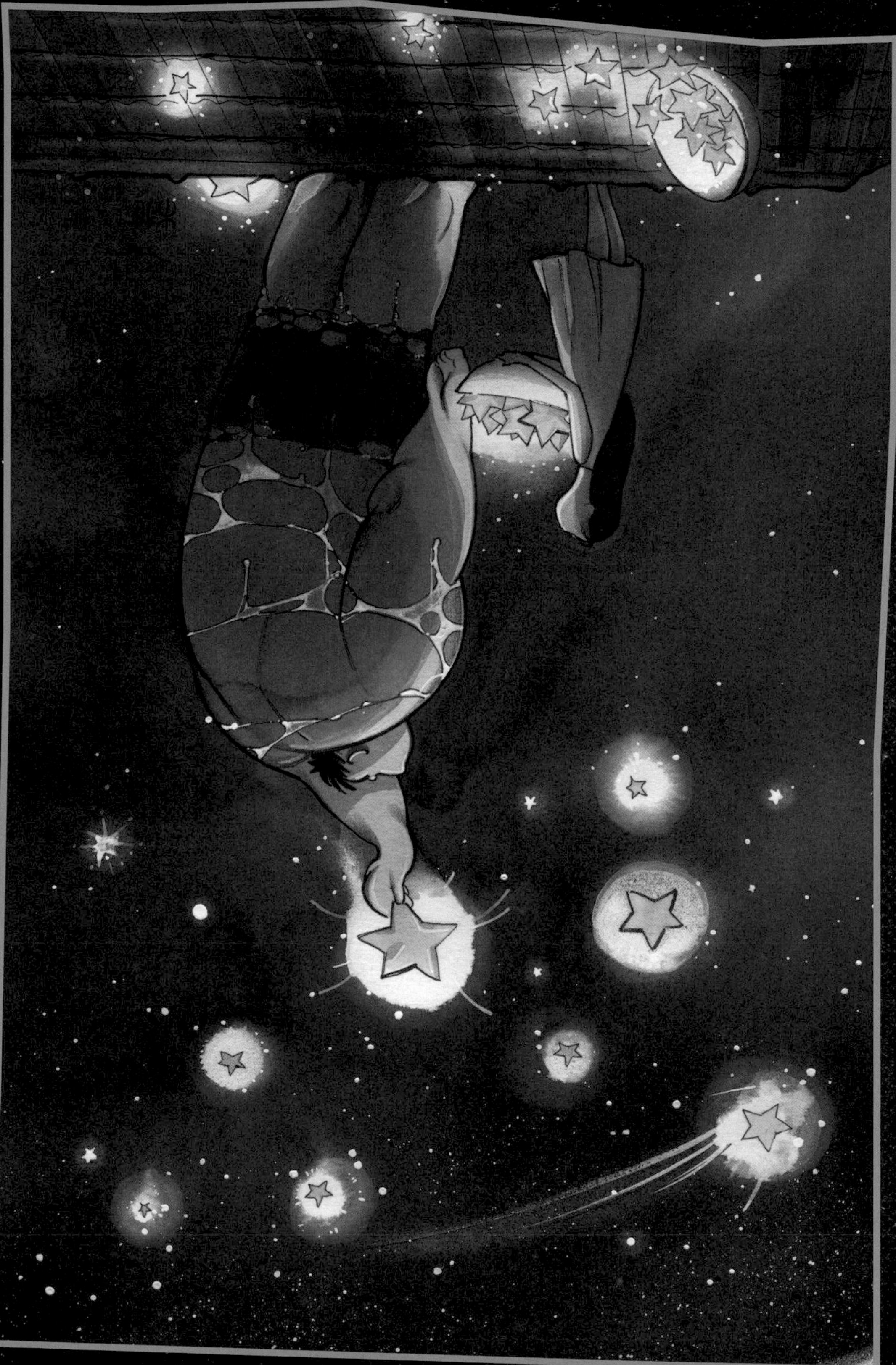

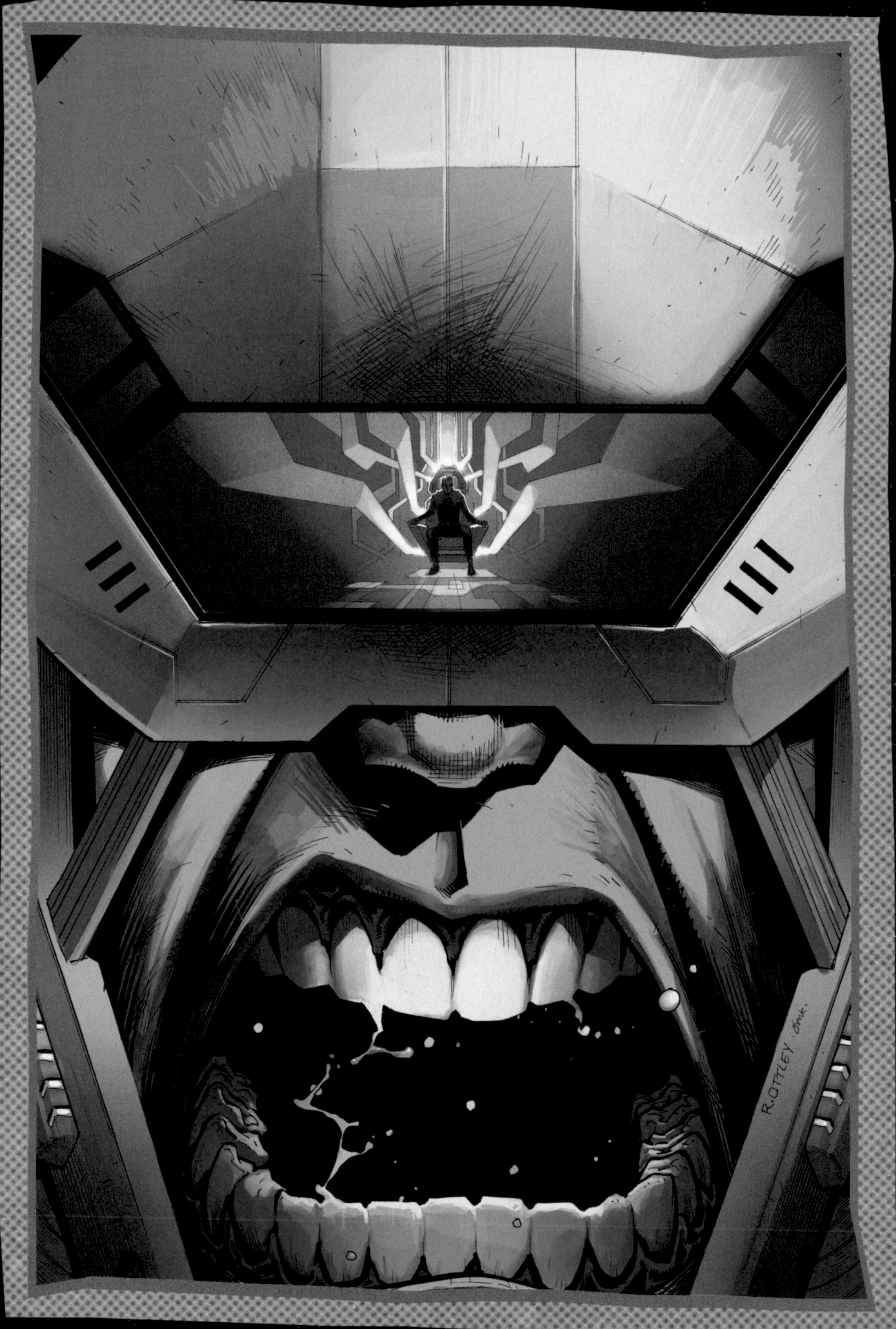
R. OTTLEY

HULK
NUMBER 2

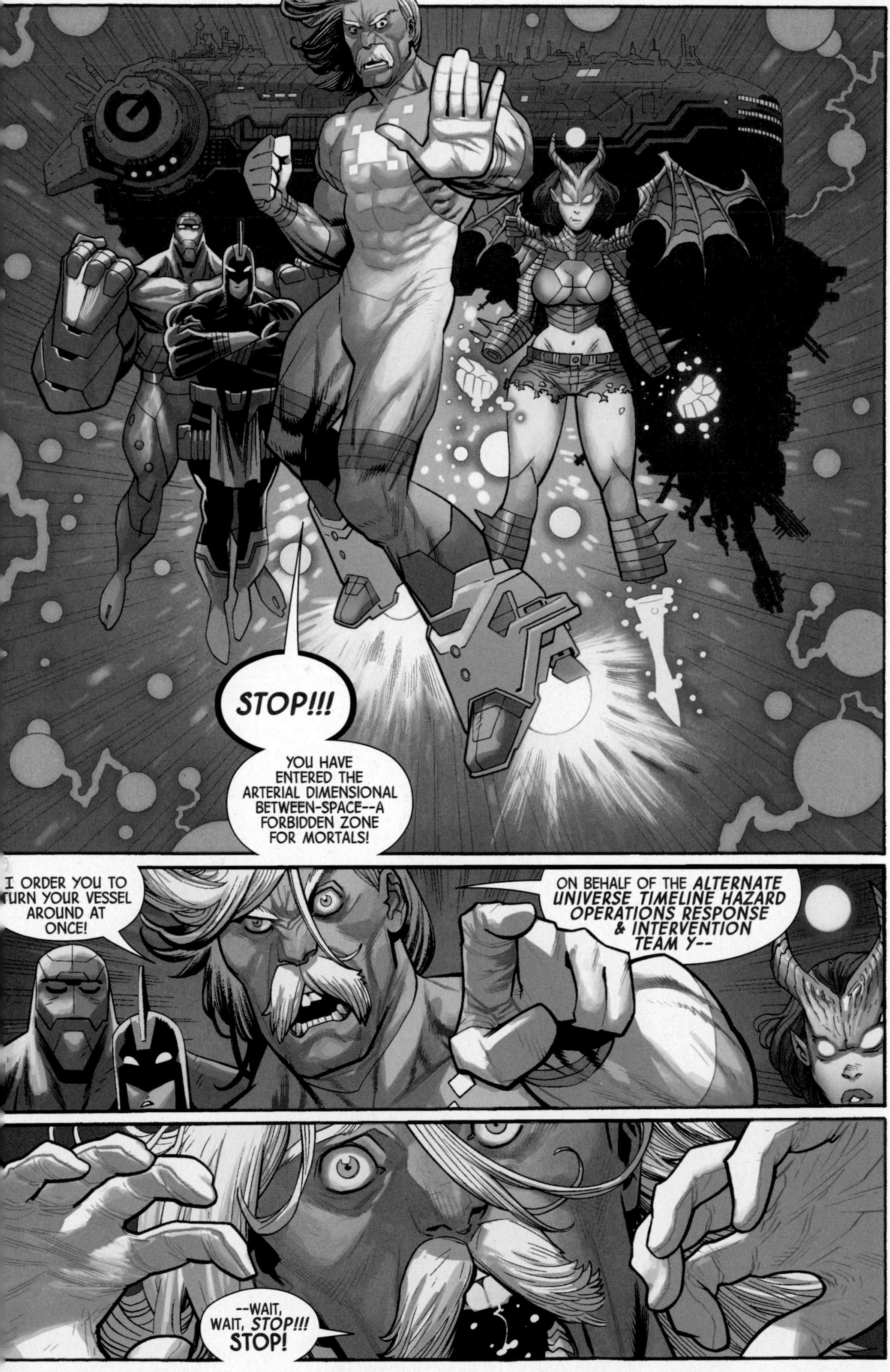
STOP!!!
YOU HAVE ENTERED THE ARTERIAL DIMENSIONAL BETWEEN-SPACE--A FORBIDDEN ZONE FOR MORTALS!
I ORDER YOU TO TURN YOUR VESSEL AROUND AT ONCE!
ON BEHALF OF THE ALTERNATE UNIVERSE TIMELINE HAZARD OPERATIONS RESPONSE & INTERVENTION TEAM Y--
--WAIT, WAIT, STOP!!! STOP!

WOMOP

ALERT! ALERT!!!

BOOOM

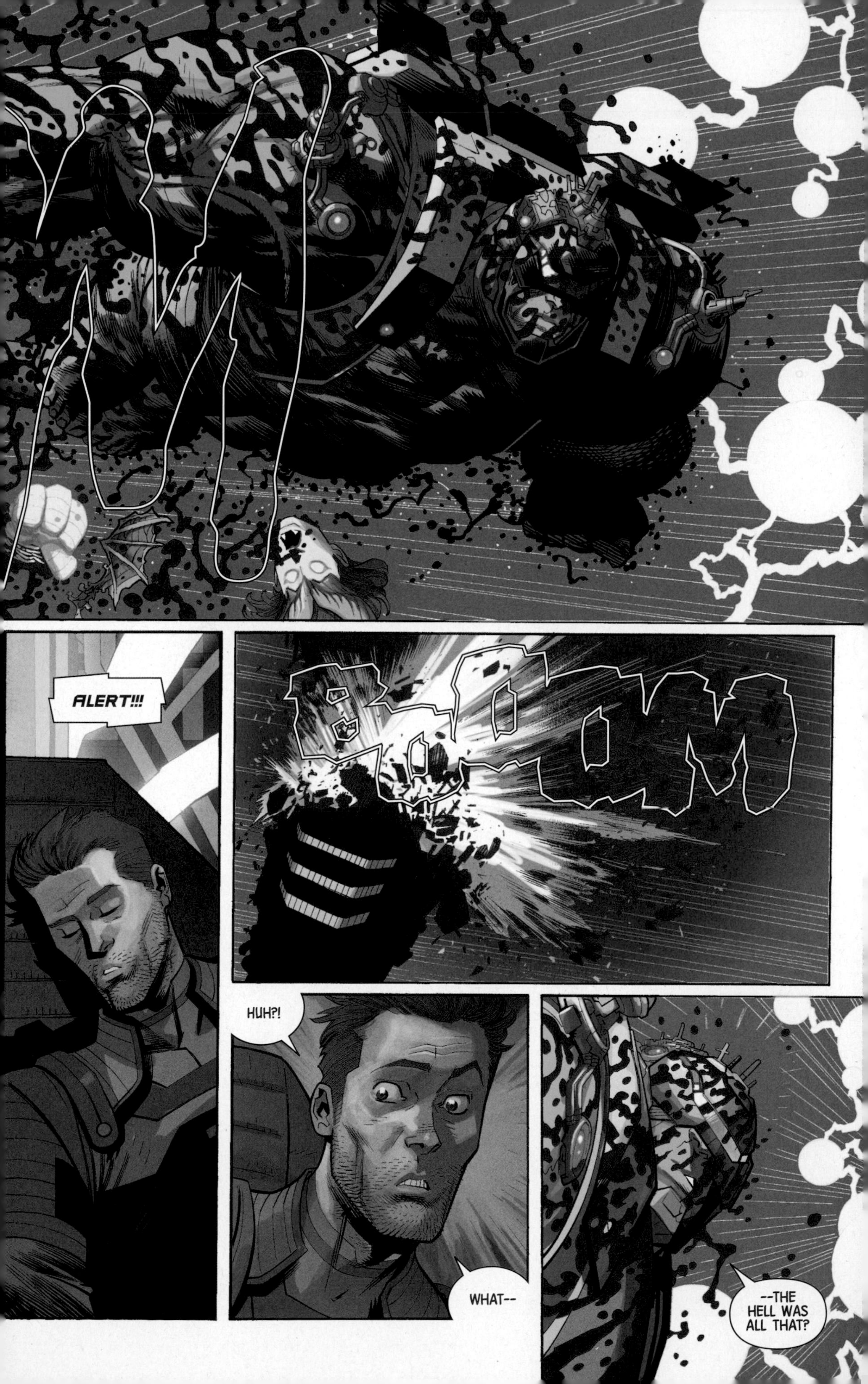
ALERT!!!
BOOM
HUH?!
WHAT--
--THE HELL WAS ALL THAT?

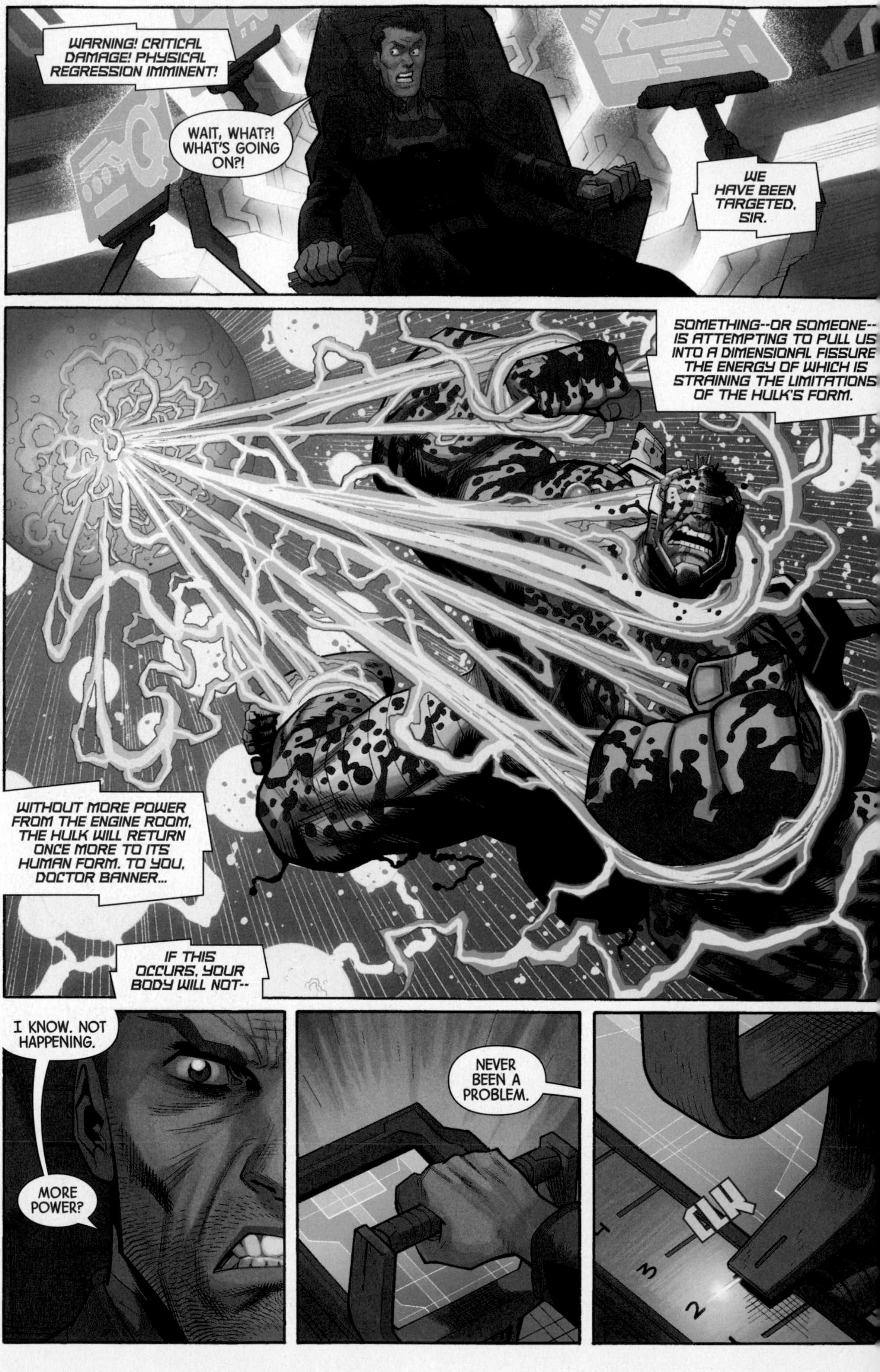
WARNING! CRITICAL DAMAGE! PHYSICAL REGRESSION IMMINENT!
WAIT, WHAT?! WHAT'S GOING ON?!
WE HAVE BEEN TARGETED, SIR.
SOMETHING--OR SOMEONE--IS ATTEMPTING TO PULL US INTO A DIMENSIONAL FISSURE THE ENERGY OF WHICH IS STRAINING THE LIMITATIONS OF THE HULK'S FORM.
WITHOUT MORE POWER FROM THE ENGINE ROOM, THE HULK WILL RETURN ONCE MORE TO ITS HUMAN FORM. TO YOU, DOCTOR BANNER...
IF THIS OCCURS, YOUR BODY WILL NOT--
I KNOW. NOT HAPPENING.
MORE POWER?
NEVER BEEN A PROBLEM.
CLR
1
3
2

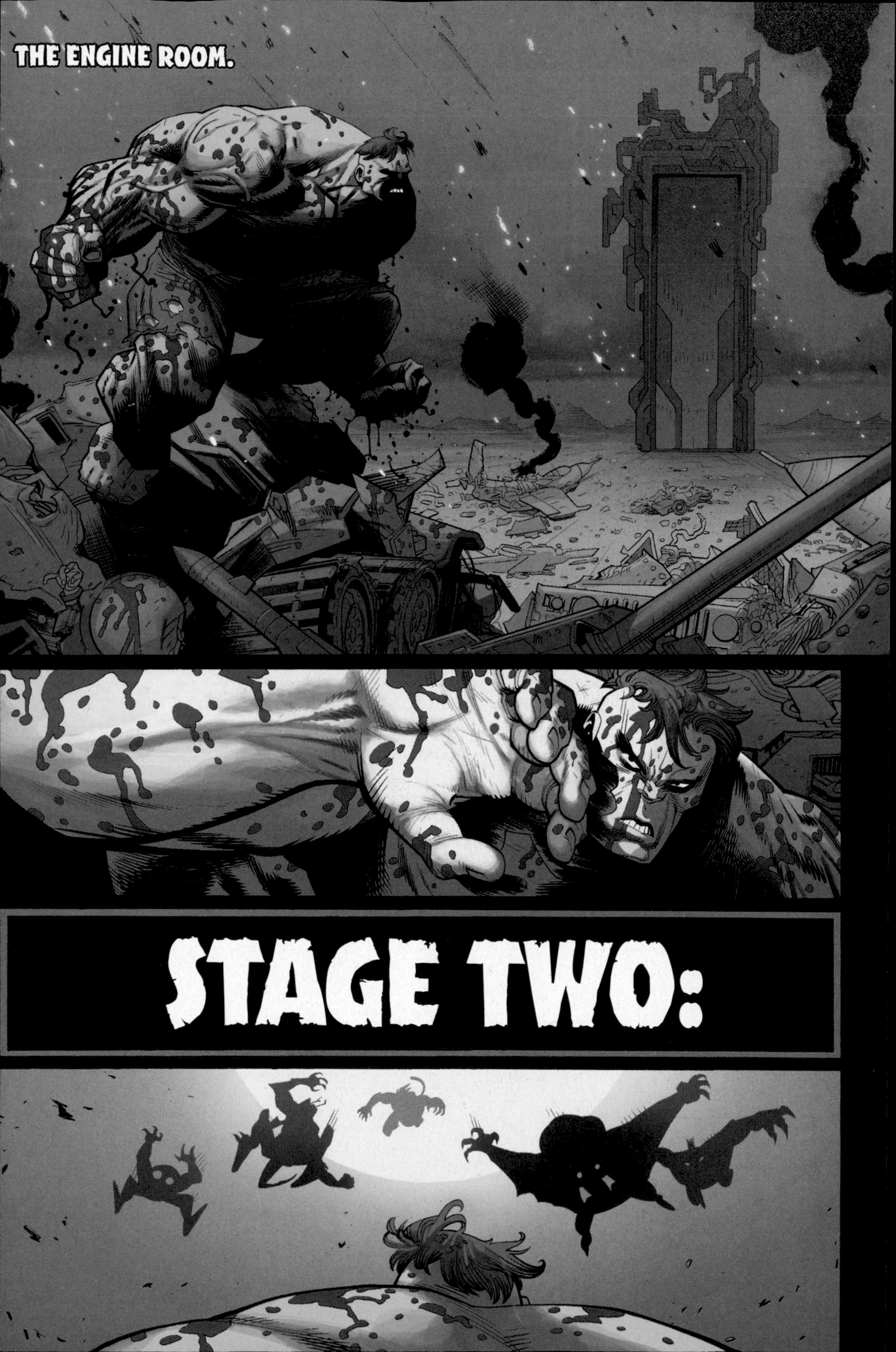
THE ENGINE ROOM.
STAGE TWO:

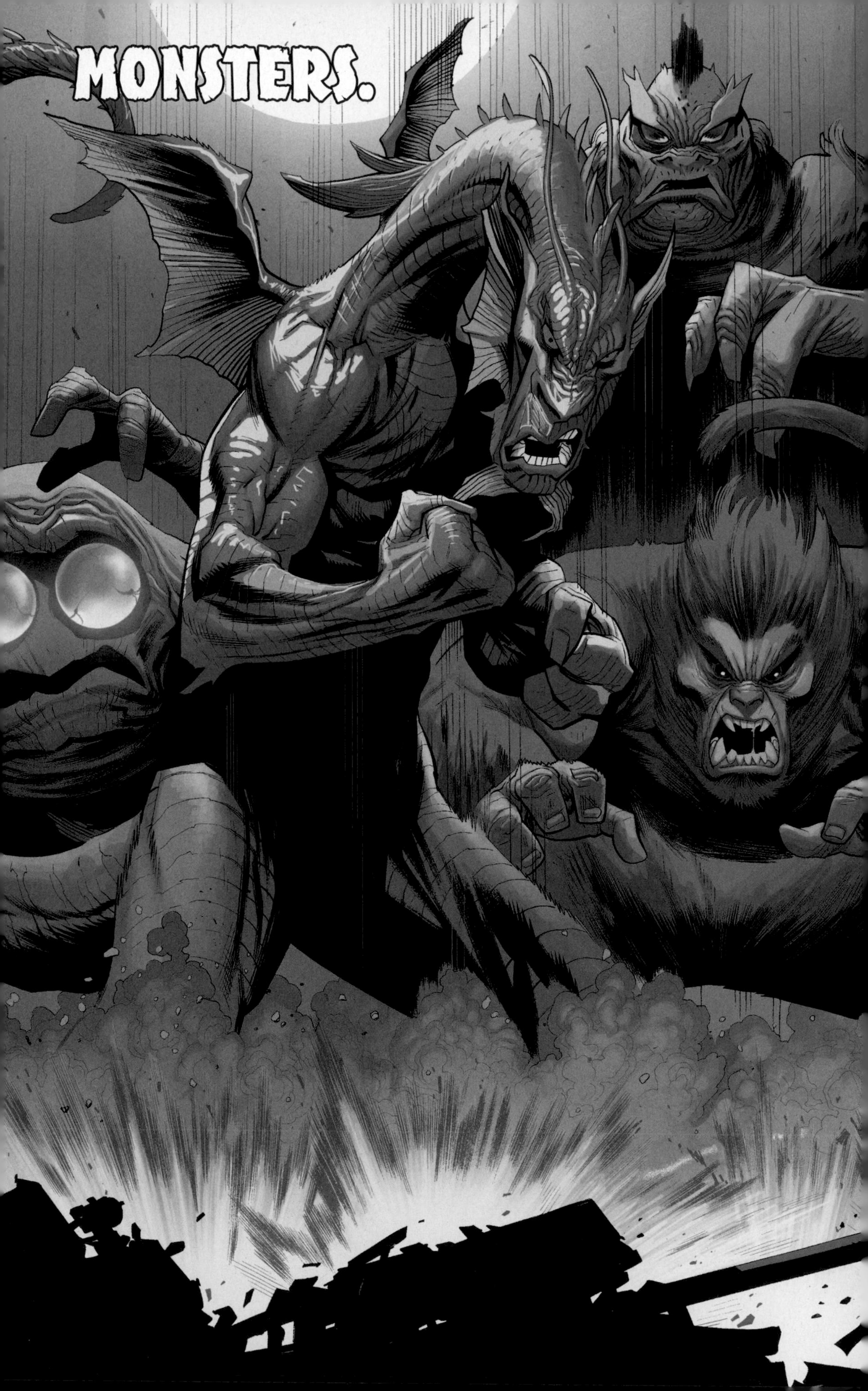
MONSTERS.

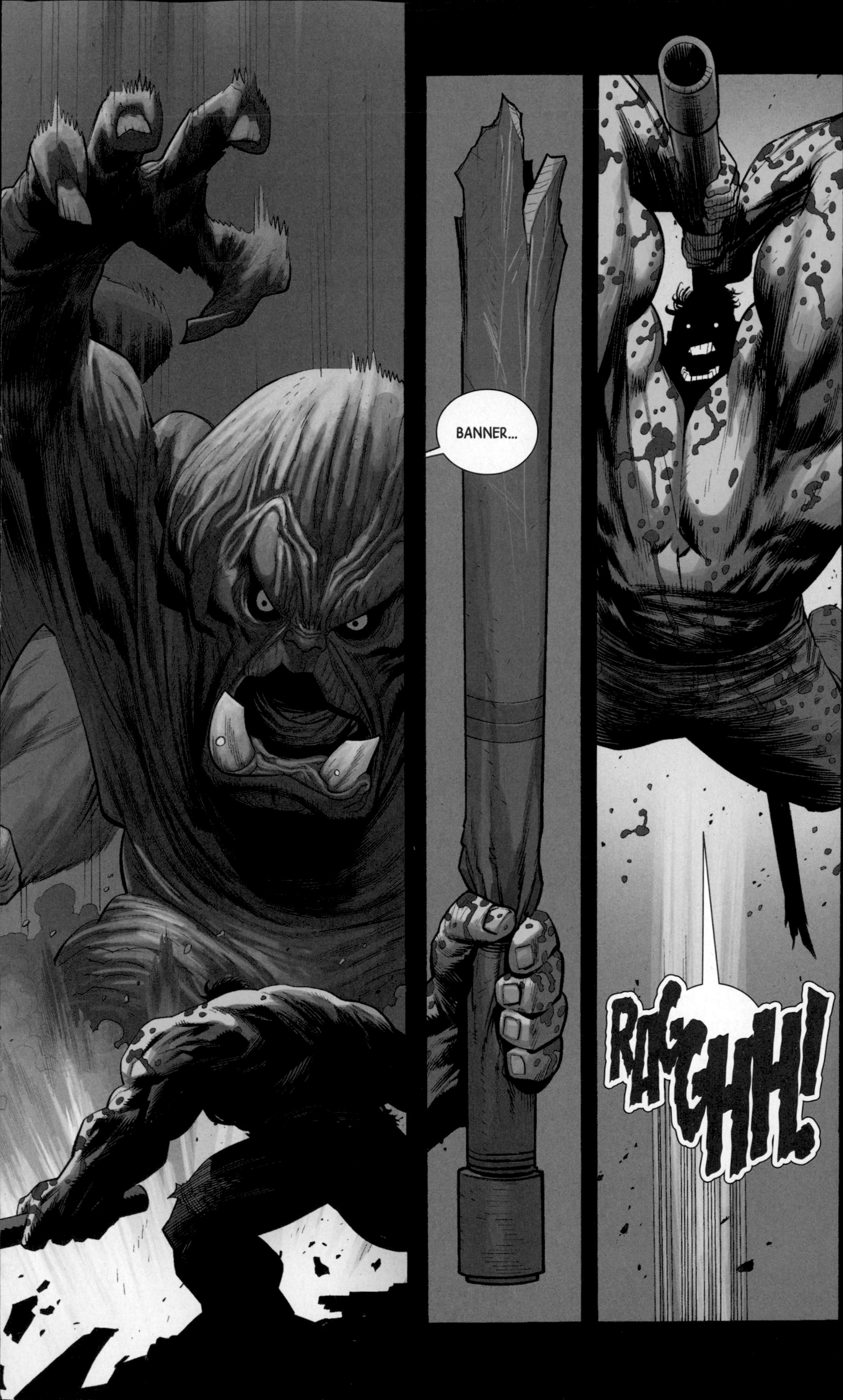
BANNER...
RAGHH!

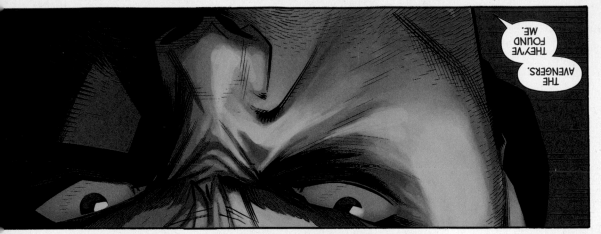

THE AVENGERS. THEY'VE FOUND ME.

GAMMA RADIATION, SIR.

SCANNED? FOR WHAT?

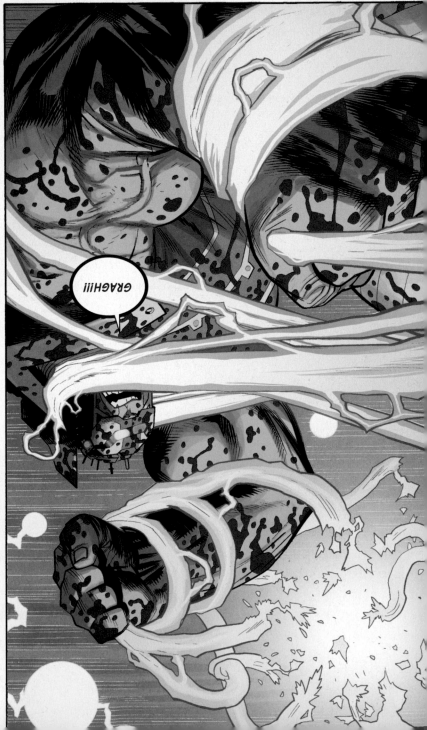

GRAGH!!!

THE ORIGIN OF THE ENERGY IS UNKNOWN.

BUT ACCORDING TO OUR SENSORS...

"...WE ARE BEING SCANNED.

OKAY, NOW WHAT THE HELL IS THIS THING ATTACKING US?

YES, SIR. ENGINES AT TWENTY PERCENT AND HOLDING.

BETTER?

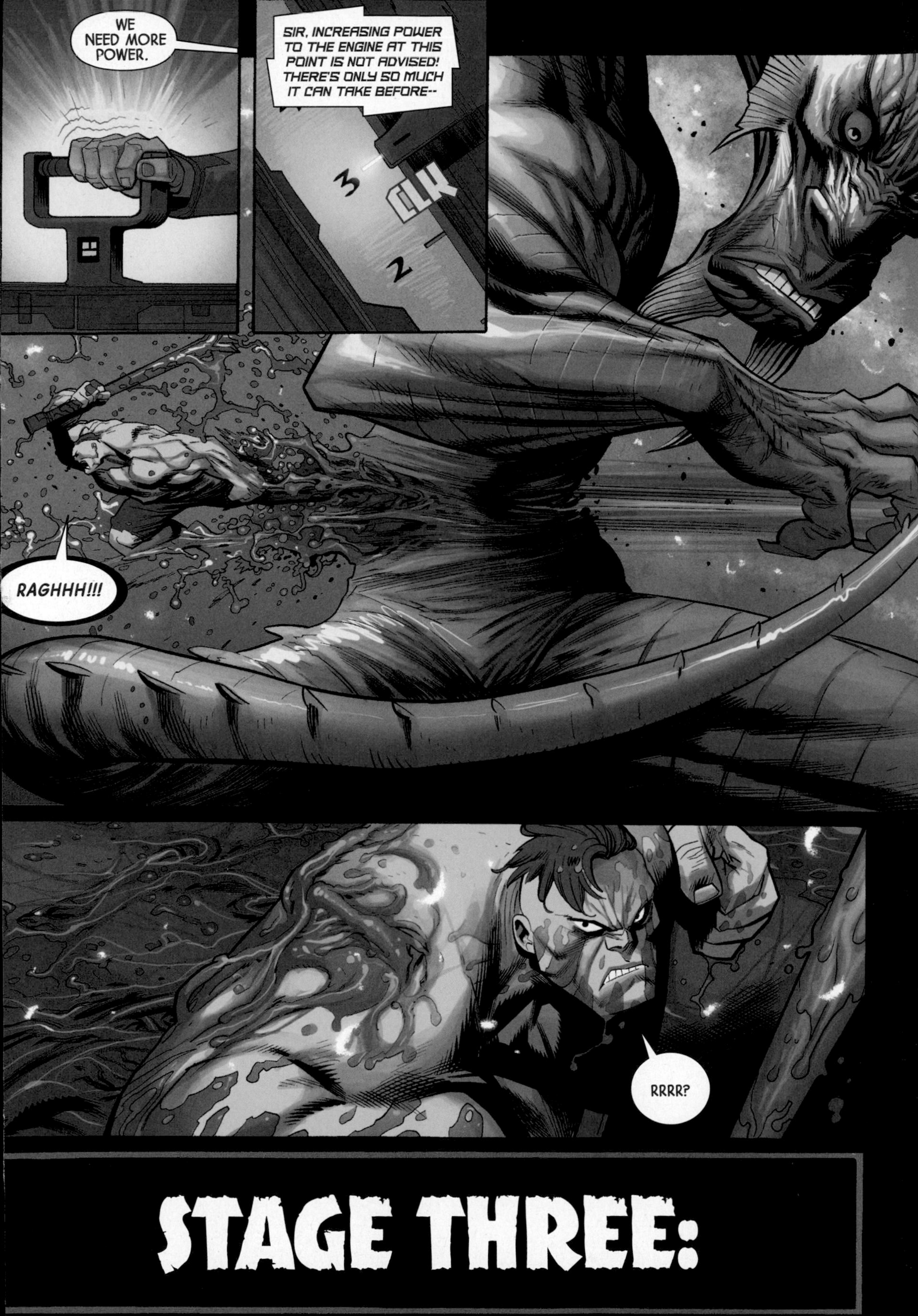
WE NEED MORE POWER.
SIR, INCREASING POWER TO THE ENGINE AT THIS POINT IS NOT ADVISED! THERE'S ONLY SO MUCH IT CAN TAKE BEFORE--
3
CLR
2
RAGHHH!!!
RRRR?
STAGE THREE:

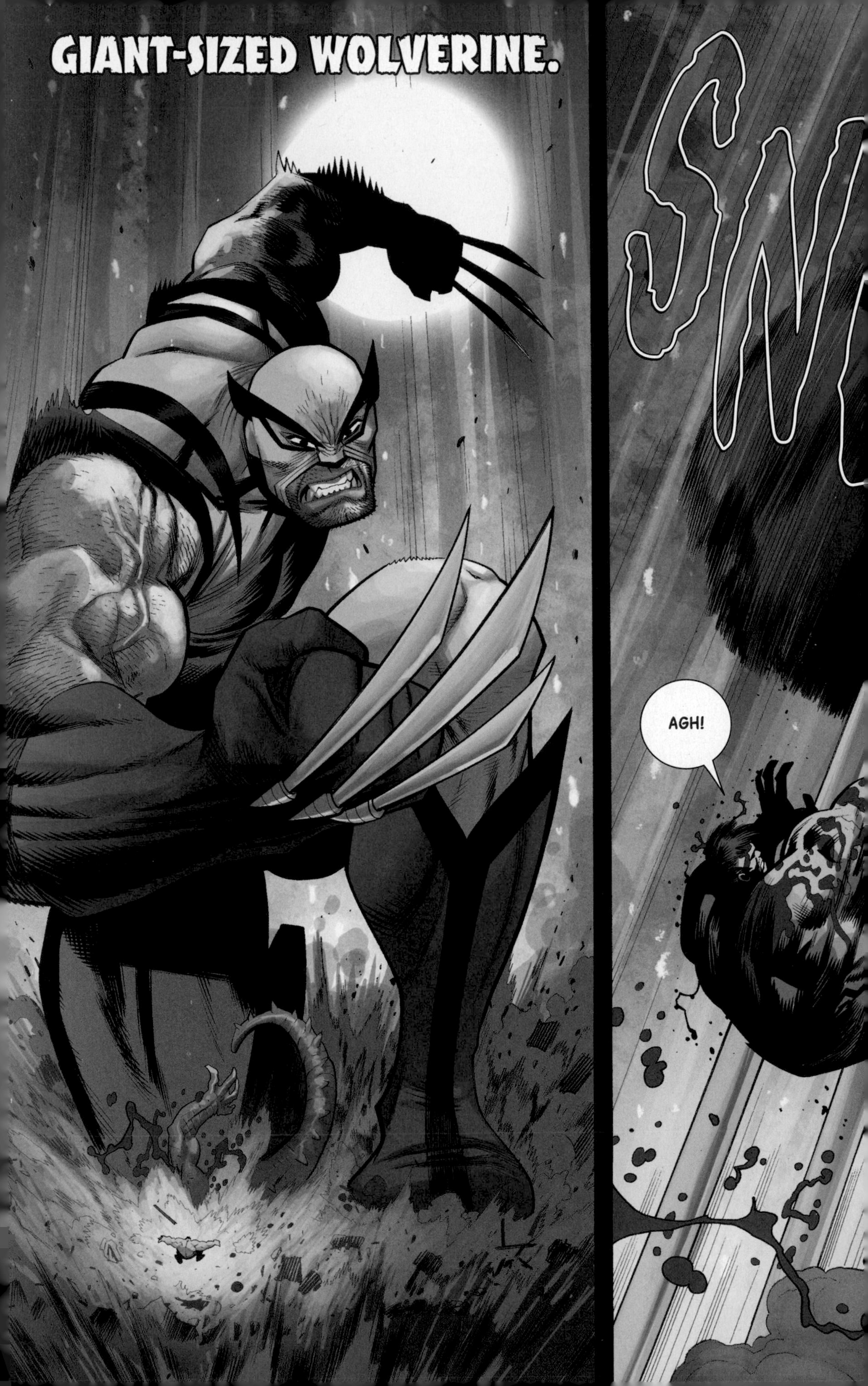
GIANT-SIZED WOLVERINE.
SN
AGH!

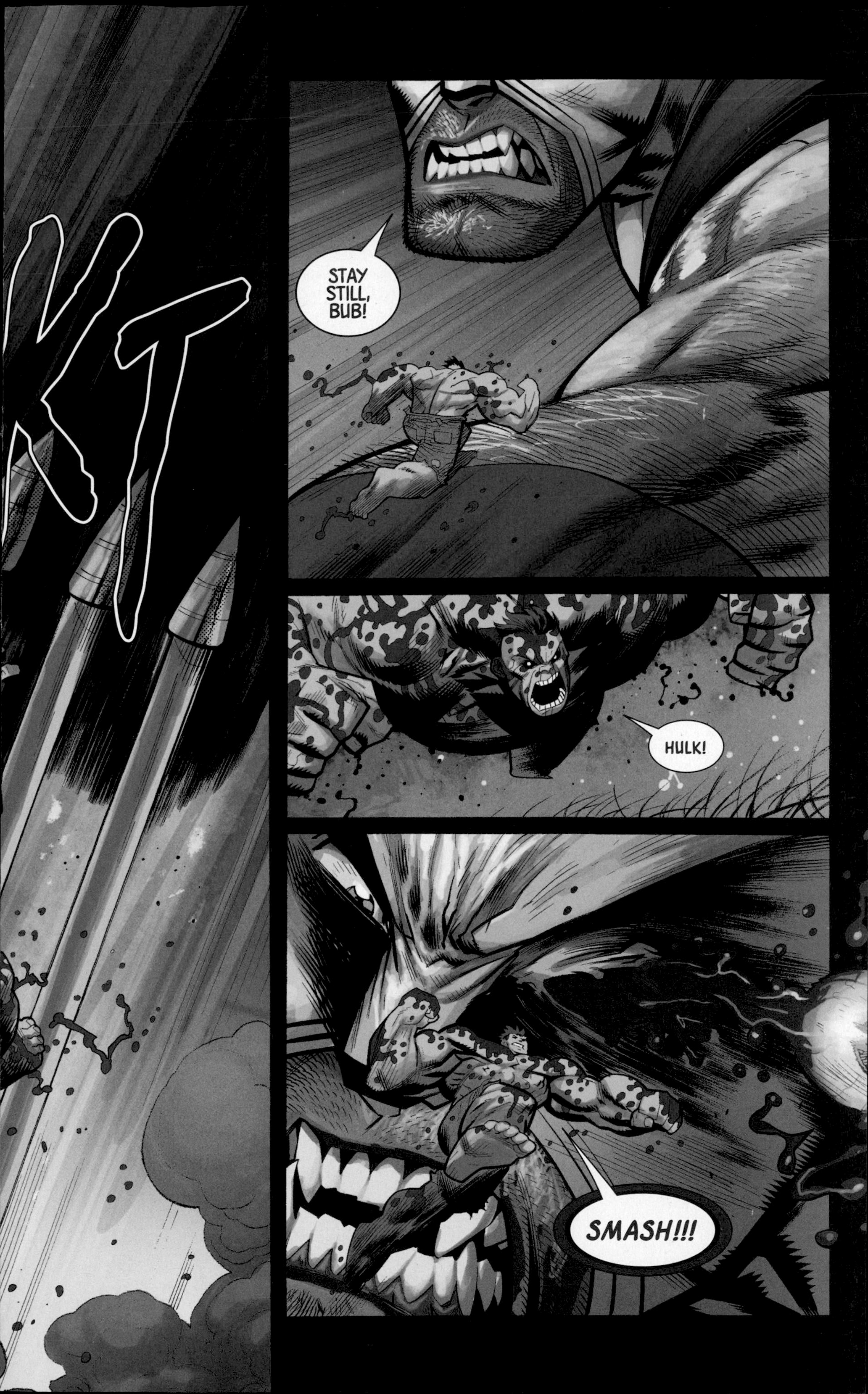
STAY STILL, BUB!
HULK!
SMASH!!!

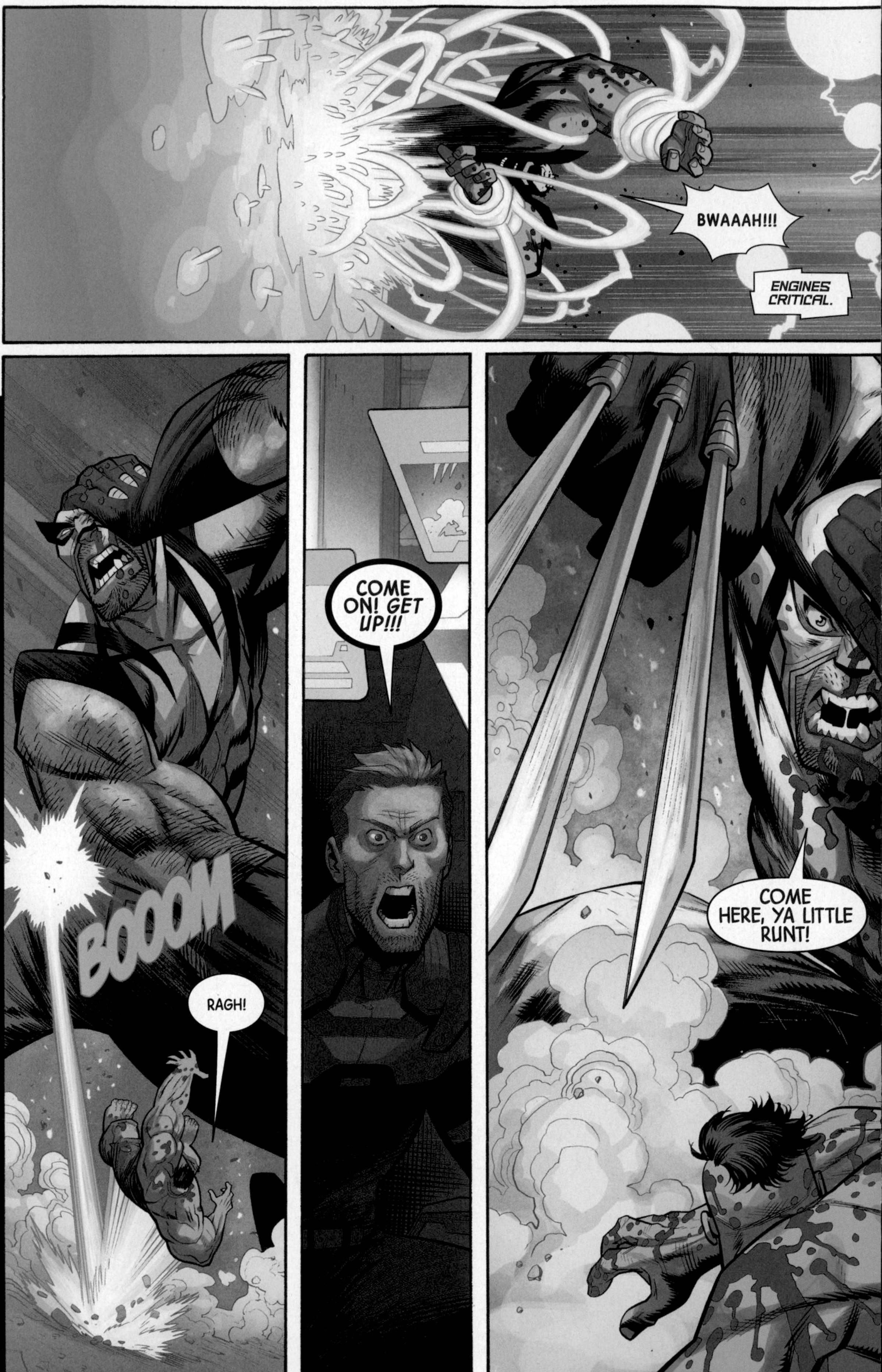
BWAAAH!!!
ENGINES CRITICAL.
BOOOM
RAGH!
COME ON! GET UP!!!
COME HERE, YA LITTLE RUNT!

YOU'RE GOING TO BREAK HIM.
HAGH!!!
SNIKT
YOU'RE WRONG, BETTY.
AGHH!!!
KRAK
HULK!!!
HE'S THE STRONGEST ONE THERE IS.

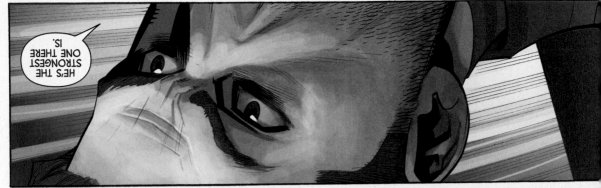

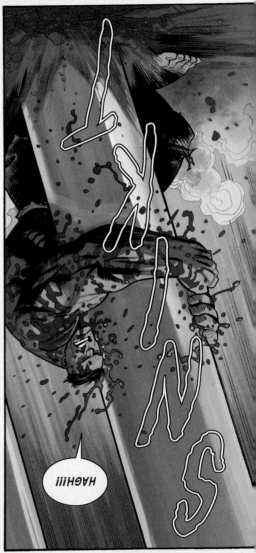

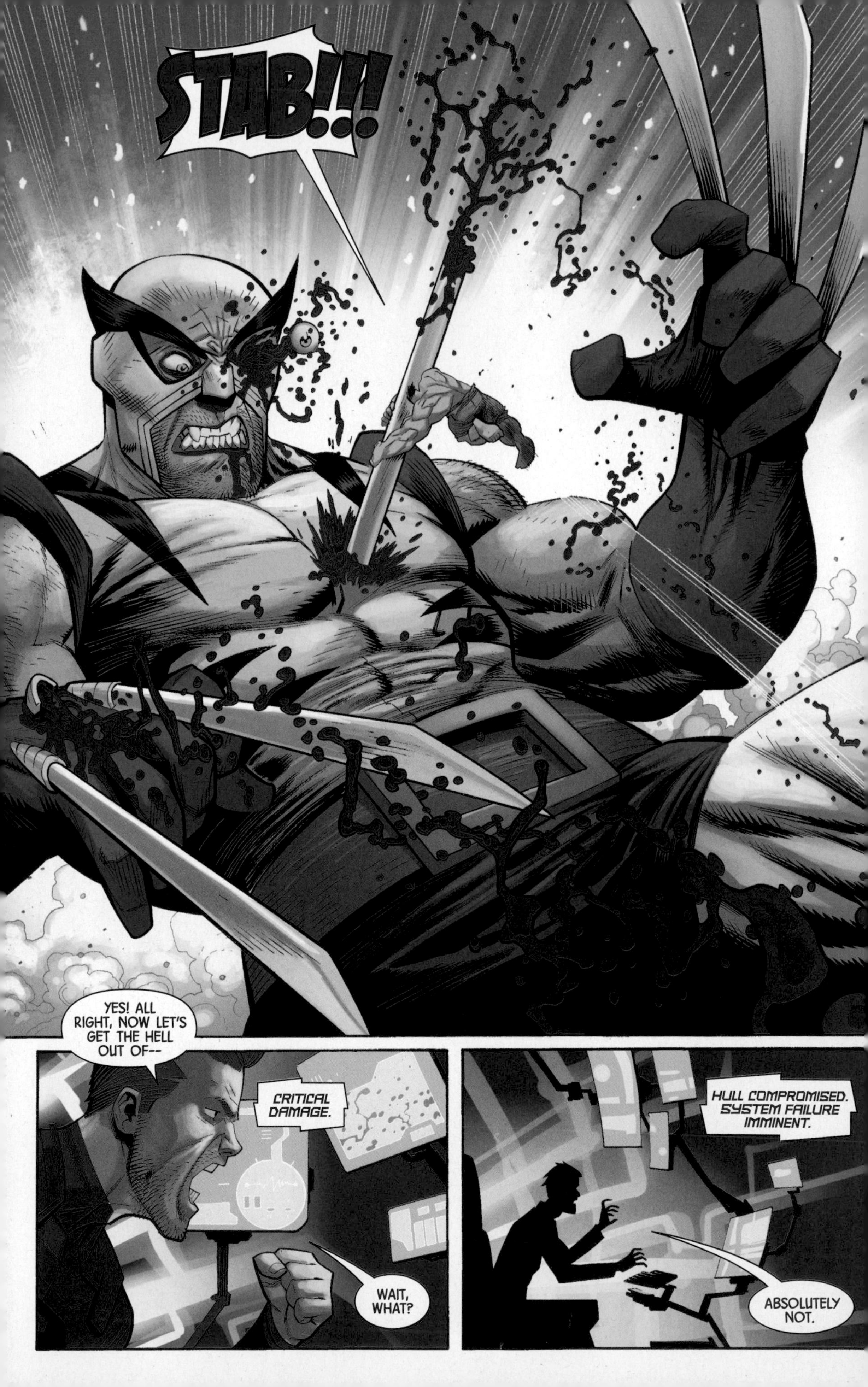
STAB!!!
YES! ALL RIGHT, NOW LET'S GET THE HELL OUT OF--
CRITICAL DAMAGE.
WAIT, WHAT?
HULL COMPROMISED. SYSTEM FAILURE IMMINENT.
ABSOLUTELY NOT.

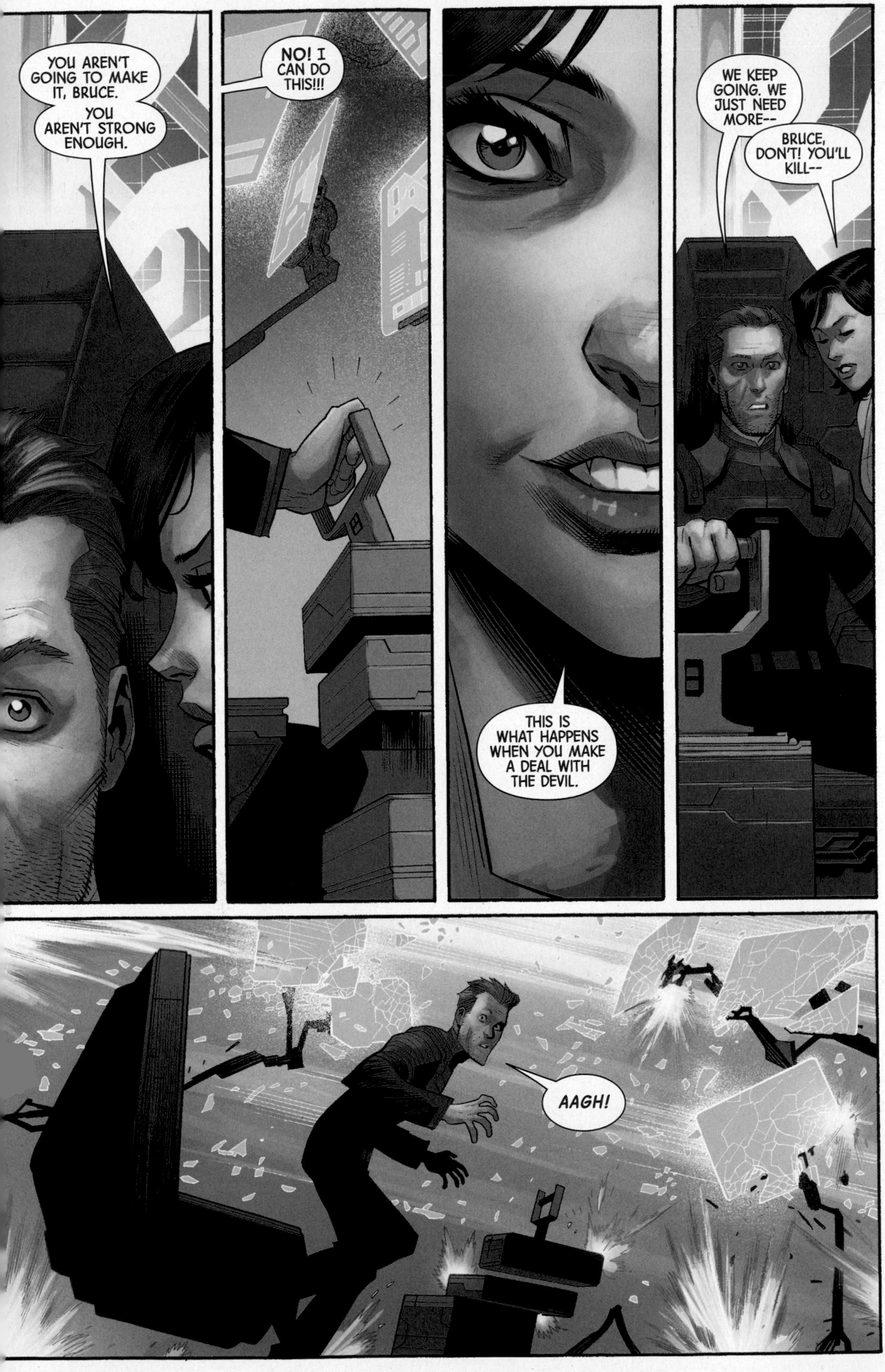
YOU AREN'T GOING TO MAKE IT, BRUCE.
YOU AREN'T STRONG ENOUGH.
NO! I CAN DO THIS!!!
THIS IS WHAT HAPPENS WHEN YOU MAKE A DEAL WITH THE DEVIL.
WE KEEP GOING. WE JUST NEED MORE--
BRUCE, DON'T! YOU'LL KILL--
AAGH!

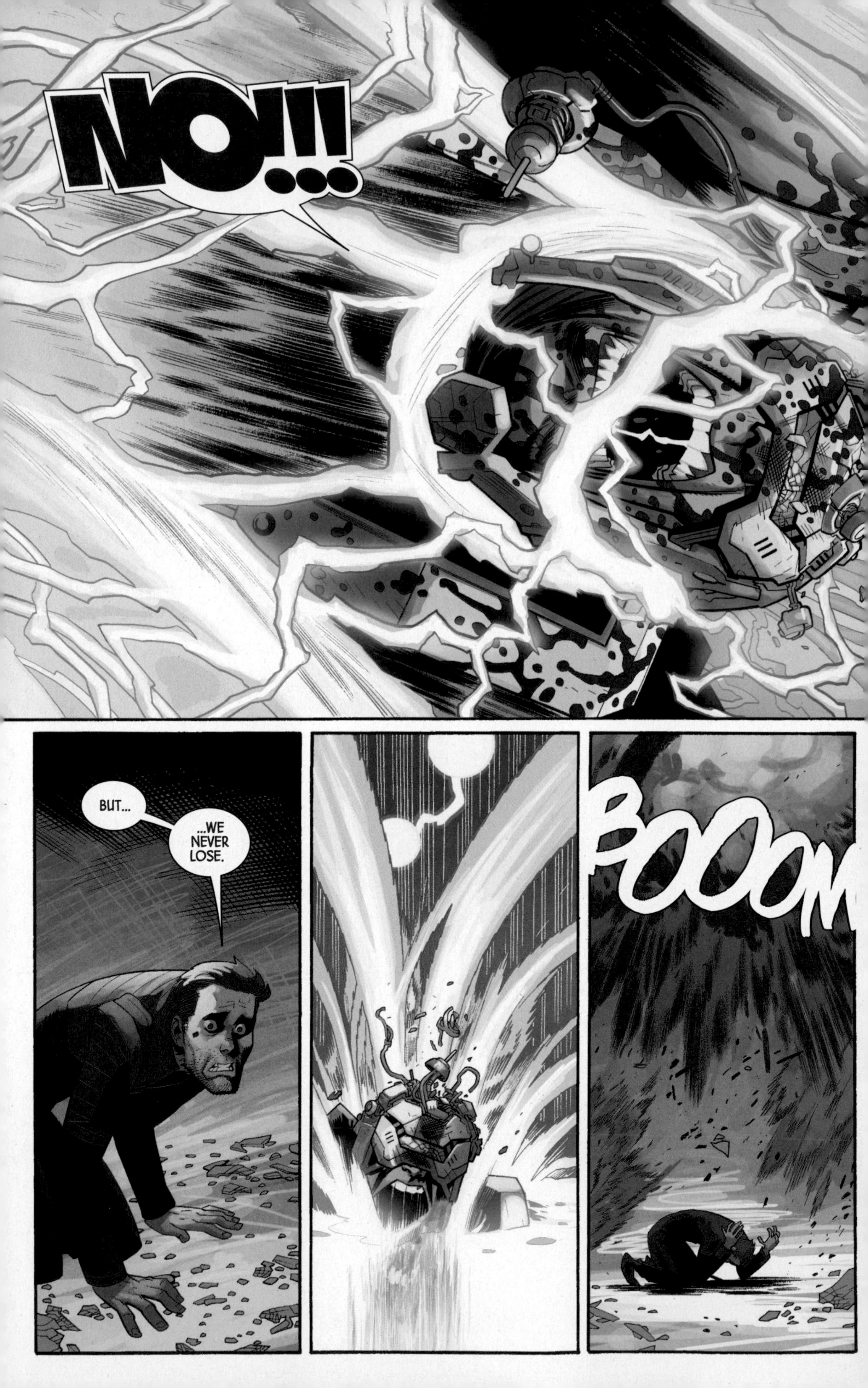
NO!!!...
BUT...
...WE NEVER LOSE.
BOOOM

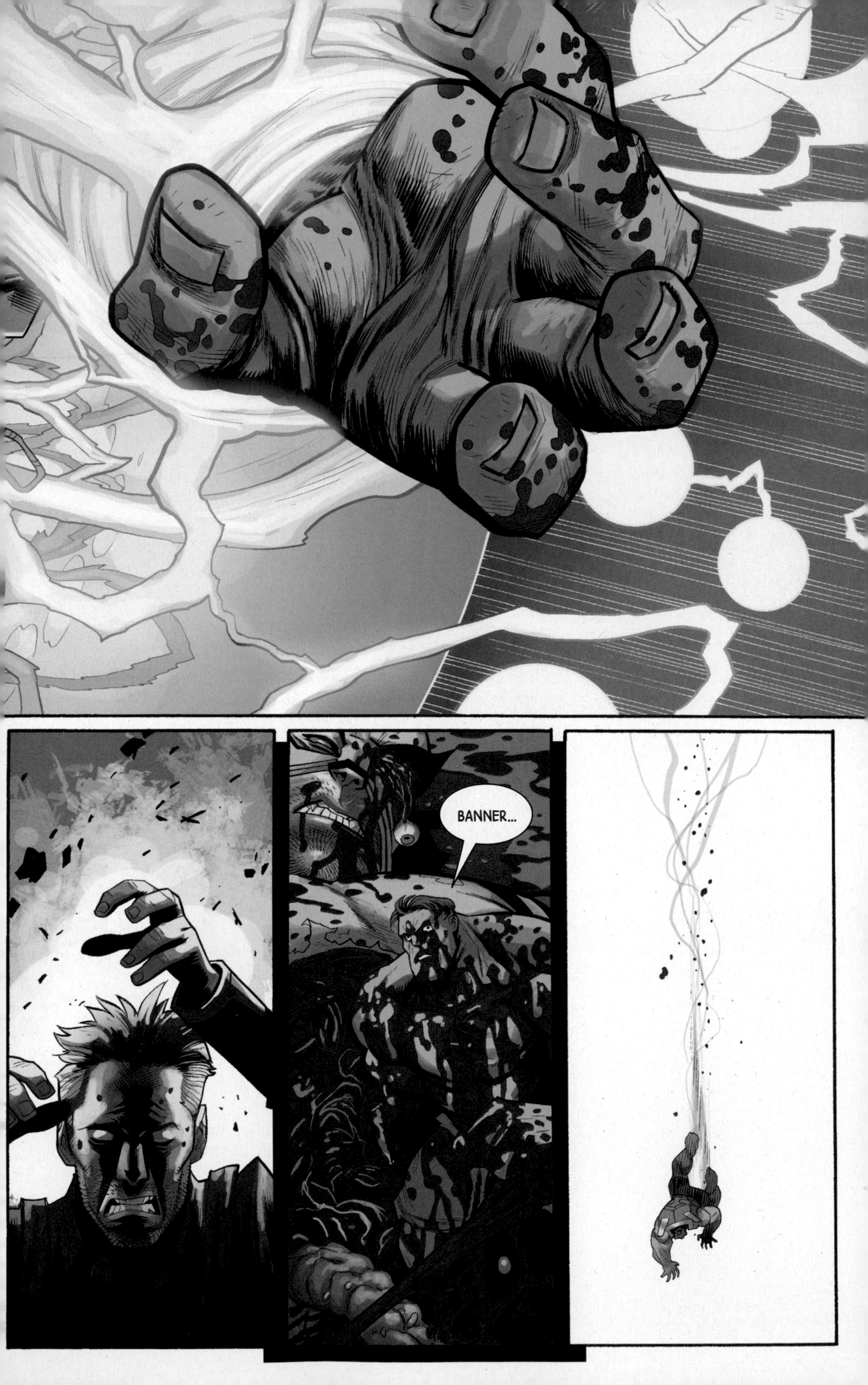
BANNER...

AGH!
WHAT...
WHAT IS THIS? WHERE ARE WE?
WH--? HEY. HEY, LET ME OUT!
LET ME OUT!!!

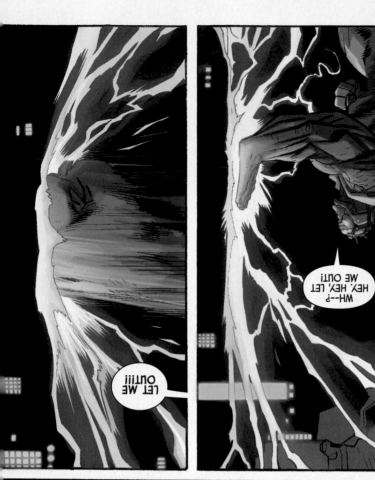

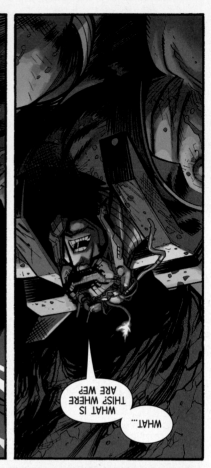

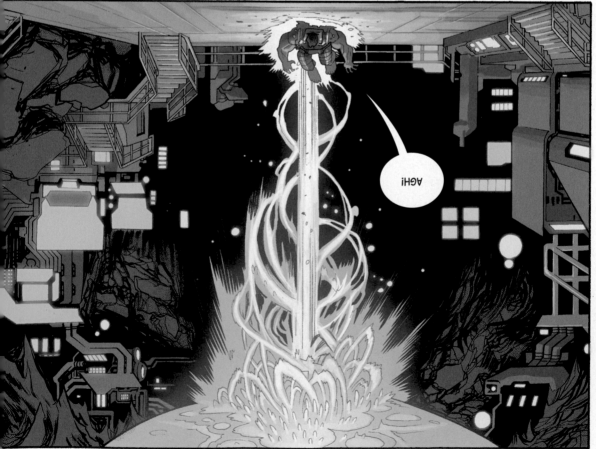

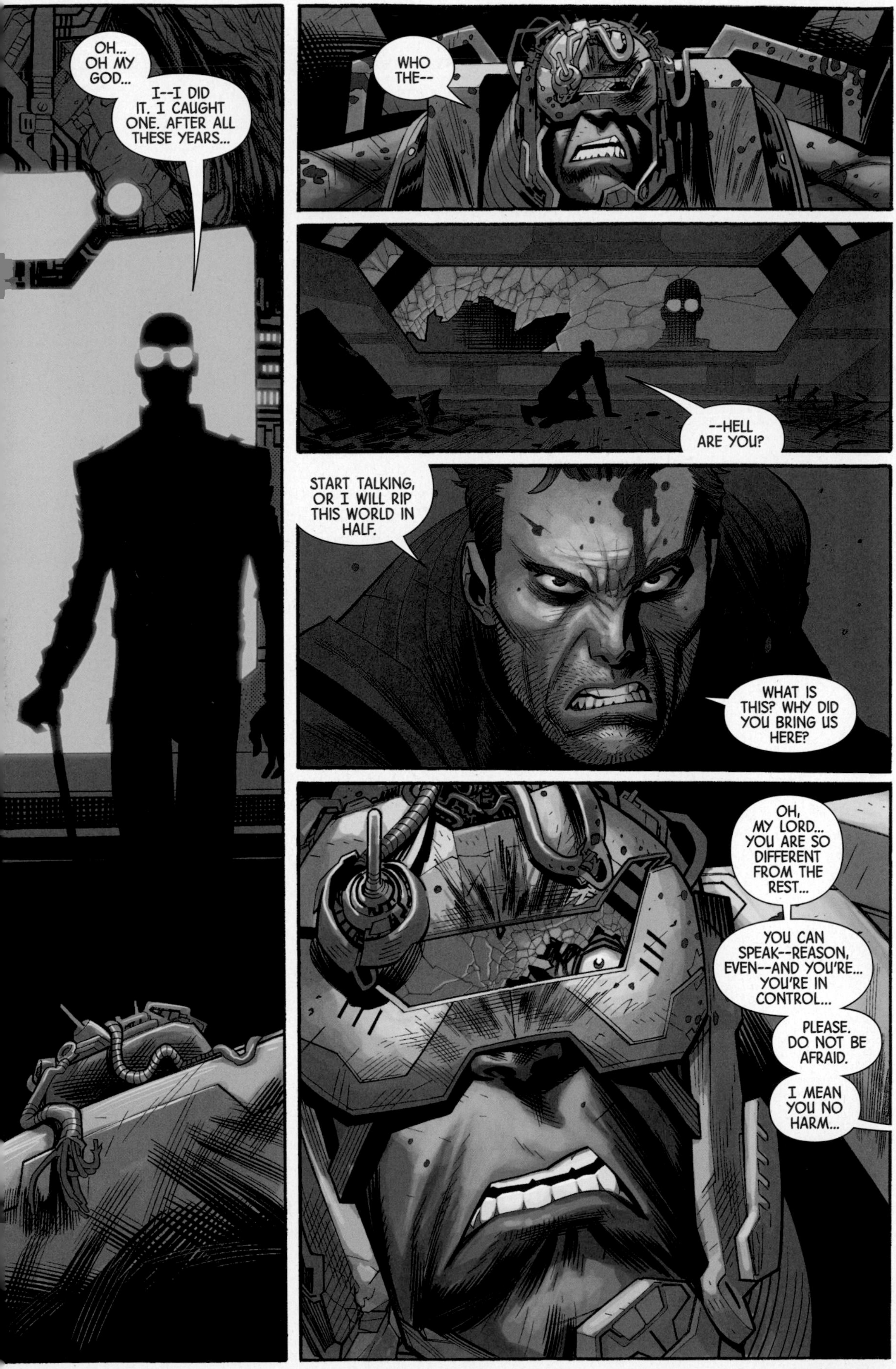
OH... OH MY GOD...
I--I DID IT. I CAUGHT ONE. AFTER ALL THESE YEARS...
WHO THE--
--HELL ARE YOU?
START TALKING, OR I WILL RIP THIS WORLD IN HALF.
WHAT IS THIS? WHY DID YOU BRING US HERE?
OH, MY LORD... YOU ARE SO DIFFERENT FROM THE REST...
YOU CAN SPEAK--REASON, EVEN--AND YOU'RE... YOU'RE IN CONTROL...
PLEASE. DO NOT BE AFRAID.
I MEAN YOU NO HARM...

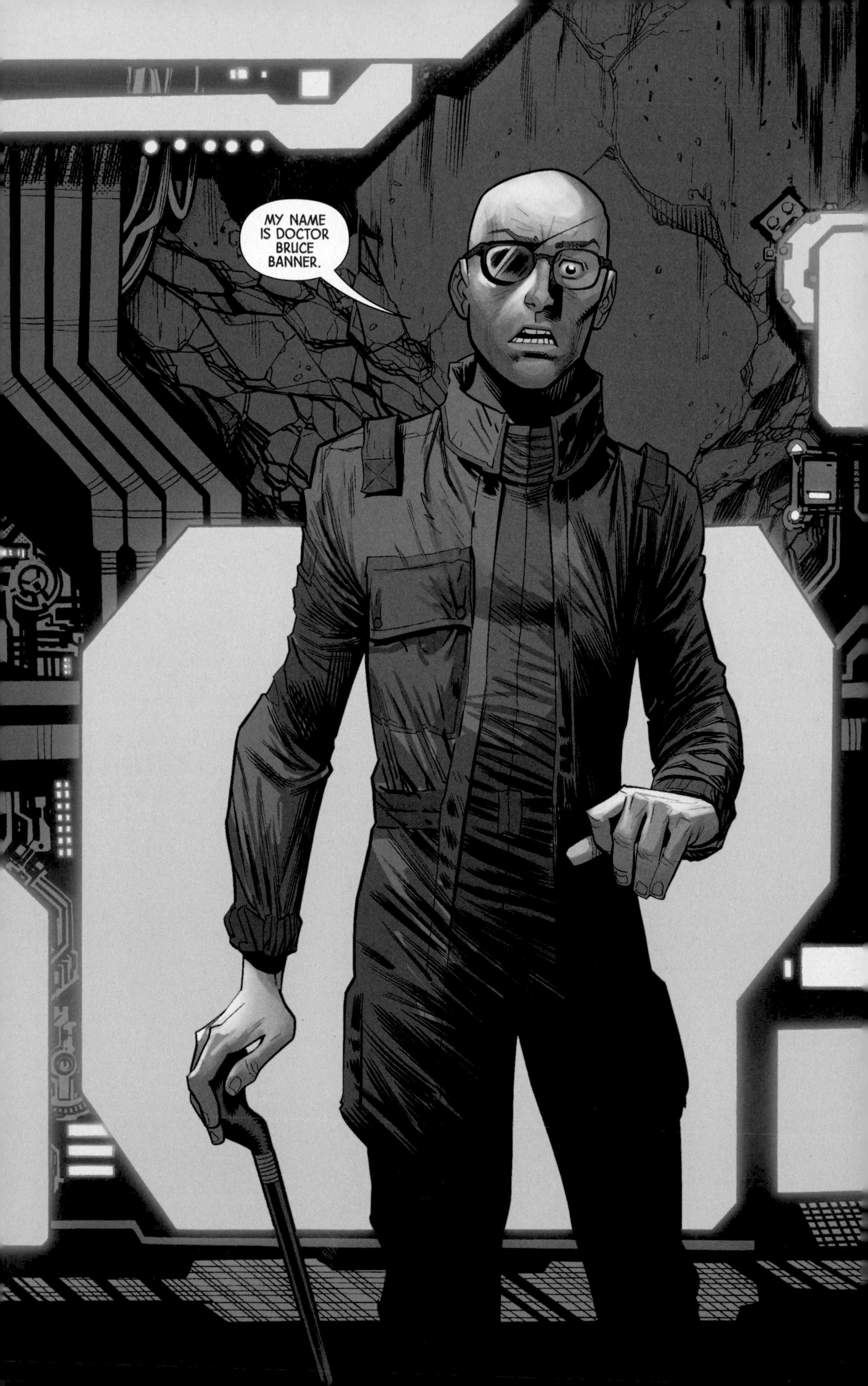
MY NAME IS DOCTOR BRUCE BANNER.

#1 VARIANT BY **ARTHUR ADAMS** & **LAURA MARTIN**

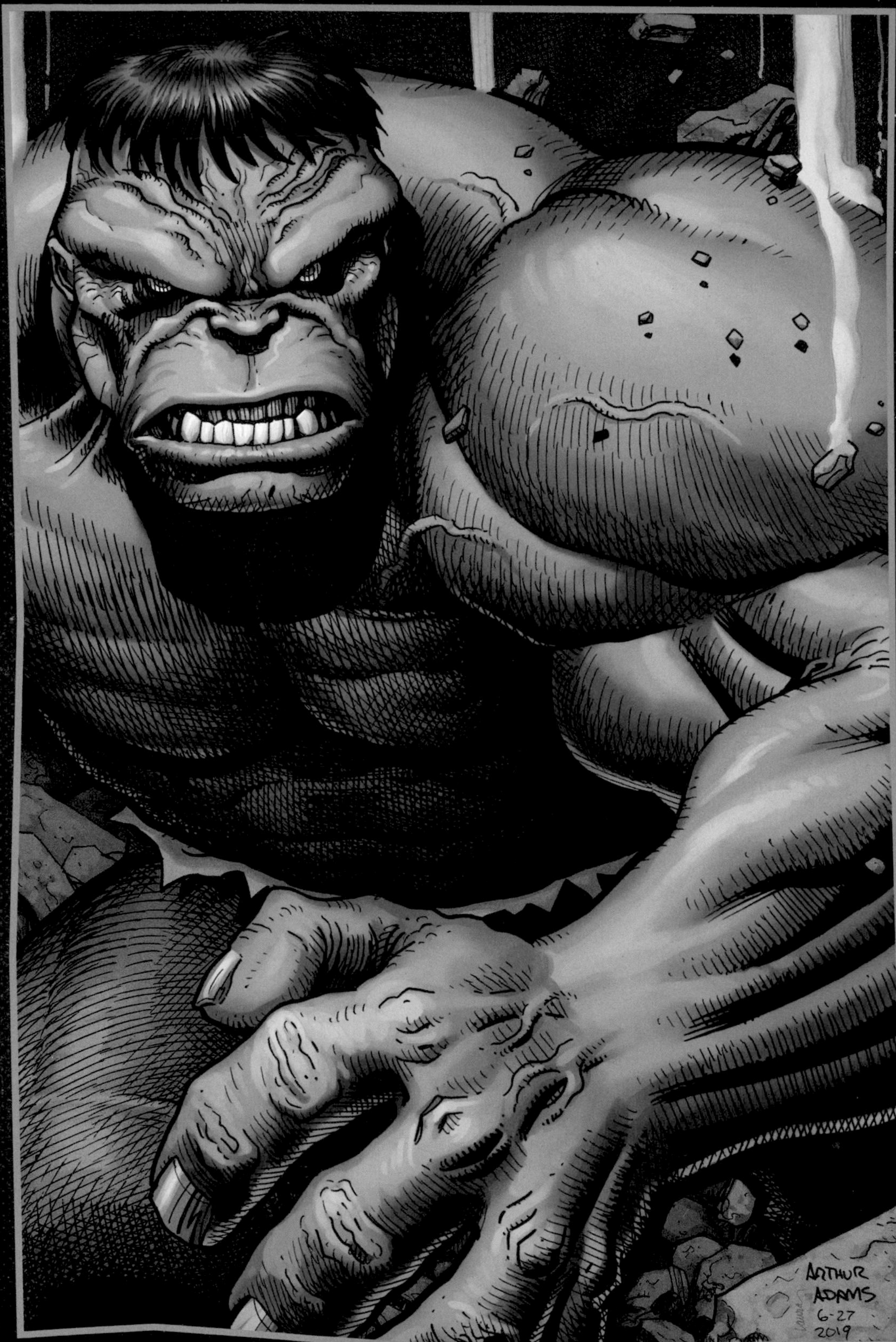
ARTHUR ADAMS 6-27 2019

R. OTTLEY

HULK
NUMBER 3

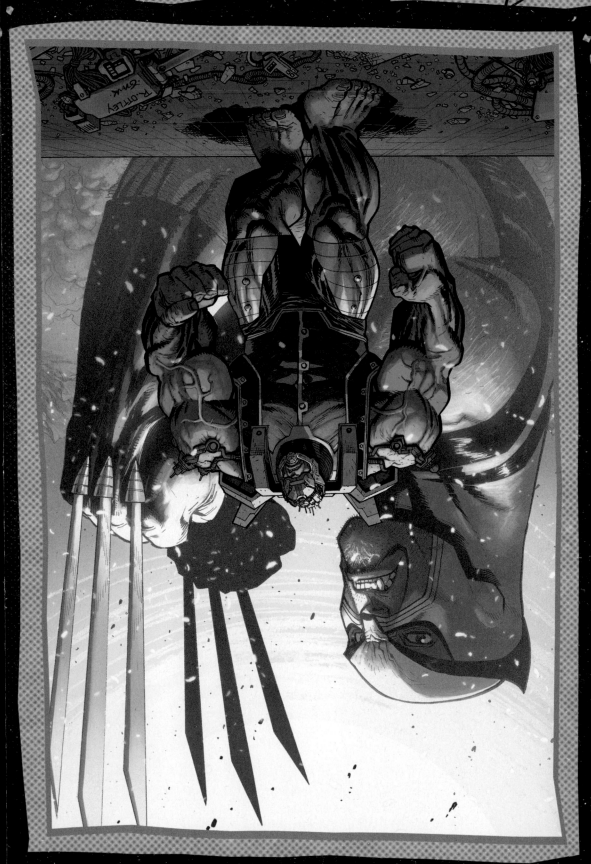

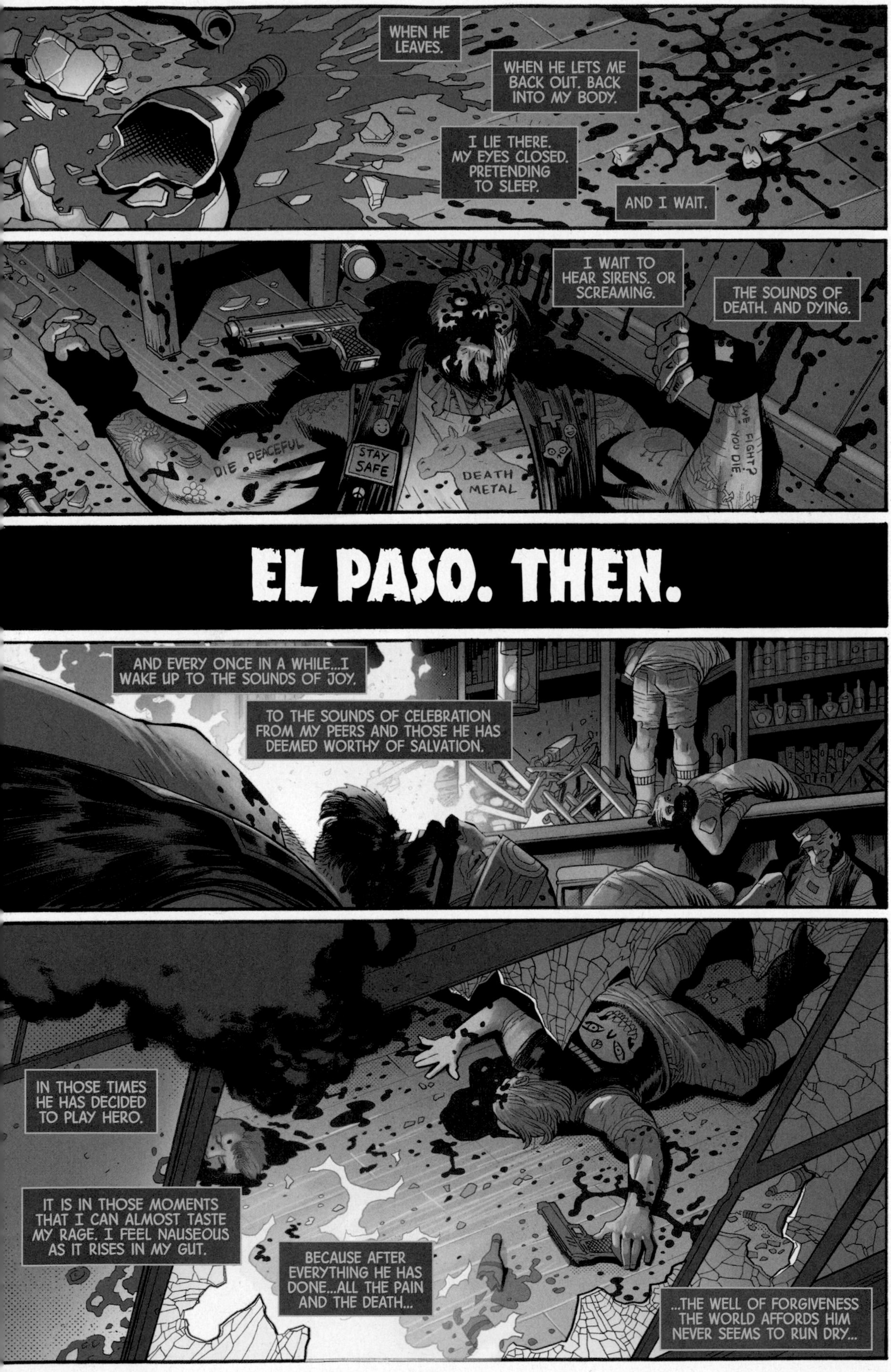
WHEN HE LEAVES.
WHEN HE LETS ME BACK OUT. BACK INTO MY BODY.
I LIE THERE. MY EYES CLOSED. PRETENDING TO SLEEP.
AND I WAIT.
I WAIT TO HEAR SIRENS. OR SCREAMING.
THE SOUNDS OF DEATH. AND DYING.
DIE PEACEFUL
STAY SAFE
DEATH METAL
WE FIGHT? YOU DIE
EL PASO. THEN.
AND EVERY ONCE IN A WHILE...I WAKE UP TO THE SOUNDS OF JOY.
TO THE SOUNDS OF CELEBRATION FROM MY PEERS AND THOSE HE HAS DEEMED WORTHY OF SALVATION.
IN THOSE TIMES HE HAS DECIDED TO PLAY HERO.
IT IS IN THOSE MOMENTS THAT I CAN ALMOST TASTE MY RAGE. I FEEL NAUSEOUS AS IT RISES IN MY GUT.
BECAUSE AFTER EVERYTHING HE HAS DONE...ALL THE PAIN AND THE DEATH...
...THE WELL OF FORGIVENESS THE WORLD AFFORDS HIM NEVER SEEMS TO RUN DRY...

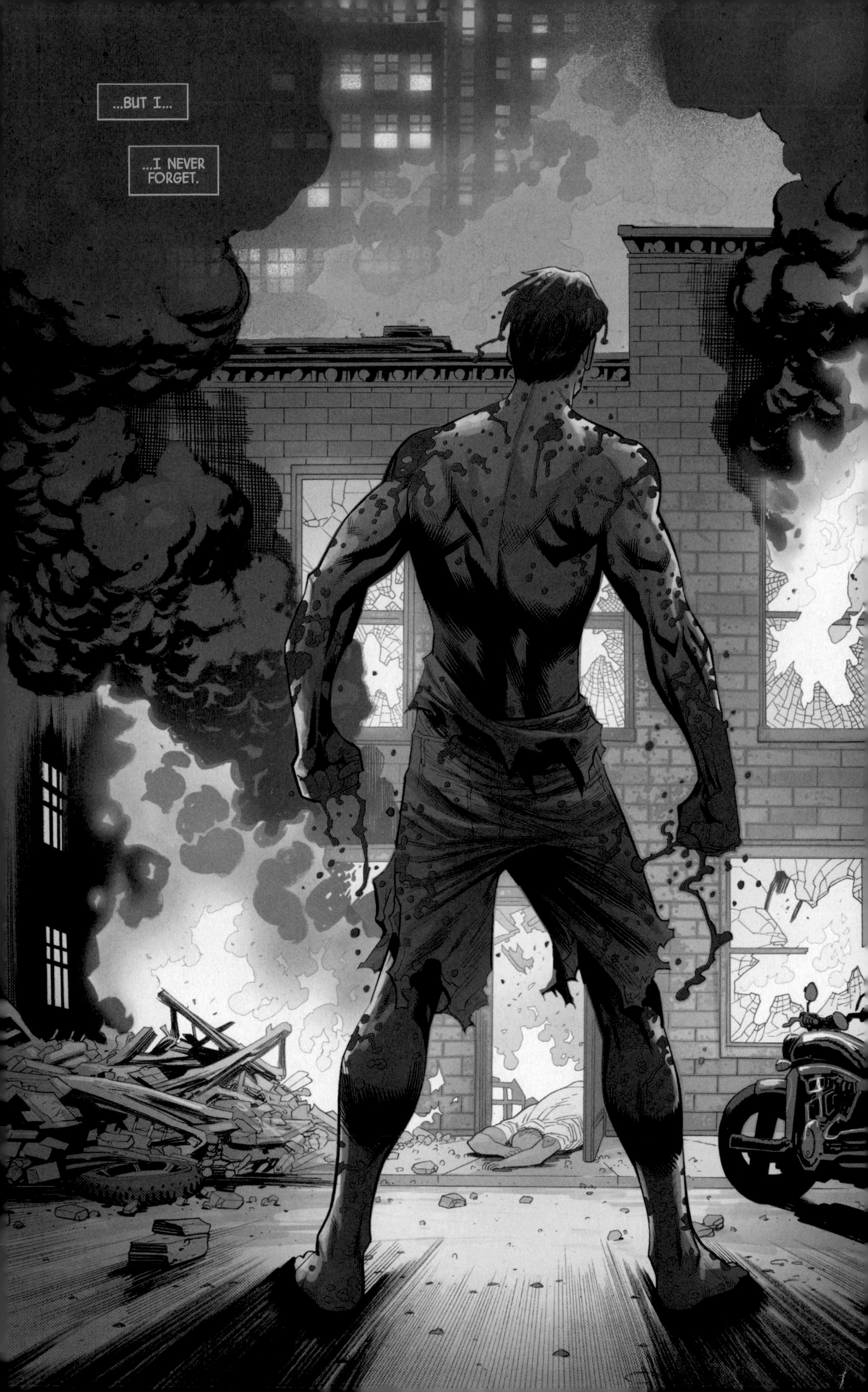
...BUT I...
...I NEVER FORGET.

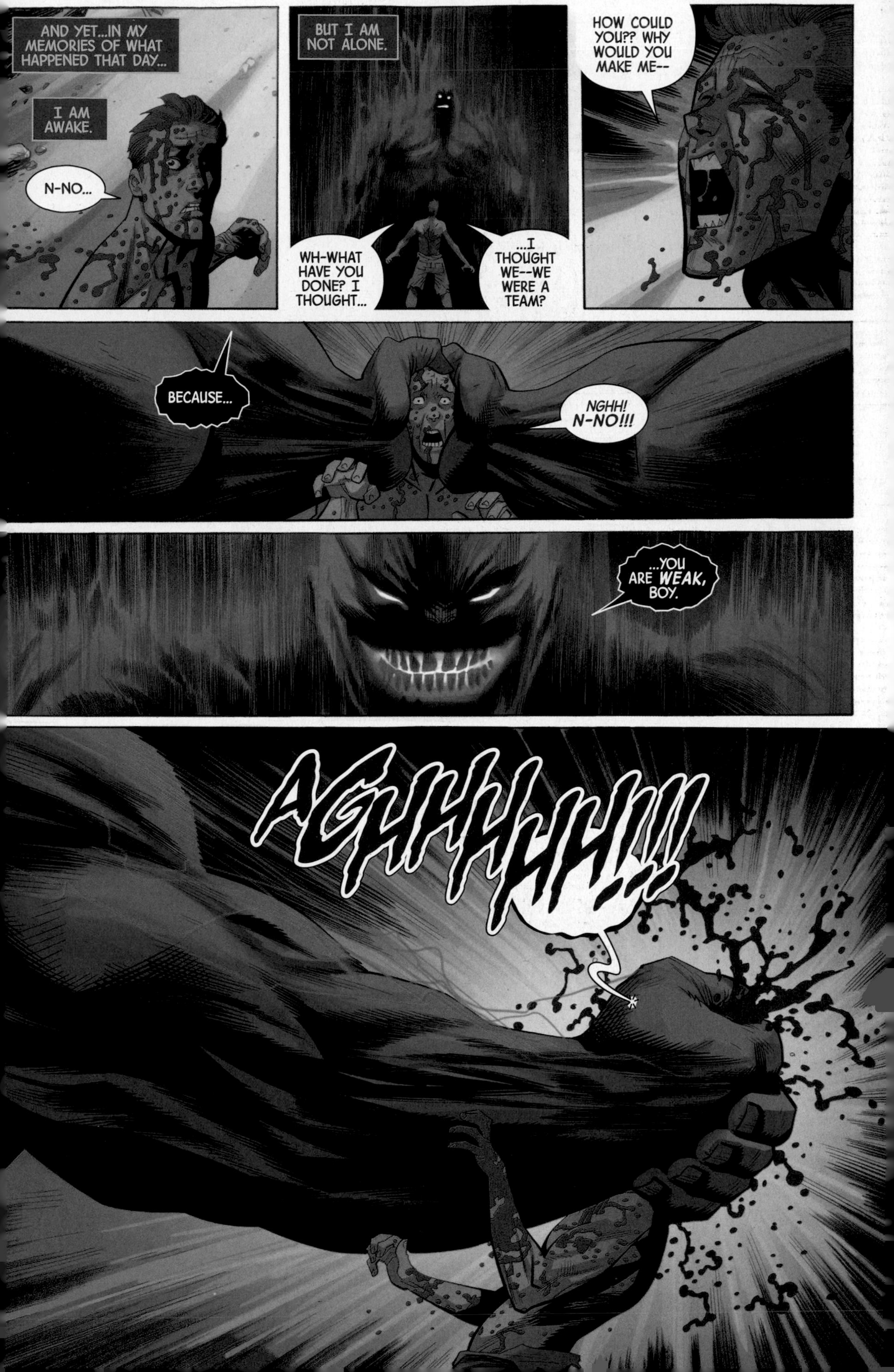
AND YET...IN MY MEMORIES OF WHAT HAPPENED THAT DAY...
I AM AWAKE.
N-NO...
BUT I AM NOT ALONE.
WH-WHAT HAVE YOU DONE? I THOUGHT...
...I THOUGHT WE--WE WERE A TEAM?
HOW COULD YOU?? WHY WOULD YOU MAKE ME--
BECAUSE...
NGHH! N-NO!!!
...YOU ARE WEAK, BOY.
AGHHHHH!!!

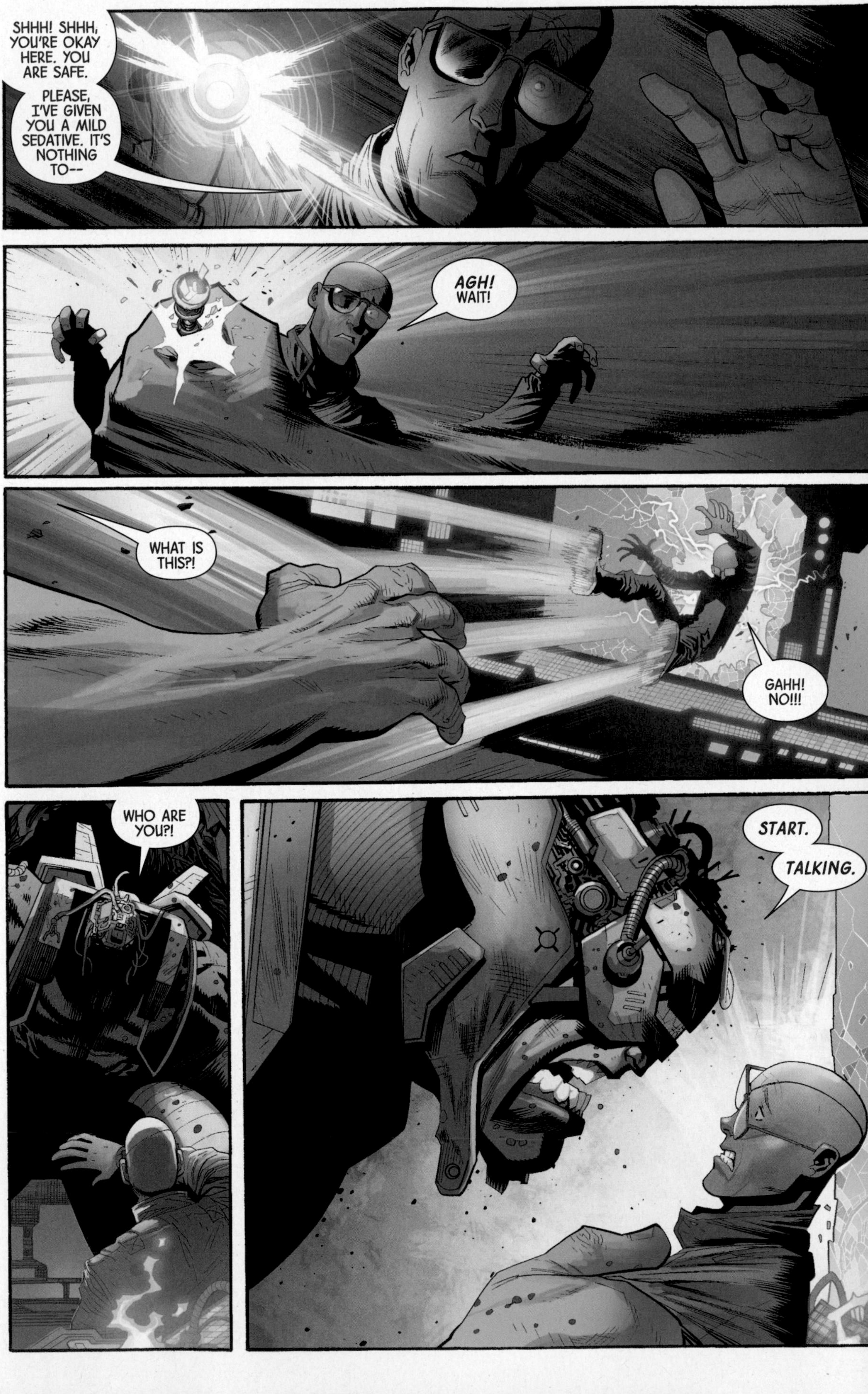
SHHH! SHHH, YOU'RE OKAY HERE. YOU ARE SAFE.
PLEASE, I'VE GIVEN YOU A MILD SEDATIVE. IT'S NOTHING TO--
AGH! WAIT!
WHAT IS THIS?!
GAHH! NO!!!
WHO ARE YOU?!
START.
TALKING.

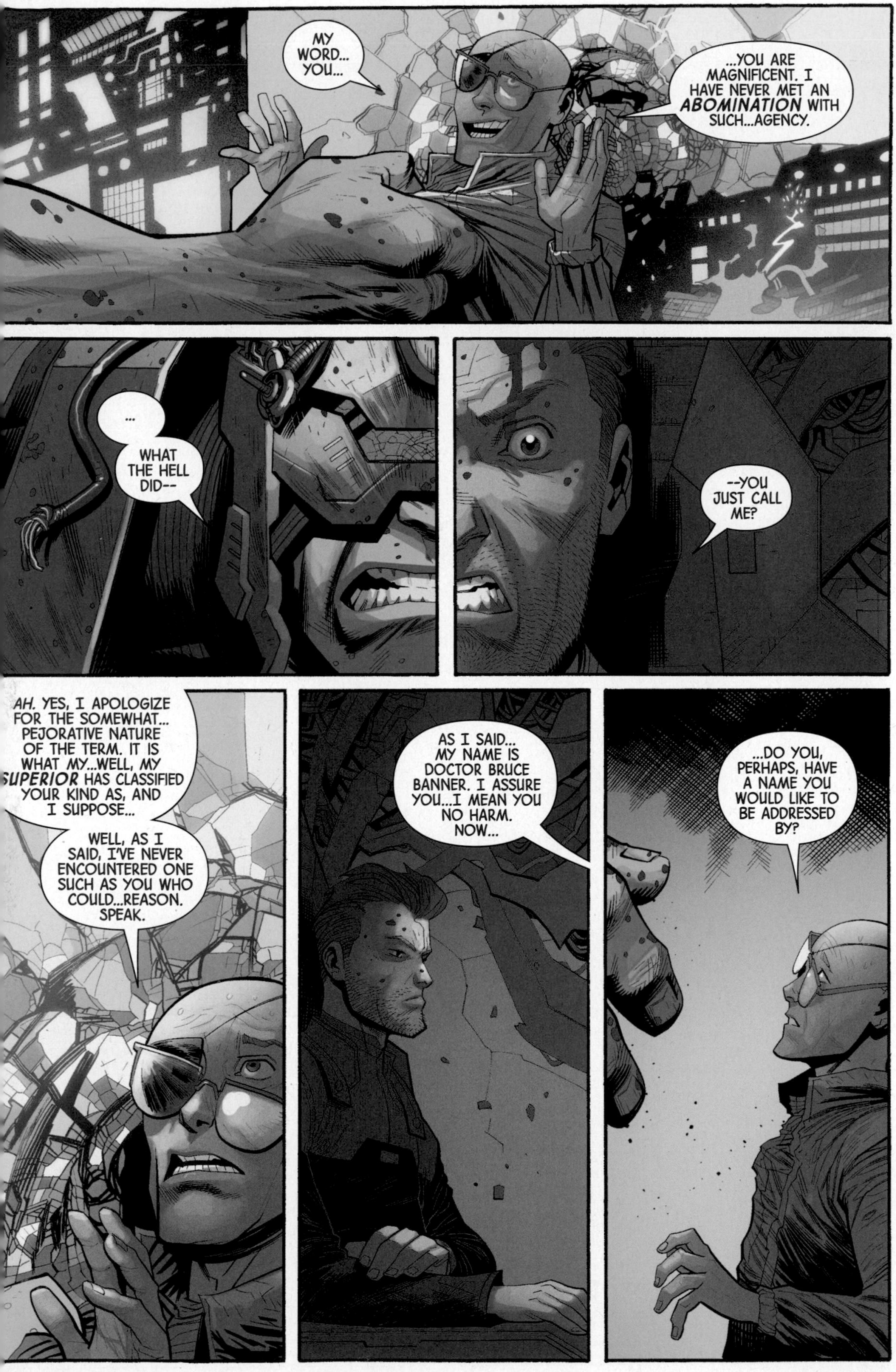
MY WORD... YOU...
...YOU ARE MAGNIFICENT. I HAVE NEVER MET AN ABOMINATION WITH SUCH...AGENCY.
... WHAT THE HELL DID--
--YOU JUST CALL ME?
AH. YES, I APOLOGIZE FOR THE SOMEWHAT... PEJORATIVE NATURE OF THE TERM. IT IS WHAT MY...WELL, MY SUPERIOR HAS CLASSIFIED YOUR KIND AS, AND I SUPPOSE...
WELL, AS I SAID, I'VE NEVER ENCOUNTERED ONE SUCH AS YOU WHO COULD...REASON. SPEAK.
AS I SAID... MY NAME IS DOCTOR BRUCE BANNER. I ASSURE YOU...I MEAN YOU NO HARM. NOW...
...DO YOU, PERHAPS, HAVE A NAME YOU WOULD LIKE TO BE ADDRESSED BY?

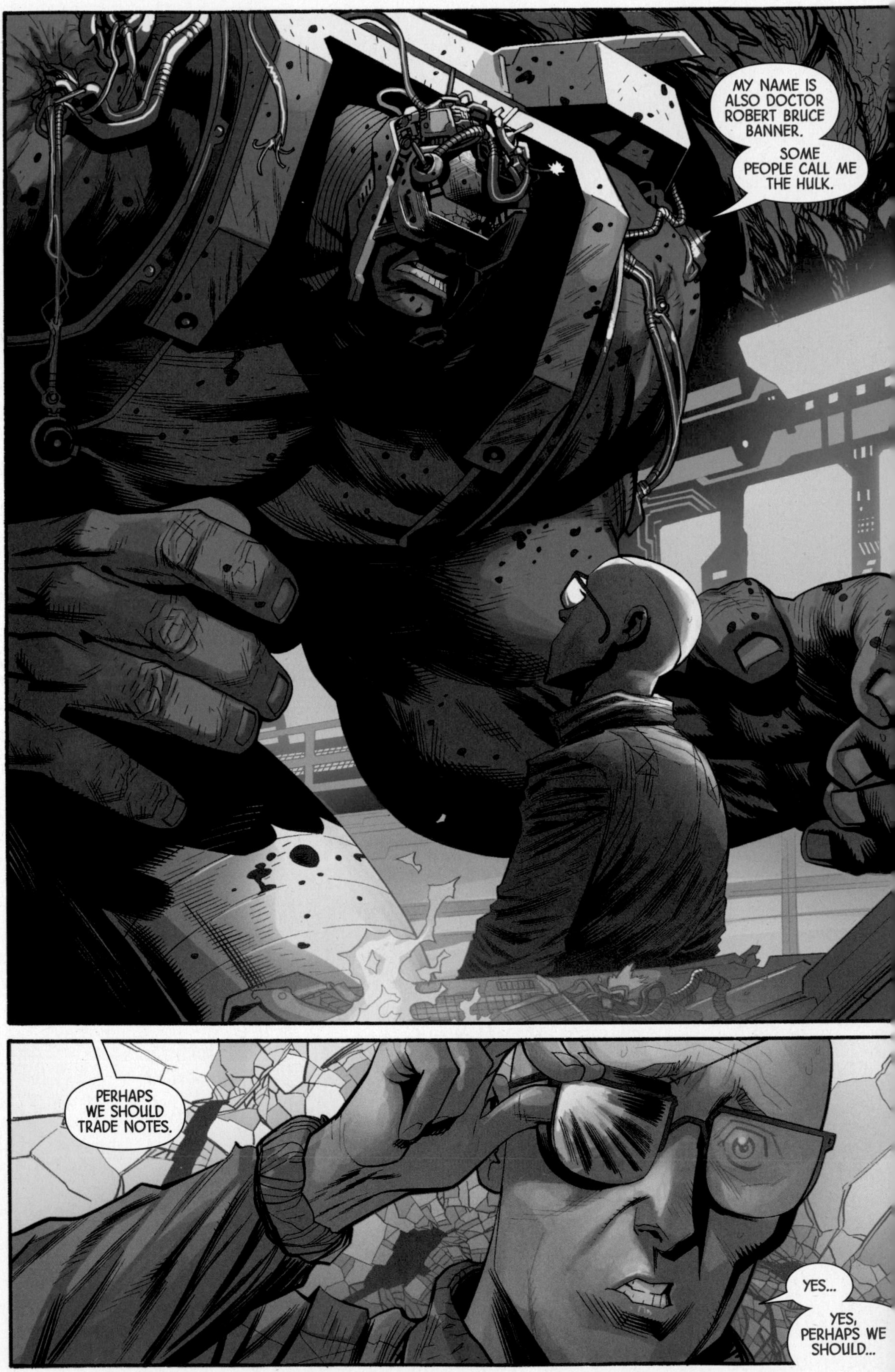
MY NAME IS ALSO DOCTOR ROBERT BRUCE BANNER.
SOME PEOPLE CALL ME THE HULK.
PERHAPS WE SHOULD TRADE NOTES.
YES...
YES, PERHAPS WE SHOULD...

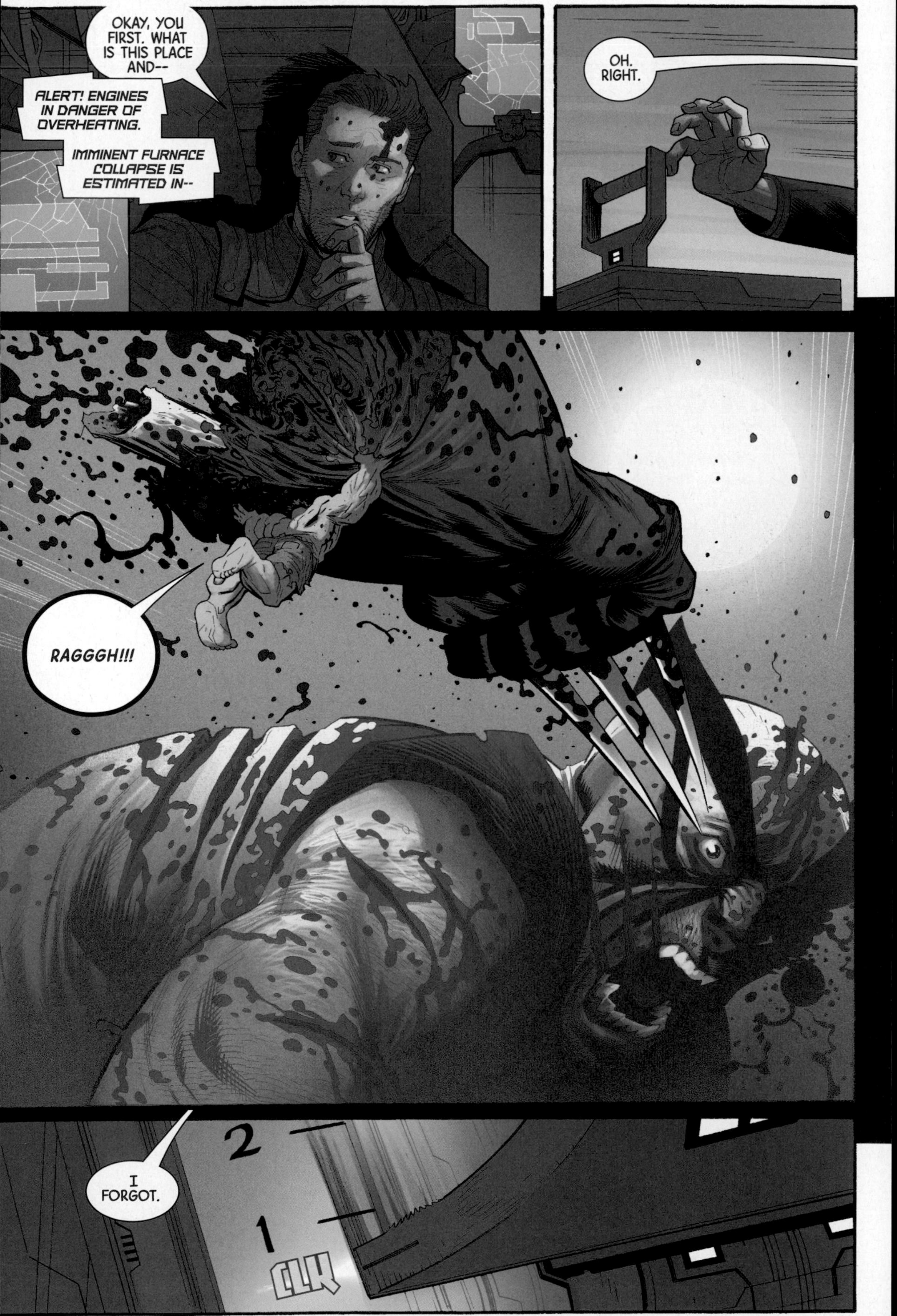
OKAY, YOU FIRST. WHAT IS THIS PLACE AND--
ALERT! ENGINES IN DANGER OF OVERHEATING.
IMMINENT FURNACE COLLAPSE IS ESTIMATED IN--
OH. RIGHT.
RAGGGH!!!
2
I FORGOT.
1
CLK

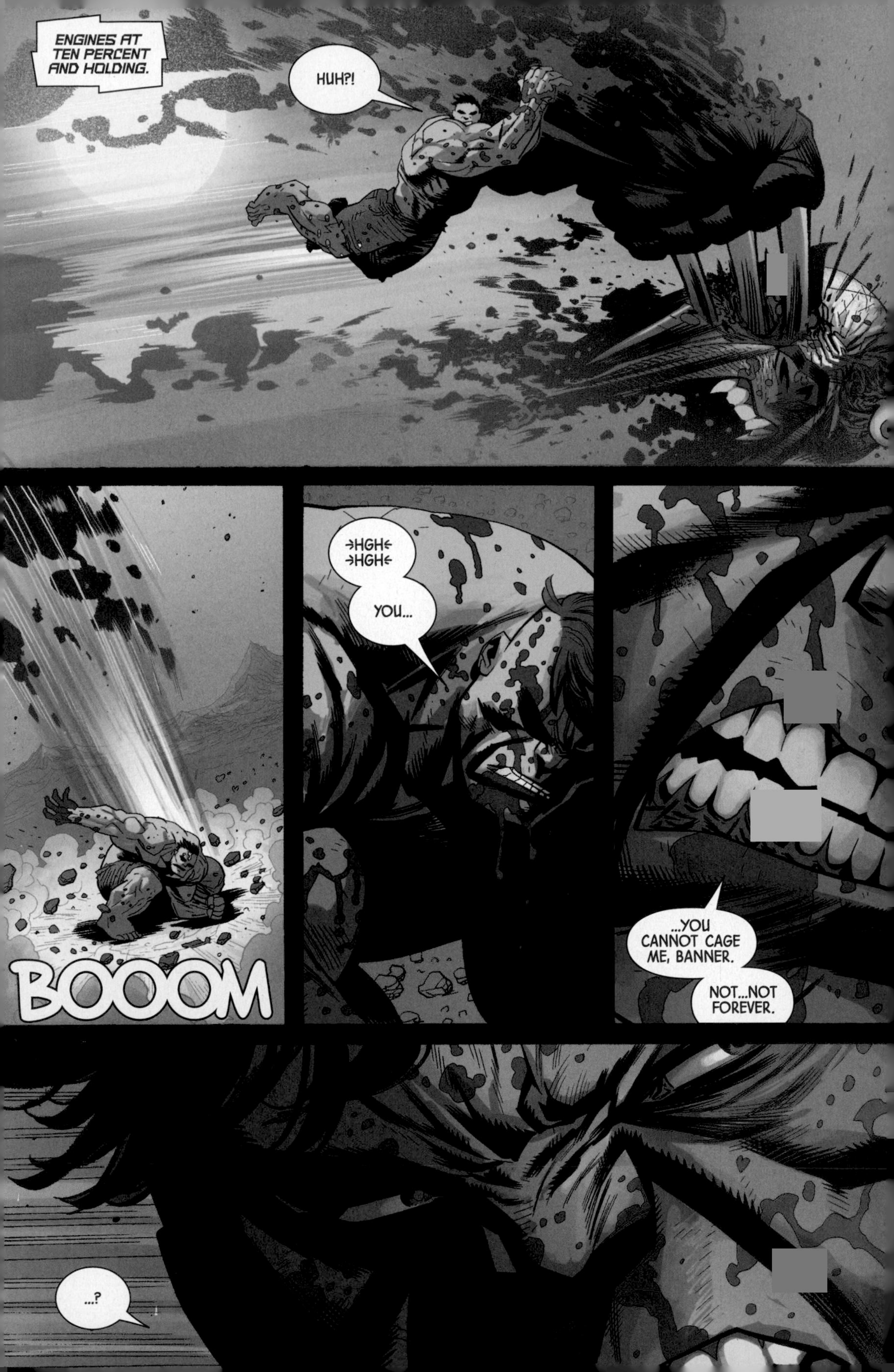
ENGINES AT TEN PERCENT AND HOLDING.
HUH?!
BOOOM
→HGH← →HGH←
YOU...
...YOU CANNOT CAGE ME, BANNER.
NOT...NOT FOREVER.
...?

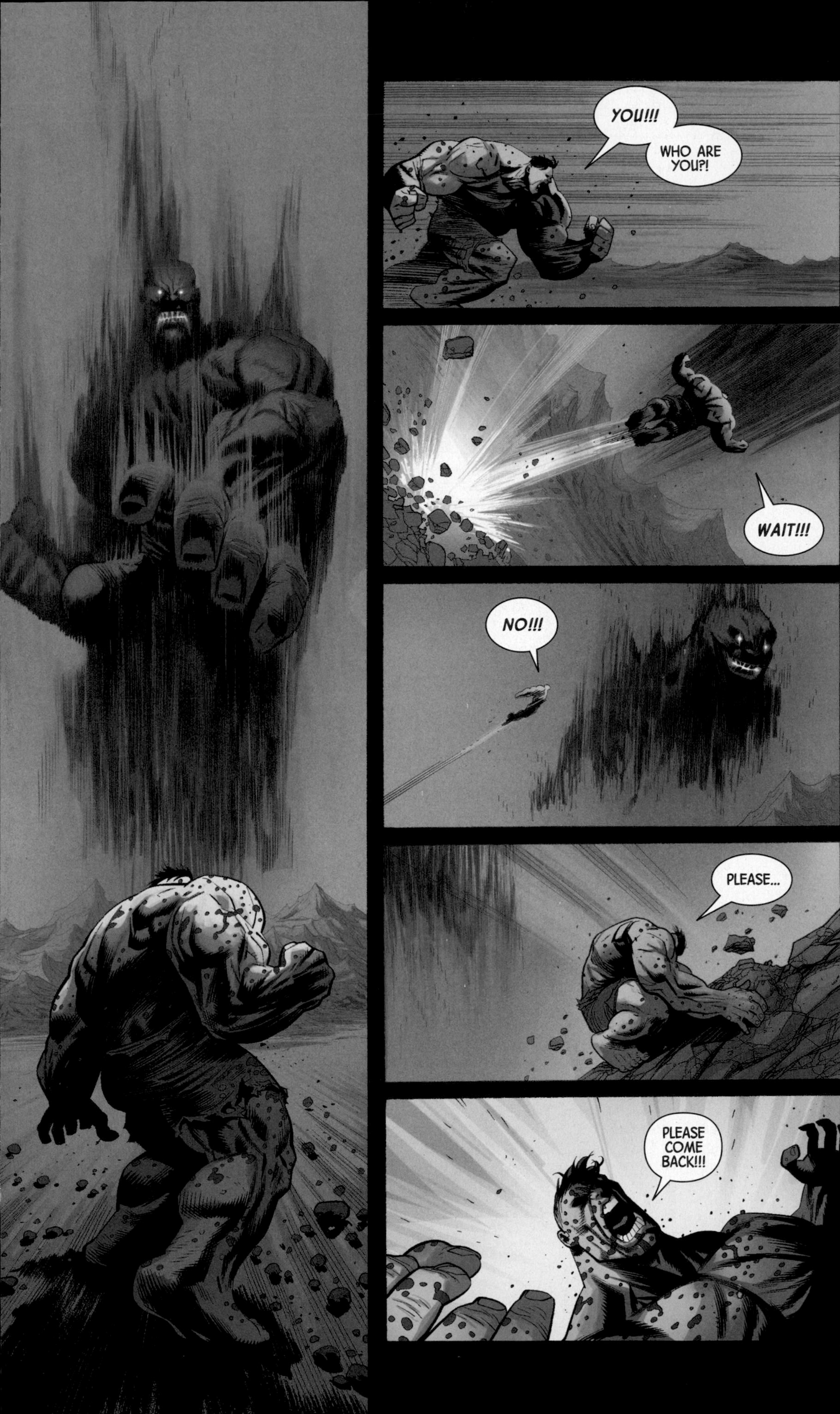
YOU!!!
WHO ARE YOU?!
WAIT!!!
NO!!!
PLEASE...
PLEASE COME BACK!!!

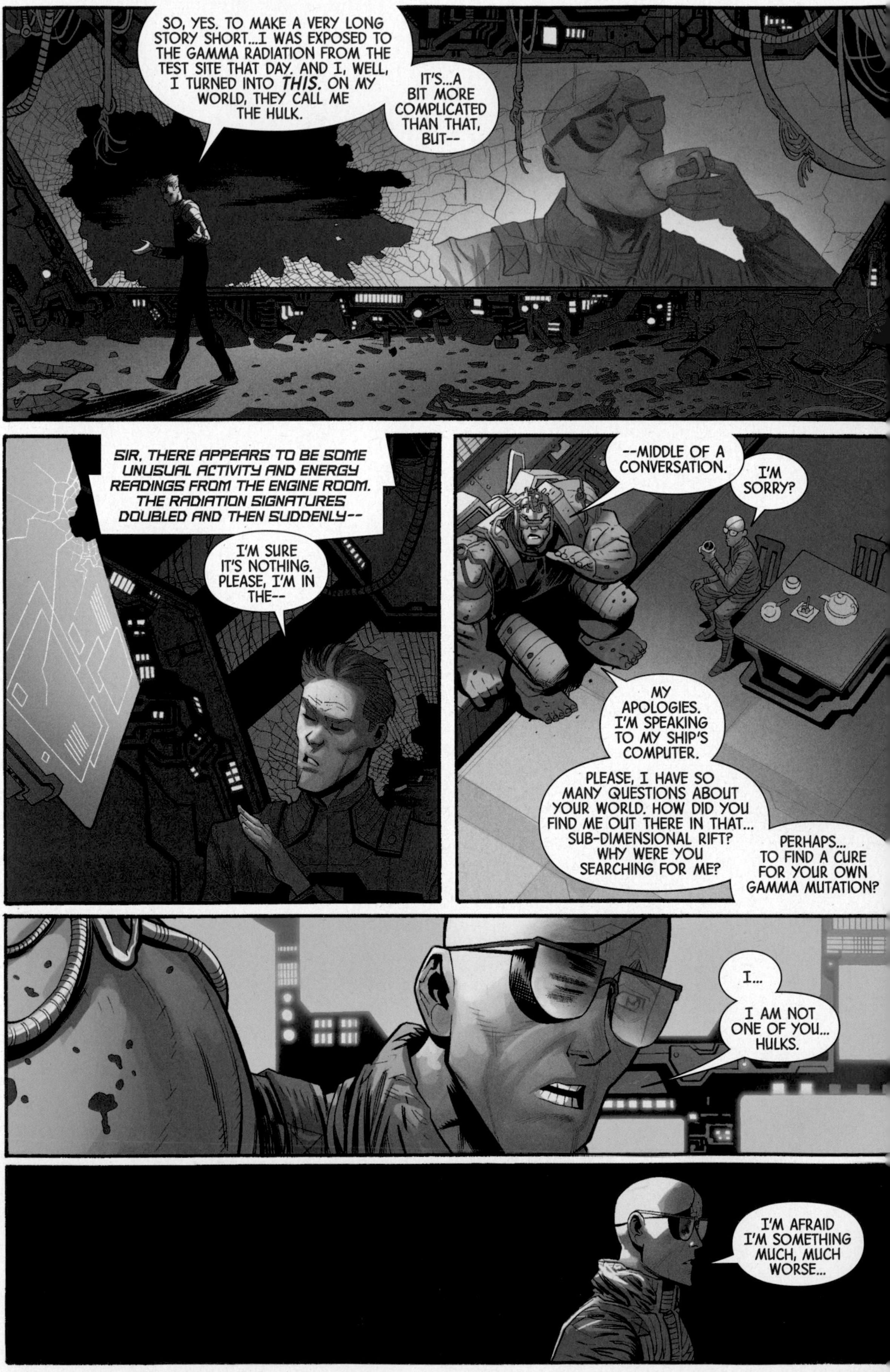
SO, YES. TO MAKE A VERY LONG STORY SHORT...I WAS EXPOSED TO THE GAMMA RADIATION FROM THE TEST SITE THAT DAY. AND I, WELL, I TURNED INTO *THIS.* ON MY WORLD, THEY CALL ME THE HULK.
IT'S...A BIT MORE COMPLICATED THAN THAT, BUT--
SIR, THERE APPEARS TO BE SOME UNUSUAL ACTIVITY AND ENERGY READINGS FROM THE ENGINE ROOM. THE RADIATION SIGNATURES DOUBLED AND THEN SUDDENLY--
I'M SURE IT'S NOTHING. PLEASE, I'M IN THE--
--MIDDLE OF A CONVERSATION.
I'M SORRY?
MY APOLOGIES. I'M SPEAKING TO MY SHIP'S COMPUTER.
PLEASE, I HAVE SO MANY QUESTIONS ABOUT YOUR WORLD. HOW DID YOU FIND ME OUT THERE IN THAT... SUB-DIMENSIONAL RIFT? WHY WERE YOU SEARCHING FOR ME?
PERHAPS... TO FIND A CURE FOR YOUR OWN GAMMA MUTATION?
I...
I AM NOT ONE OF YOU... HULKS.
I'M AFRAID I'M SOMETHING MUCH, MUCH WORSE...

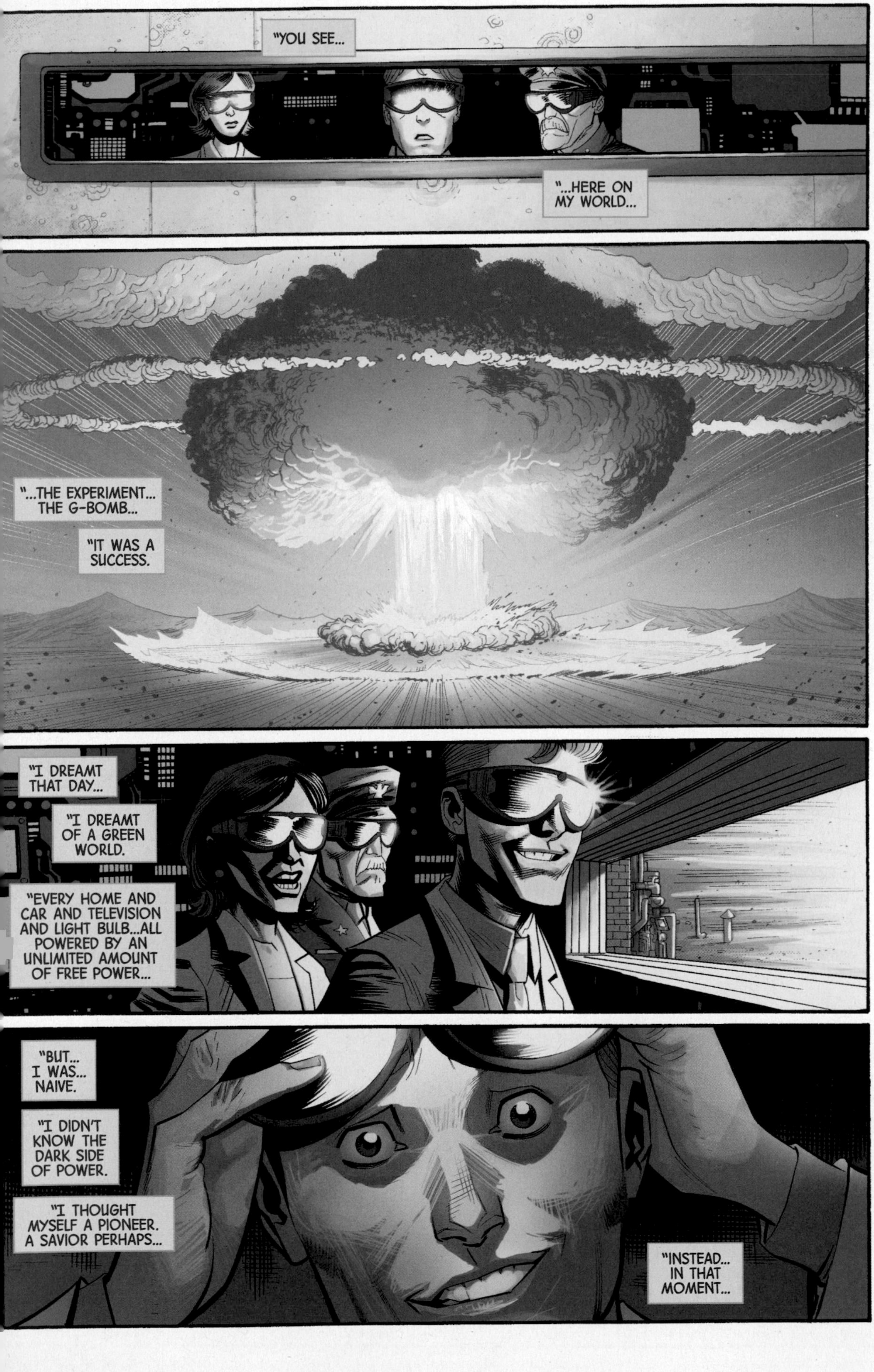
"YOU SEE...
"...HERE ON MY WORLD...
"...THE EXPERIMENT... THE G-BOMB...
"IT WAS A SUCCESS.
"I DREAMT THAT DAY...
"I DREAMT OF A GREEN WORLD.
"EVERY HOME AND CAR AND TELEVISION AND LIGHT BULB...ALL POWERED BY AN UNLIMITED AMOUNT OF FREE POWER...
"BUT... I WAS... NAIVE.
"I DIDN'T KNOW THE DARK SIDE OF POWER.
"I THOUGHT MYSELF A PIONEER. A SAVIOR PERHAPS...
"INSTEAD... IN THAT MOMENT...

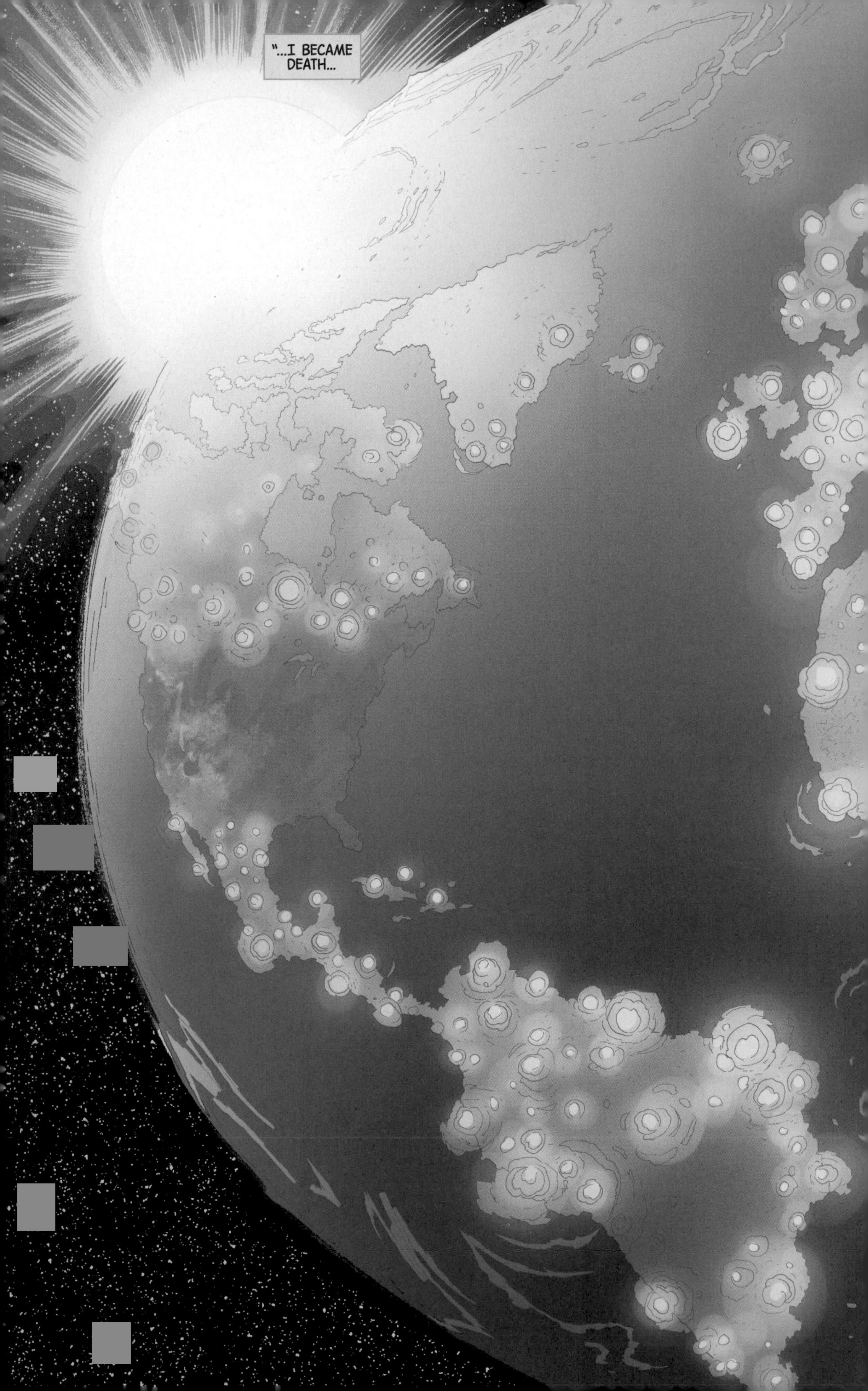
"...I BECAME DEATH...

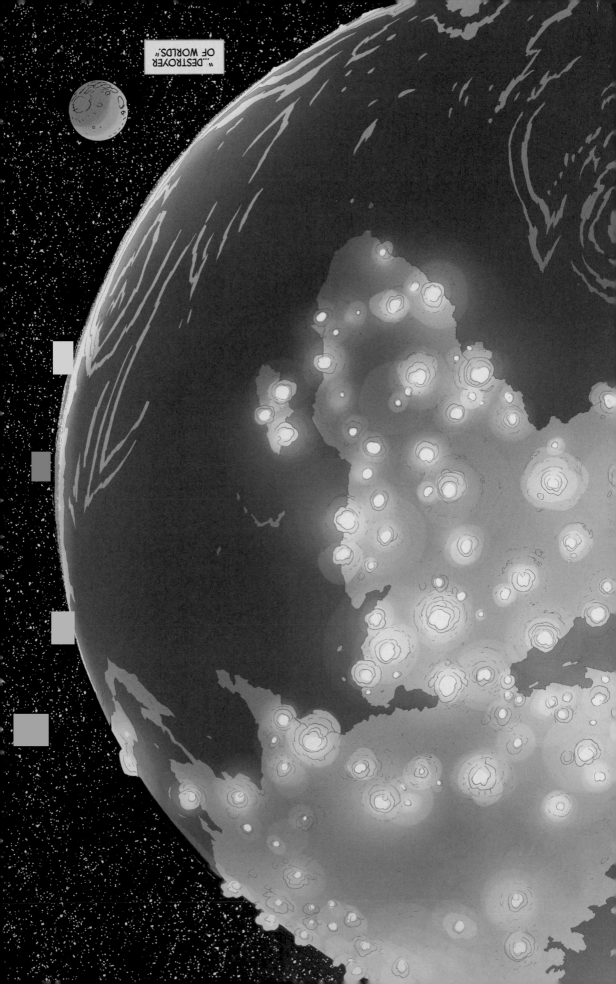

"...DESTROYER OF WORLDS."

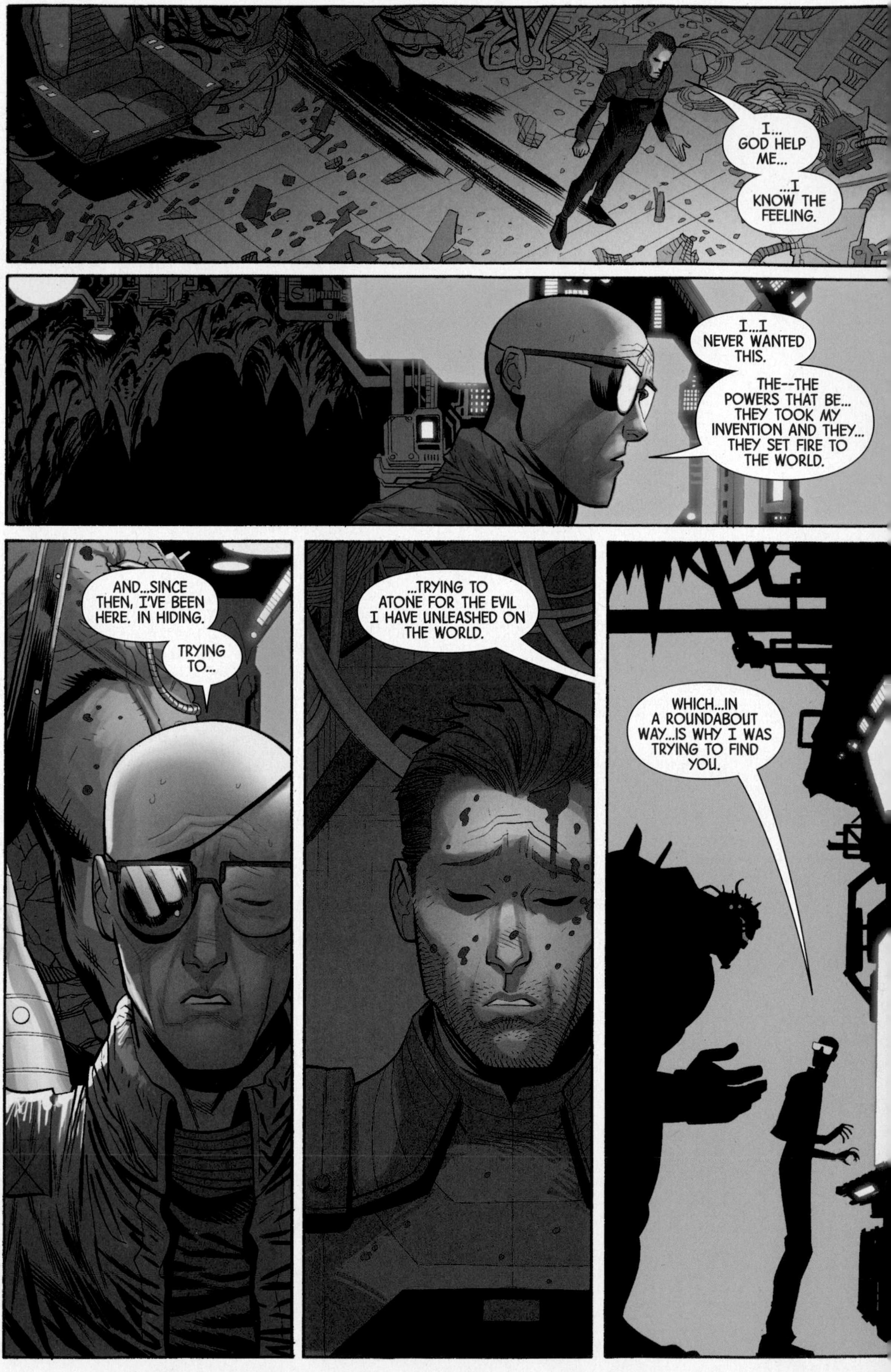
I... GOD HELP ME...
...I KNOW THE FEELING.
I...I NEVER WANTED THIS.
THE--THE POWERS THAT BE... THEY TOOK MY INVENTION AND THEY... THEY SET FIRE TO THE WORLD.
AND...SINCE THEN, I'VE BEEN HERE. IN HIDING.
TRYING TO...
...TRYING TO ATONE FOR THE EVIL I HAVE UNLEASHED ON THE WORLD.
WHICH...IN A ROUNDABOUT WAY...IS WHY I WAS TRYING TO FIND YOU.

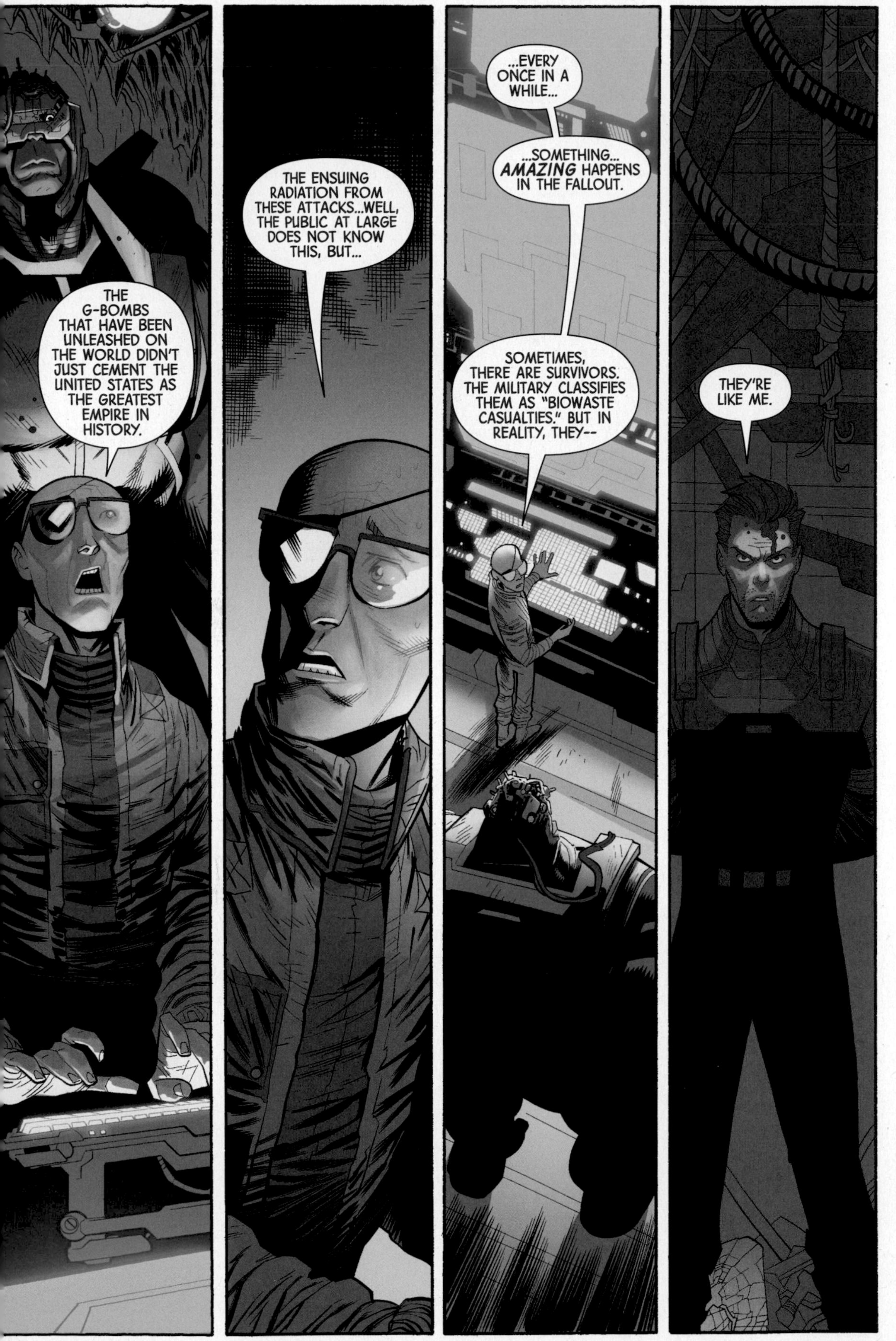
THE G-BOMBS THAT HAVE BEEN UNLEASHED ON THE WORLD DIDN'T JUST CEMENT THE UNITED STATES AS THE GREATEST EMPIRE IN HISTORY.
THE ENSUING RADIATION FROM THESE ATTACKS...WELL, THE PUBLIC AT LARGE DOES NOT KNOW THIS, BUT...
...EVERY ONCE IN A WHILE...
...SOMETHING... *AMAZING* HAPPENS IN THE FALLOUT.
SOMETIMES, THERE ARE SURVIVORS. THE MILITARY CLASSIFIES THEM AS "BIOWASTE CASUALTIES." BUT IN REALITY, THEY--
THEY'RE LIKE ME.

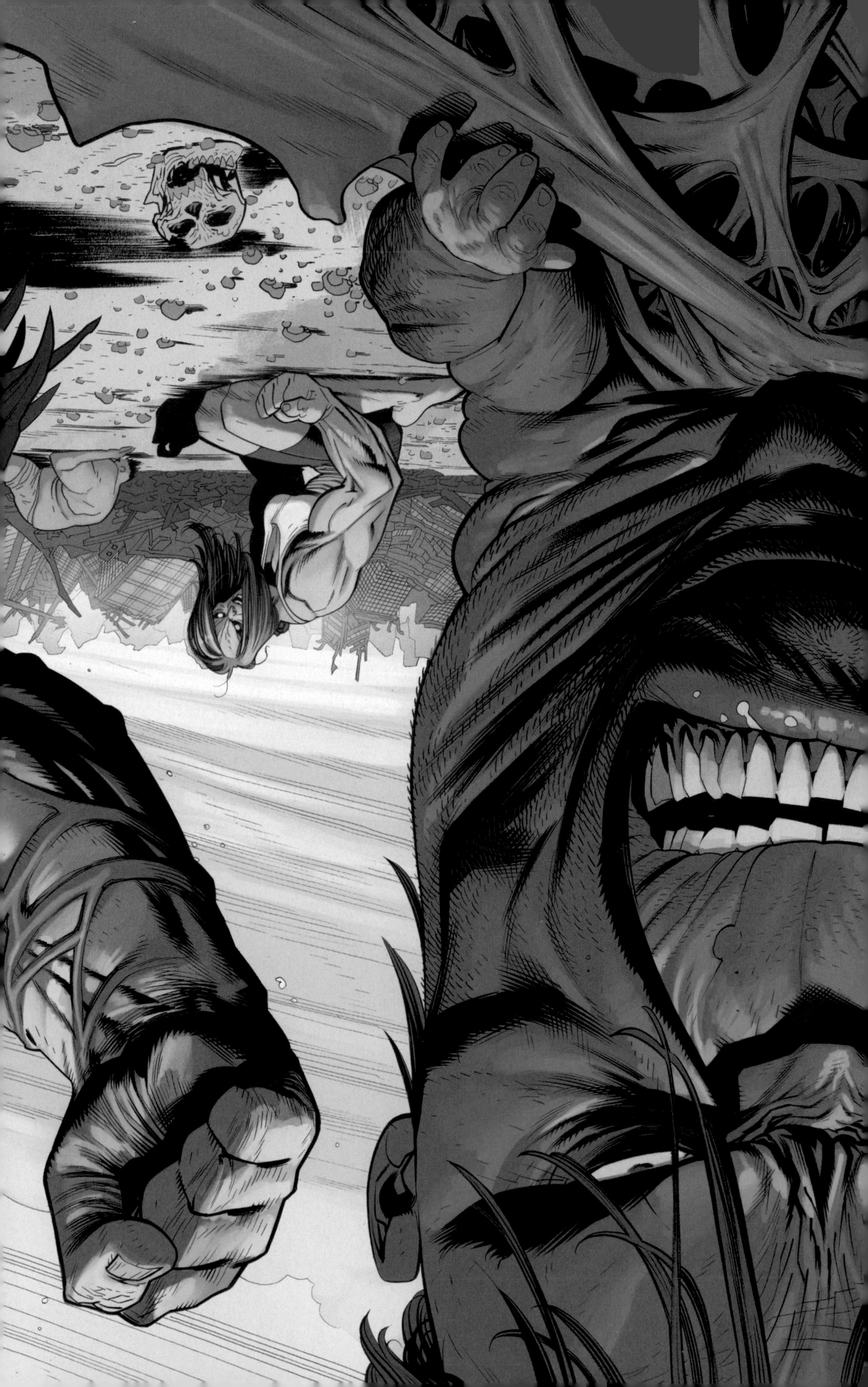

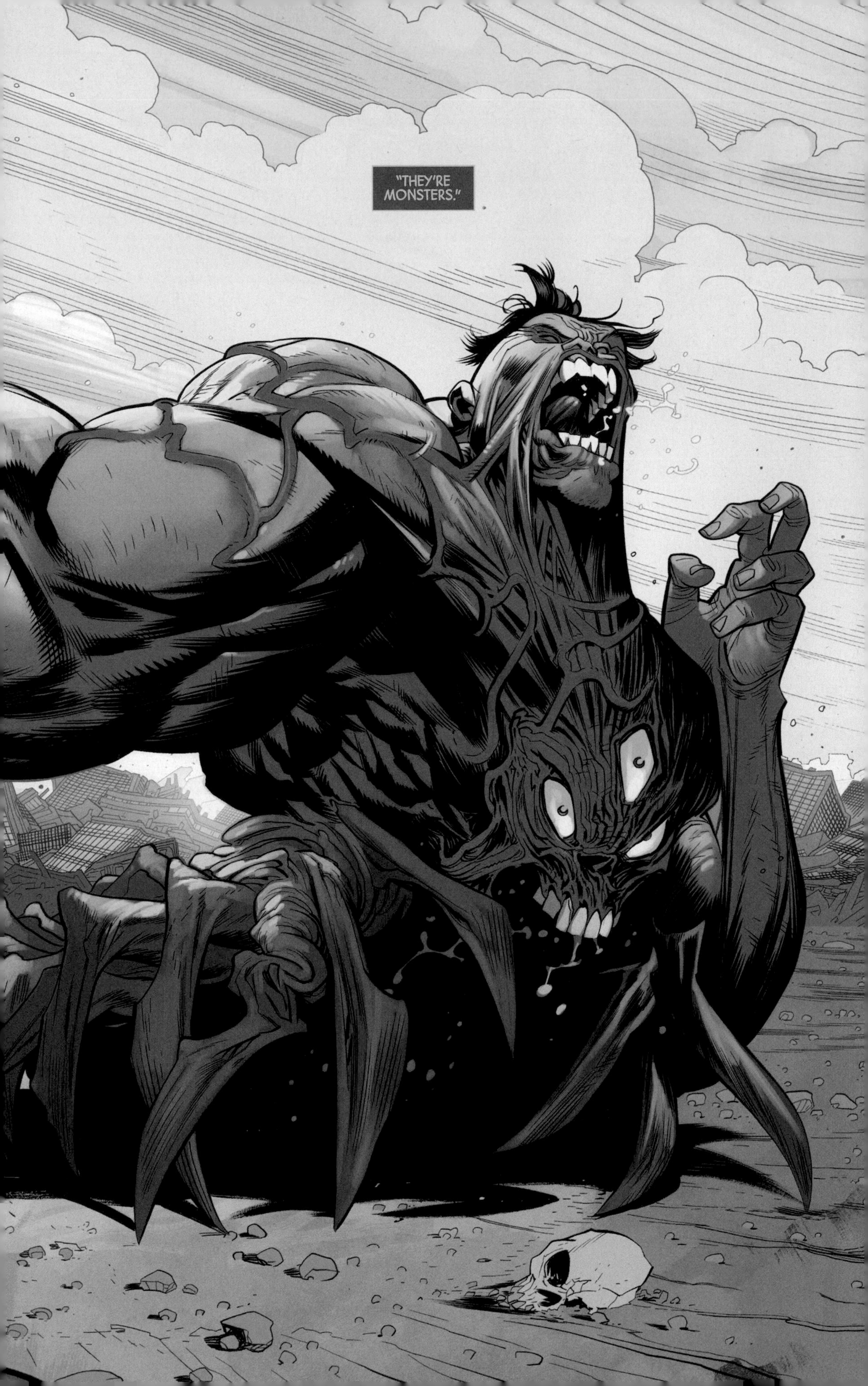
"THEY'RE MONSTERS."

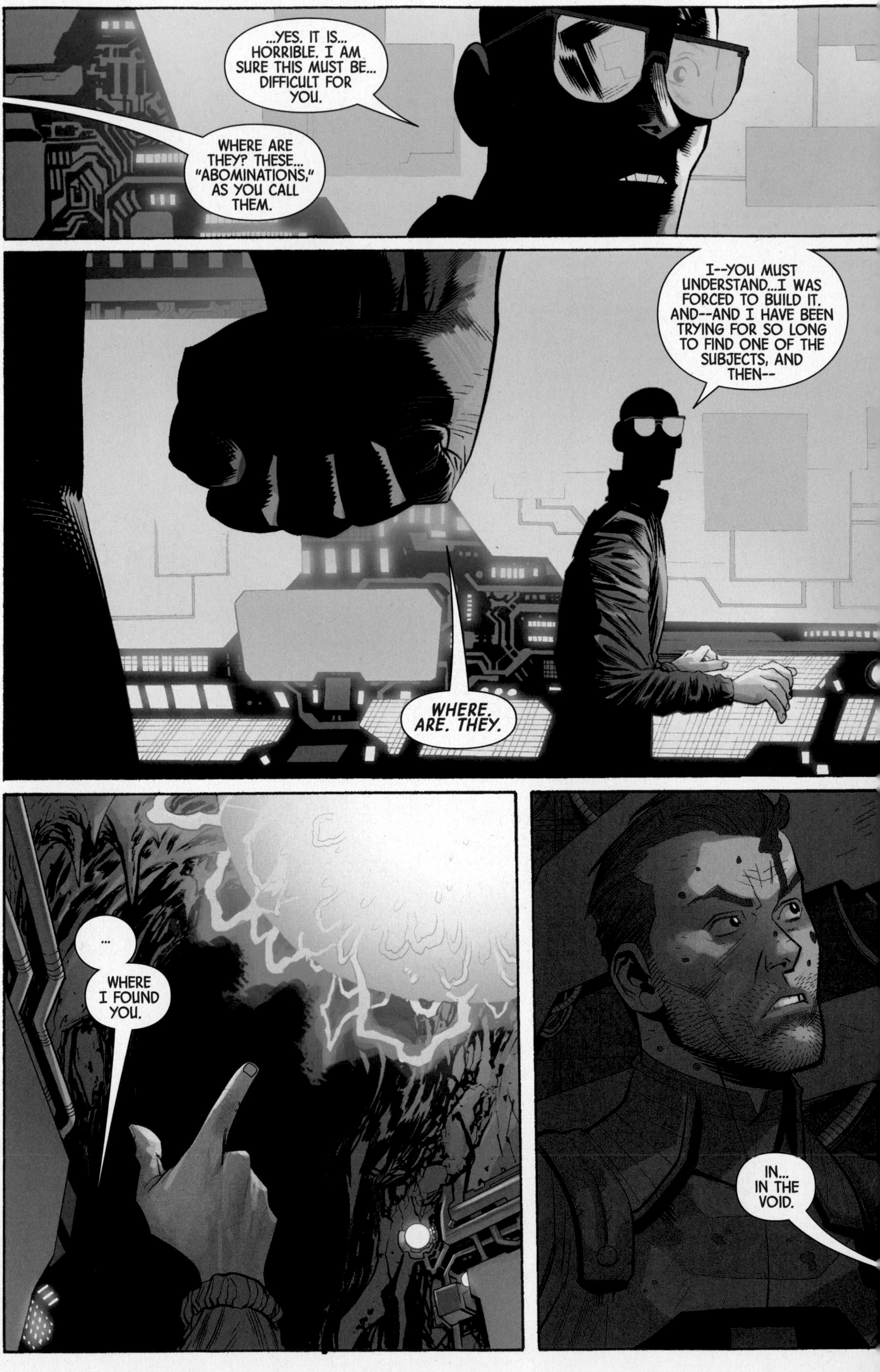
...YES. IT IS... HORRIBLE. I AM SURE THIS MUST BE... DIFFICULT FOR YOU.
WHERE ARE THEY? THESE... "ABOMINATIONS," AS YOU CALL THEM.
I--YOU MUST UNDERSTAND...I WAS FORCED TO BUILD IT. AND--AND I HAVE BEEN TRYING FOR SO LONG TO FIND ONE OF THE SUBJECTS, AND THEN--
WHERE. ARE. THEY.
...
WHERE I FOUND YOU.
IN... IN THE VOID.

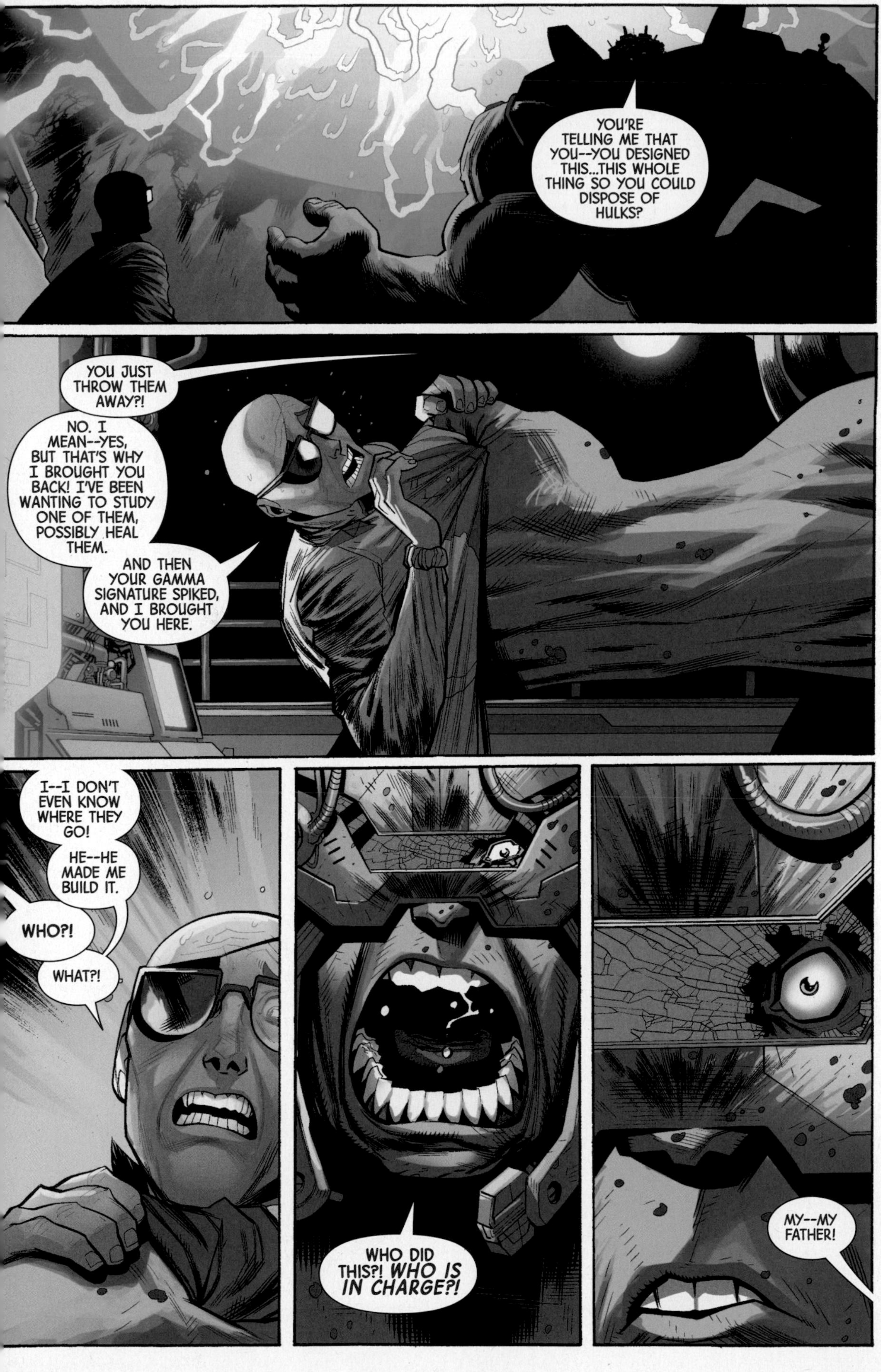
YOU'RE TELLING ME THAT YOU--YOU DESIGNED THIS...THIS WHOLE THING SO YOU COULD DISPOSE OF HULKS?
YOU JUST THROW THEM AWAY?!
NO. I MEAN--YES, BUT THAT'S WHY I BROUGHT YOU BACK! I'VE BEEN WANTING TO STUDY ONE OF THEM, POSSIBLY HEAL THEM.
AND THEN YOUR GAMMA SIGNATURE SPIKED, AND I BROUGHT YOU HERE.
I--I DON'T EVEN KNOW WHERE THEY GO!
HE--HE MADE ME BUILD IT.
WHO?!
WHAT?!
WHO DID THIS?! WHO IS IN CHARGE?!
MY--MY FATHER!

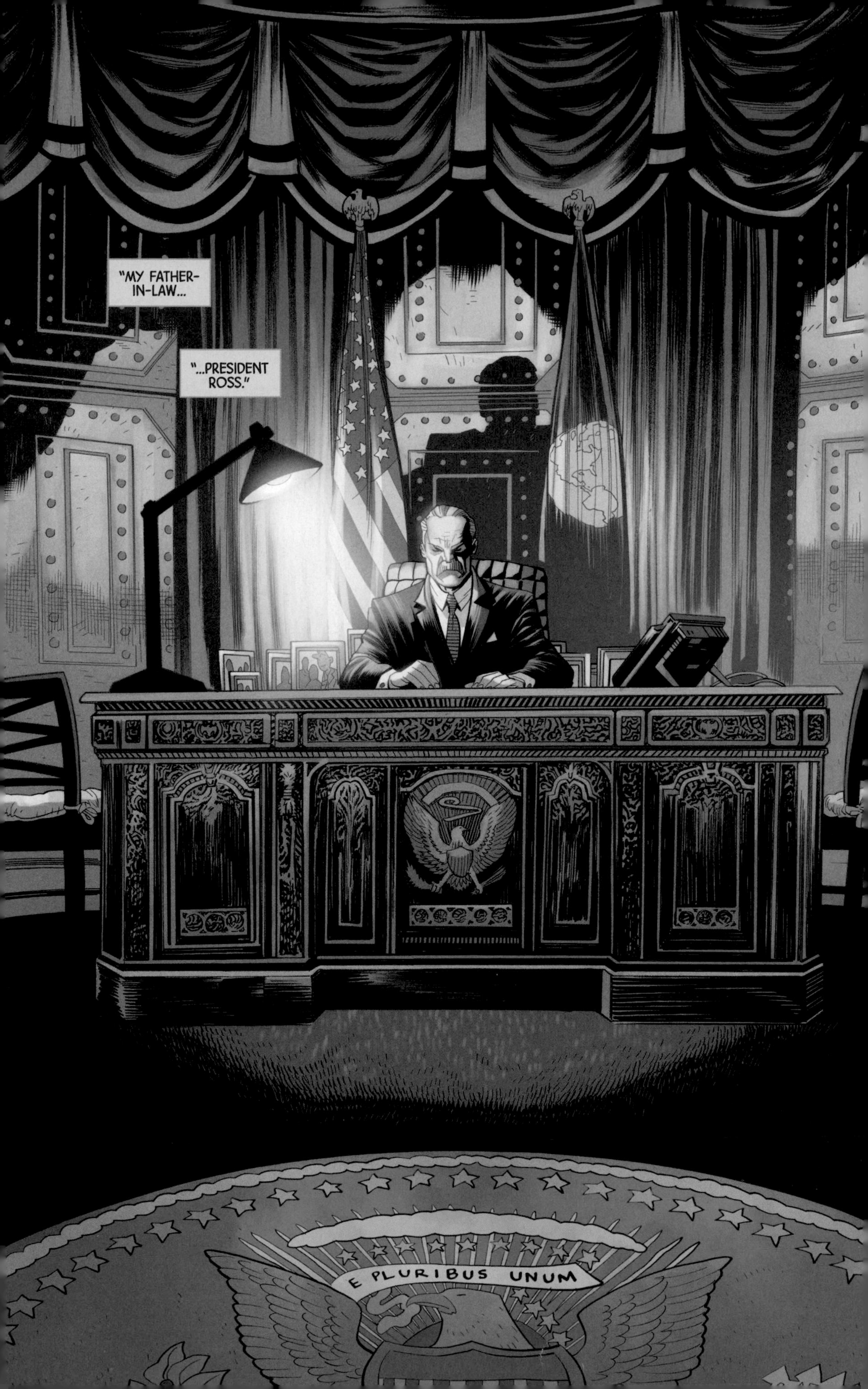
"MY FATHER-IN-LAW...
"...PRESIDENT ROSS."
E PLURIBUS UNUM

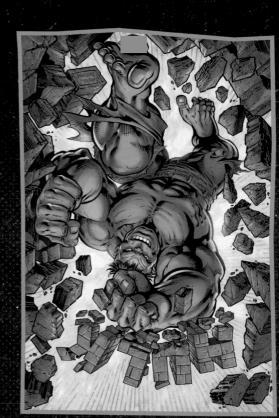

#1 VARIANT BY
DAN JURGENS, BRETT BREEDING, &
ALEX SINCLAIR

#1 VARIANT BY
ED McGUINNESS &
LAURA MARTIN

#1 INFINITY SAGA PHASE 1 VARIANT BY
JOE BENNETT, RUY JOSÉ &
JAY DAVID RAMOS

#1 VARIANT BY
SIMONE BIANCHI

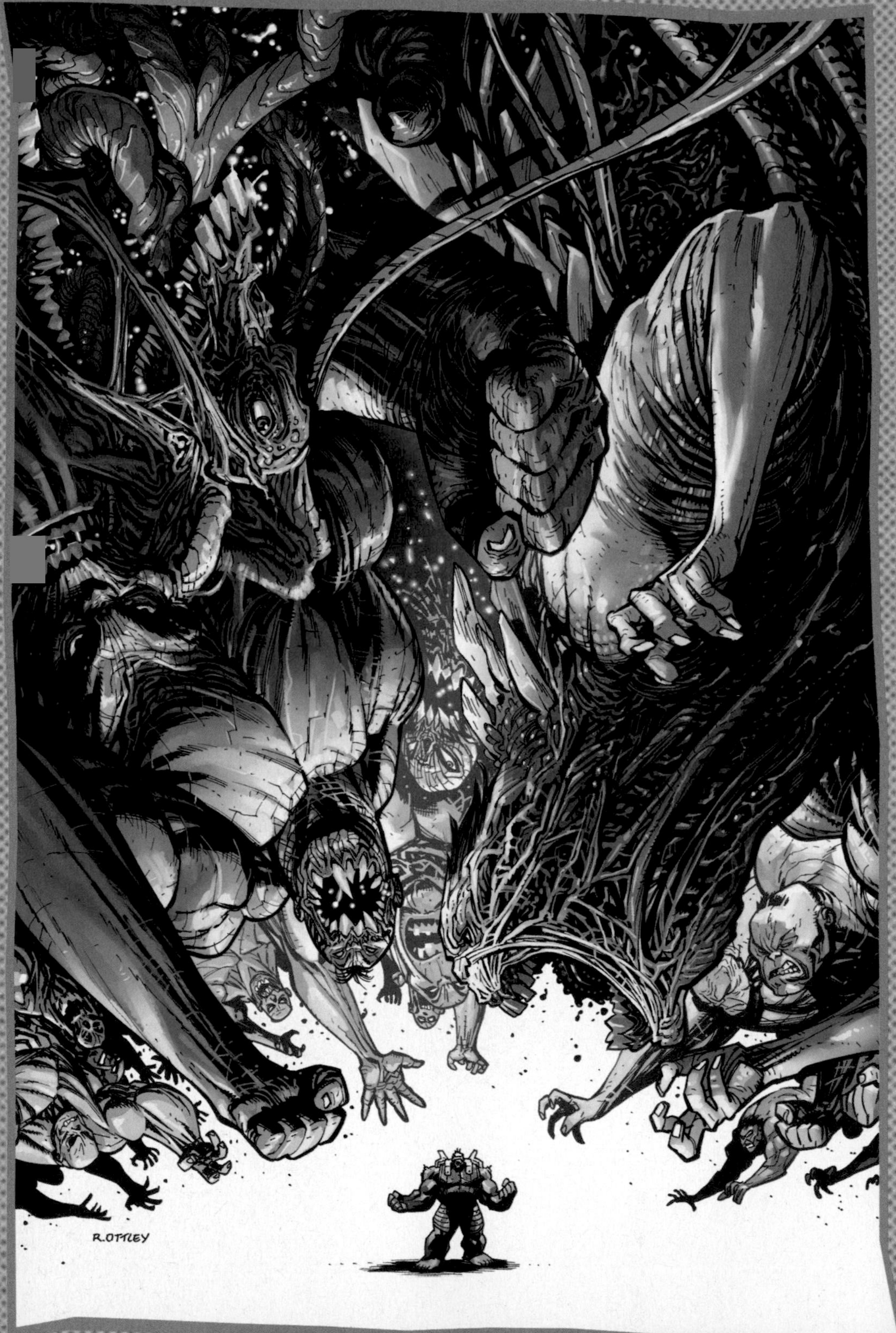
R.OTTLEY

HULK
NUMBER 4

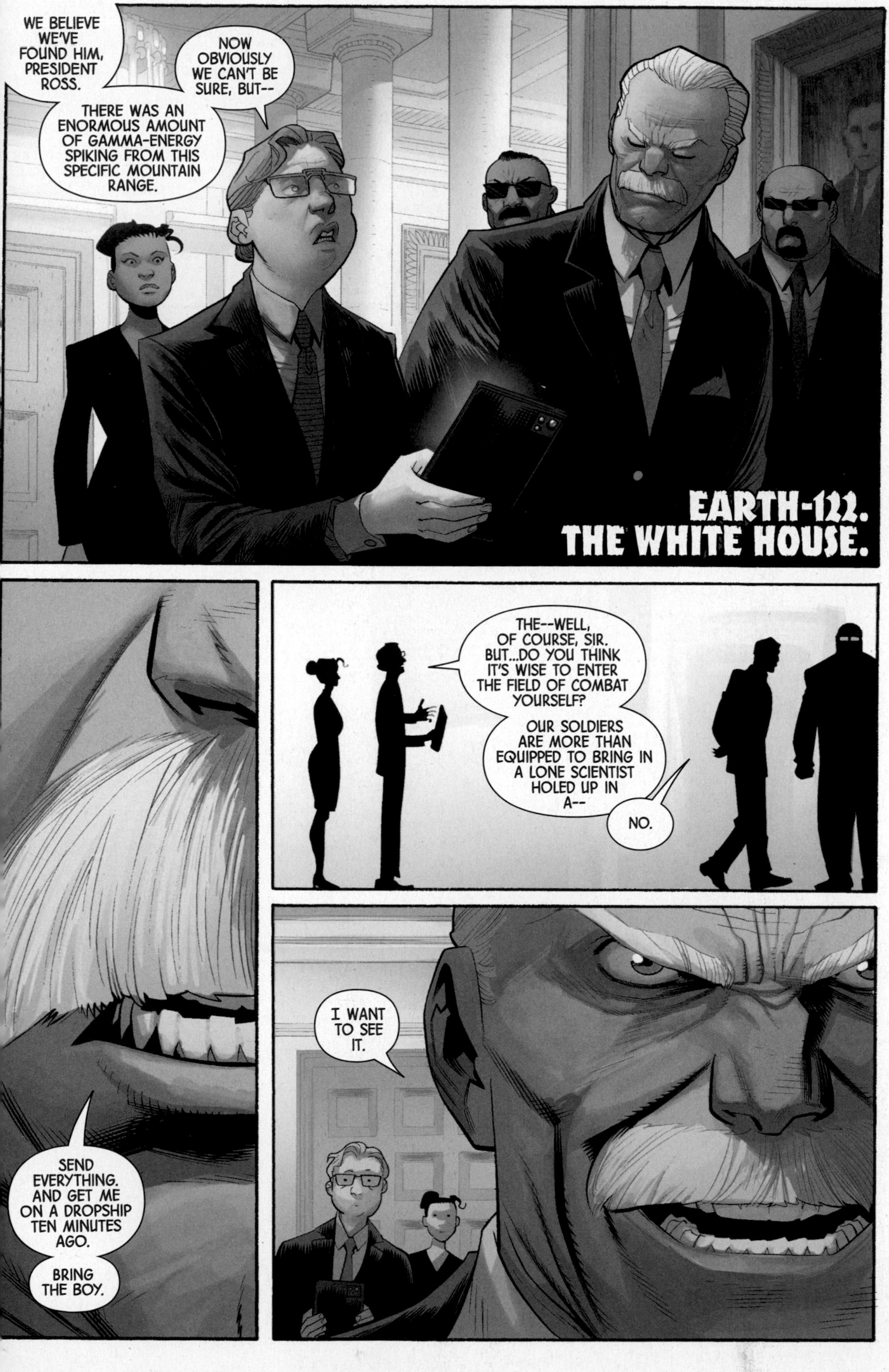
WE BELIEVE WE'VE FOUND HIM, PRESIDENT ROSS.
THERE WAS AN ENORMOUS AMOUNT OF GAMMA-ENERGY SPIKING FROM THIS SPECIFIC MOUNTAIN RANGE.
NOW OBVIOUSLY WE CAN'T BE SURE, BUT--
EARTH-122. THE WHITE HOUSE.
THE--WELL, OF COURSE, SIR. BUT...DO YOU THINK IT'S WISE TO ENTER THE FIELD OF COMBAT YOURSELF?
OUR SOLDIERS ARE MORE THAN EQUIPPED TO BRING IN A LONE SCIENTIST HOLED UP IN A--
NO.
I WANT TO SEE IT.
SEND EVERYTHING. AND GET ME ON A DROPSHIP TEN MINUTES AGO.
BRING THE BOY.

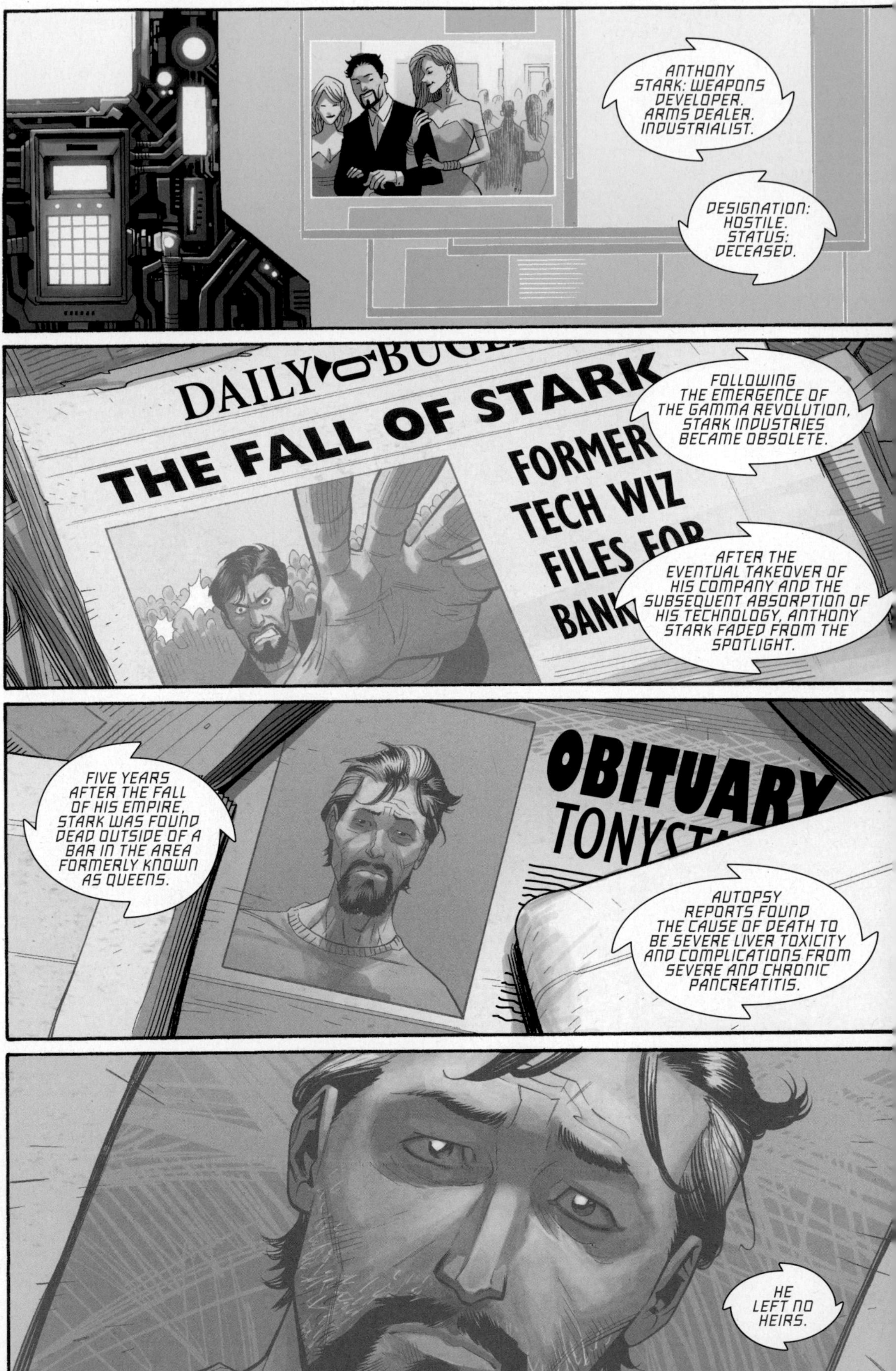
ANTHONY STARK: WEAPONS DEVELOPER. ARMS DEALER. INDUSTRIALIST.
DESIGNATION: HOSTILE. STATUS: DECEASED.
DAILY BUGLE
THE FALL OF STARK
FORMER TECH WIZ FILES FOR
FOLLOWING THE EMERGENCE OF THE GAMMA REVOLUTION, STARK INDUSTRIES BECAME OBSOLETE.
AFTER THE EVENTUAL TAKEOVER OF HIS COMPANY AND THE SUBSEQUENT ABSORPTION OF HIS TECHNOLOGY, ANTHONY STARK FADED FROM THE SPOTLIGHT.
OBITUARY
FIVE YEARS AFTER THE FALL OF HIS EMPIRE, STARK WAS FOUND DEAD OUTSIDE OF A BAR IN THE AREA FORMERLY KNOWN AS QUEENS.
AUTOPSY REPORTS FOUND THE CAUSE OF DEATH TO BE SEVERE LIVER TOXICITY AND COMPLICATIONS FROM SEVERE AND CHRONIC PANCREATITIS.
HE LEFT NO HEIRS.

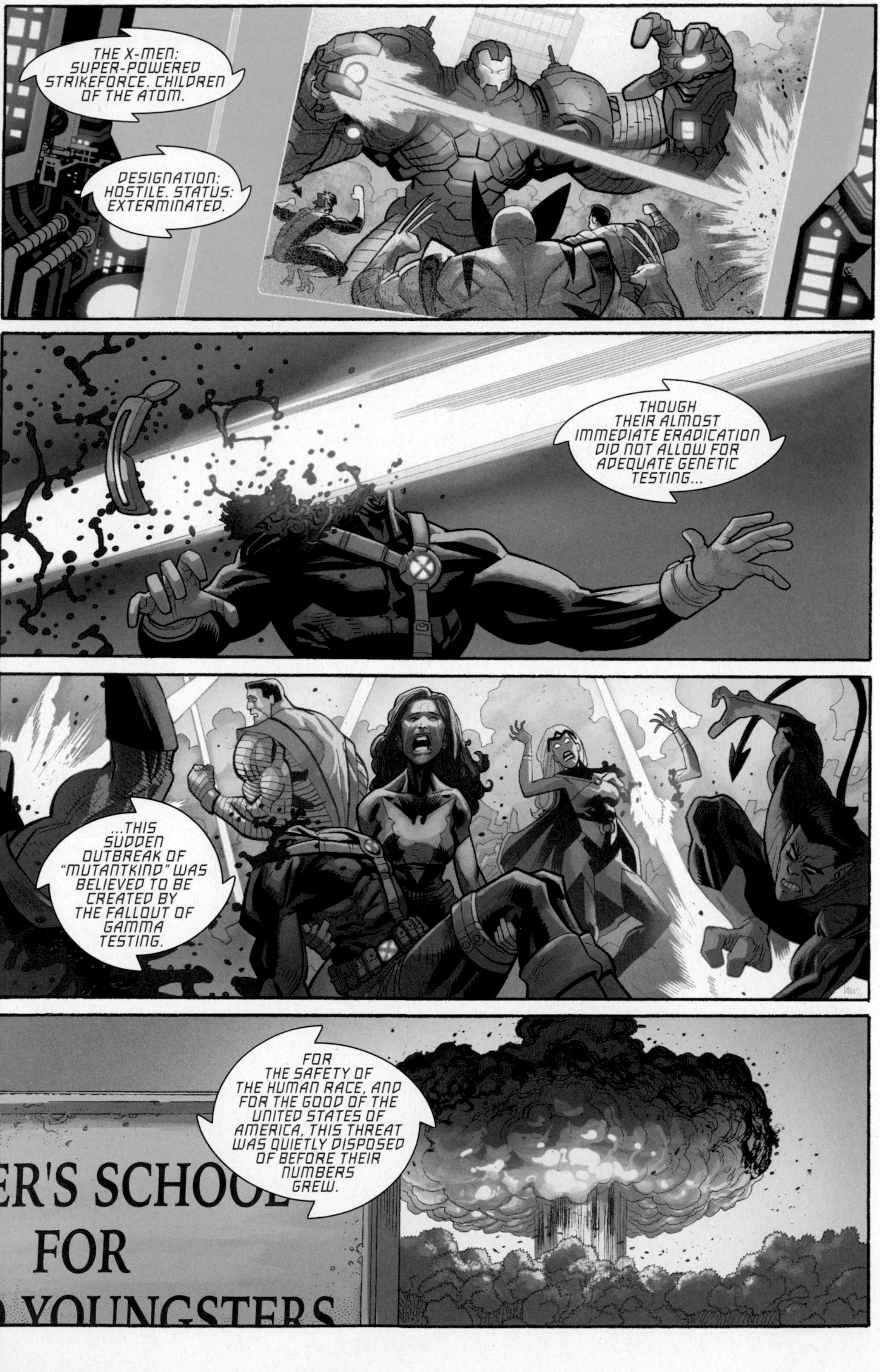
THE X-MEN: SUPER-POWERED STRIKEFORCE. CHILDREN OF THE ATOM.
DESIGNATION: HOSTILE. STATUS: EXTERMINATED.
THOUGH THEIR ALMOST IMMEDIATE ERADICATION DID NOT ALLOW FOR ADEQUATE GENETIC TESTING...
...THIS SUDDEN OUTBREAK OF "MUTANTKIND" WAS BELIEVED TO BE CREATED BY THE FALLOUT OF GAMMA TESTING.
FOR THE SAFETY OF THE HUMAN RACE, AND FOR THE GOOD OF THE UNITED STATES OF AMERICA, THIS THREAT WAS QUIETLY DISPOSED OF BEFORE THEIR NUMBERS GREW.
ER'S SCHOOL
FOR
YOUNGSTERS

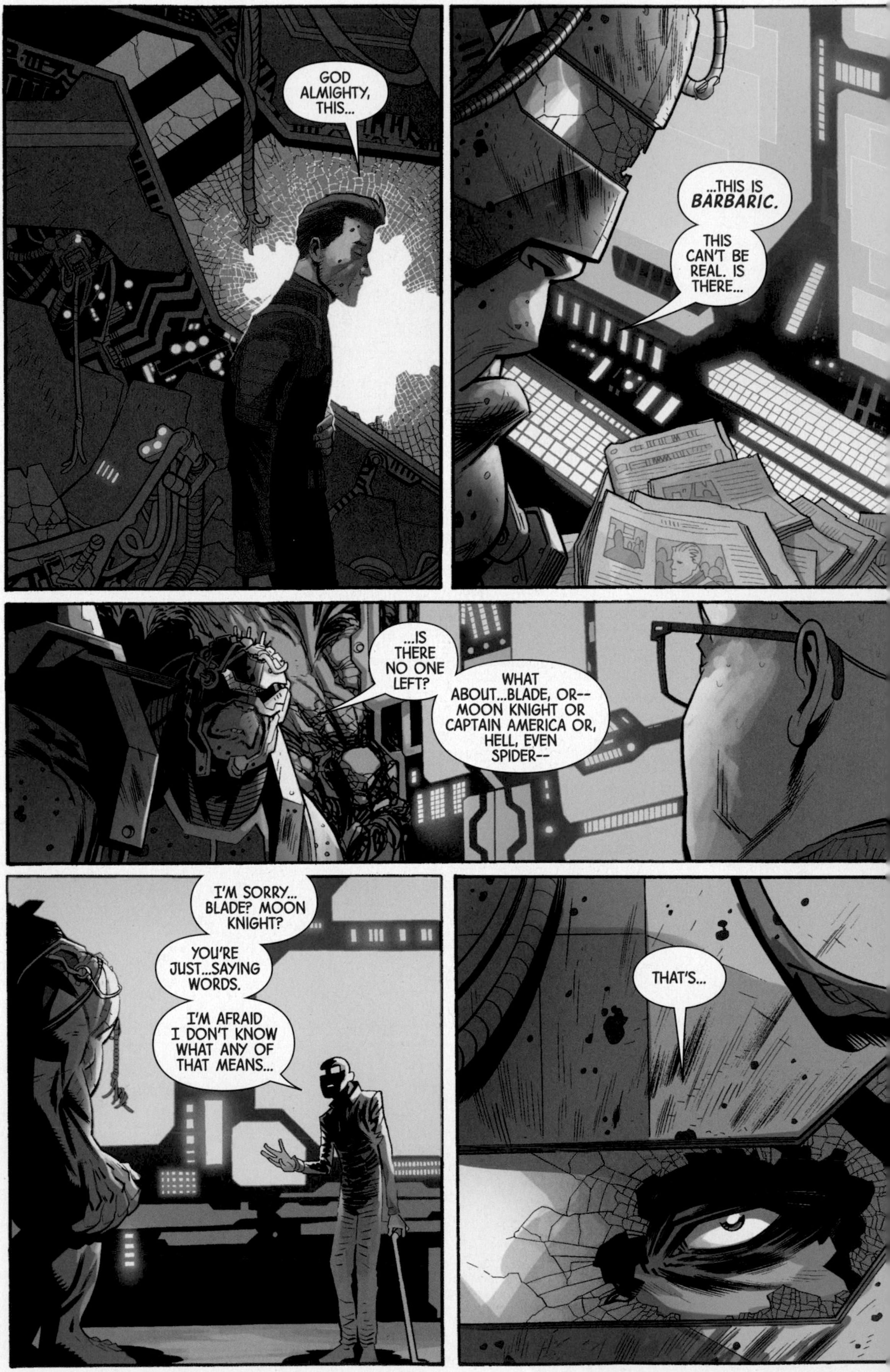
GOD ALMIGHTY, THIS...
...THIS IS *BARBARIC.*
THIS CAN'T BE REAL. IS THERE...
...IS THERE NO ONE LEFT?
WHAT ABOUT...BLADE, OR-- MOON KNIGHT OR CAPTAIN AMERICA OR, HELL, EVEN SPIDER--
I'M SORRY... BLADE? MOON KNIGHT?
YOU'RE JUST...SAYING WORDS.
I'M AFRAID I DON'T KNOW WHAT ANY OF THAT MEANS...
THAT'S...

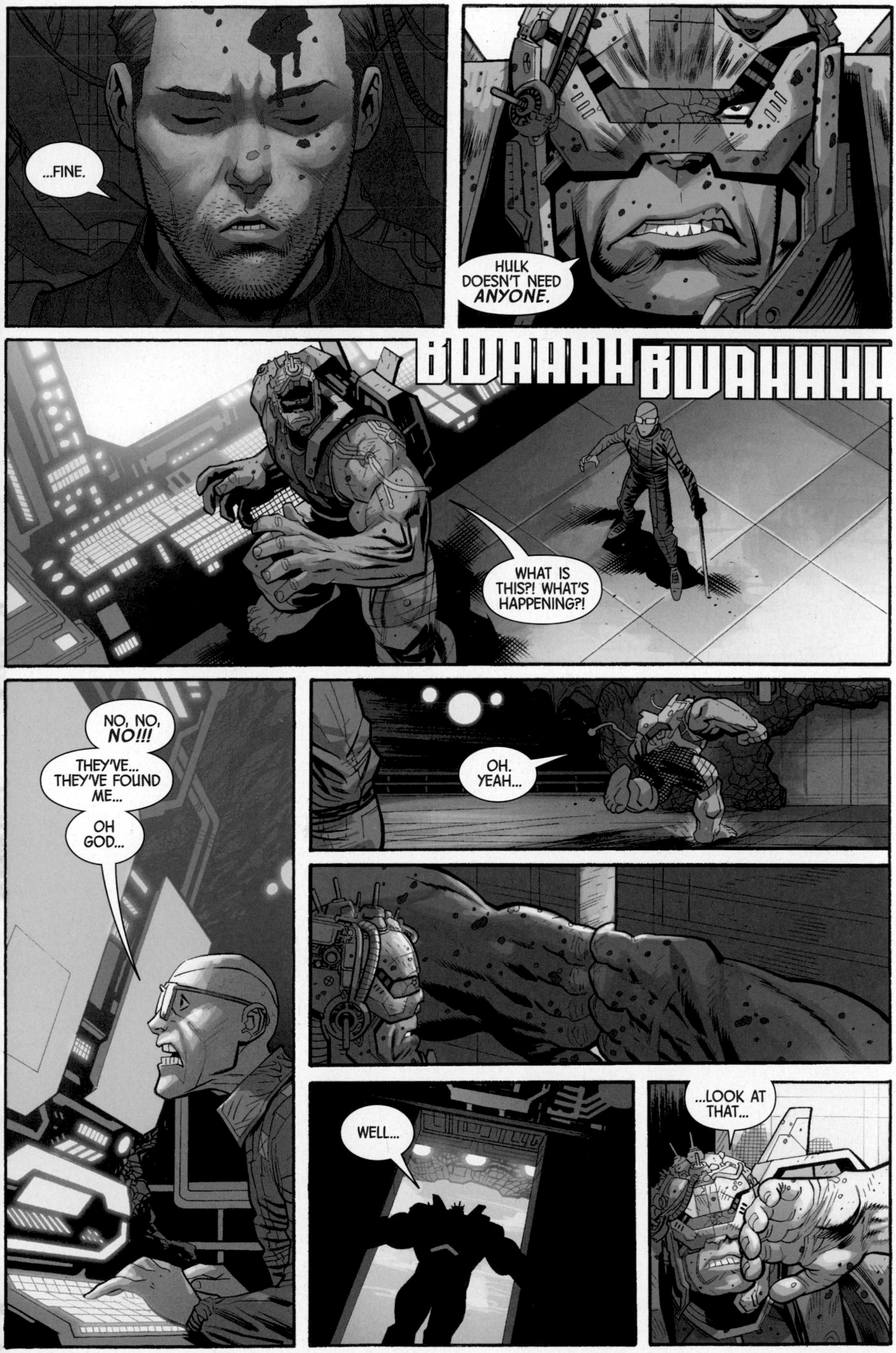
...FINE.
HULK DOESN'T NEED *ANYONE.*
BWAAAH BWAHHHH
WHAT IS THIS?! WHAT'S HAPPENING?!
NO, NO, ***NO!!!***
THEY'VE... THEY'VE FOUND ME...
OH GOD...
OH. YEAH...
WELL...
...LOOK AT THAT...

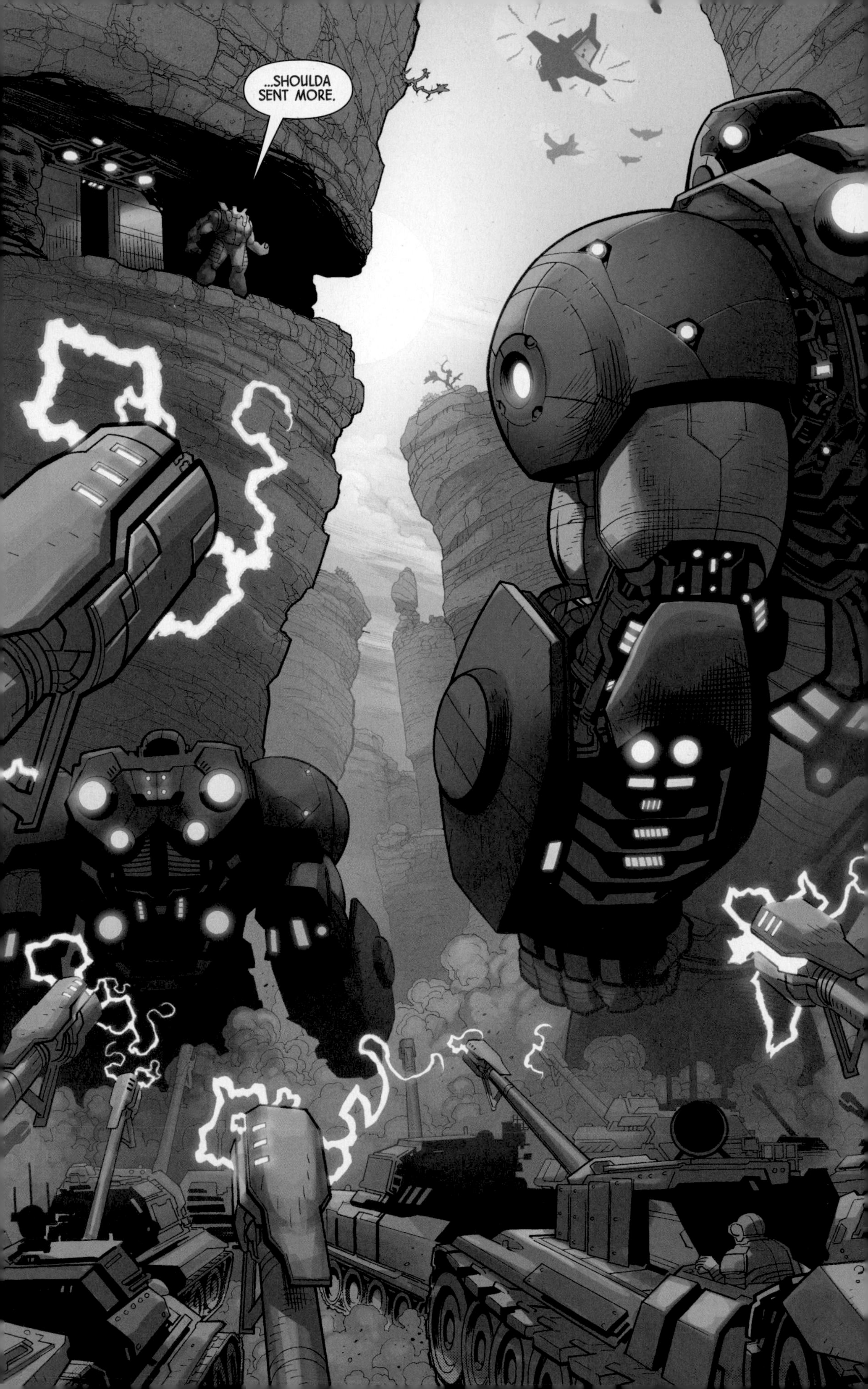
...SHOULDA SENT MORE.

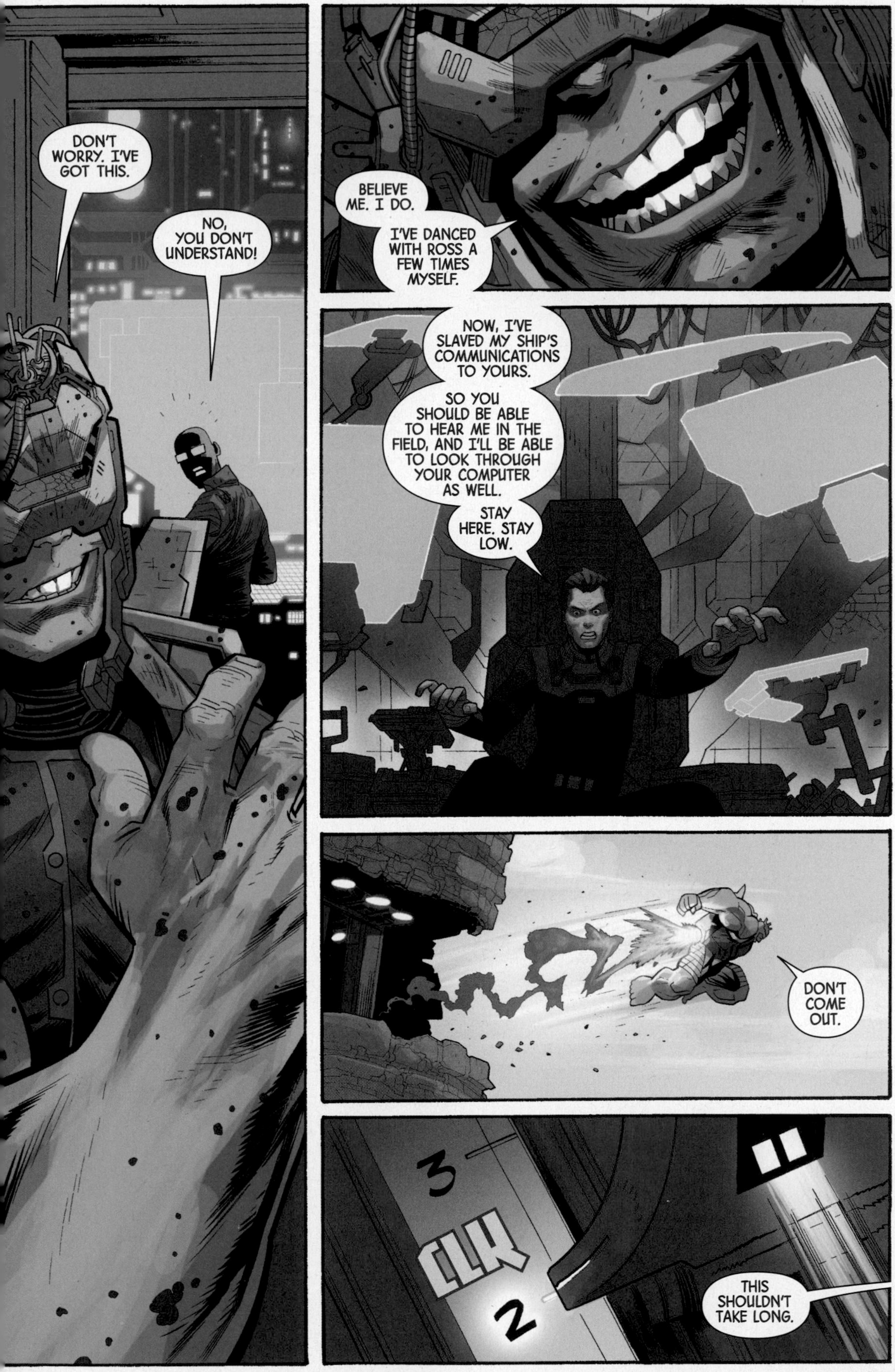
DON'T WORRY. I'VE GOT THIS.
NO, YOU DON'T UNDERSTAND!
BELIEVE ME. I DO.
I'VE DANCED WITH ROSS A FEW TIMES MYSELF.
NOW, I'VE SLAVED MY SHIP'S COMMUNICATIONS TO YOURS.
SO YOU SHOULD BE ABLE TO HEAR ME IN THE FIELD, AND I'LL BE ABLE TO LOOK THROUGH YOUR COMPUTER AS WELL.
STAY HERE. STAY LOW.
DON'T COME OUT.
3
CLR
2
THIS SHOULDN'T TAKE LONG.

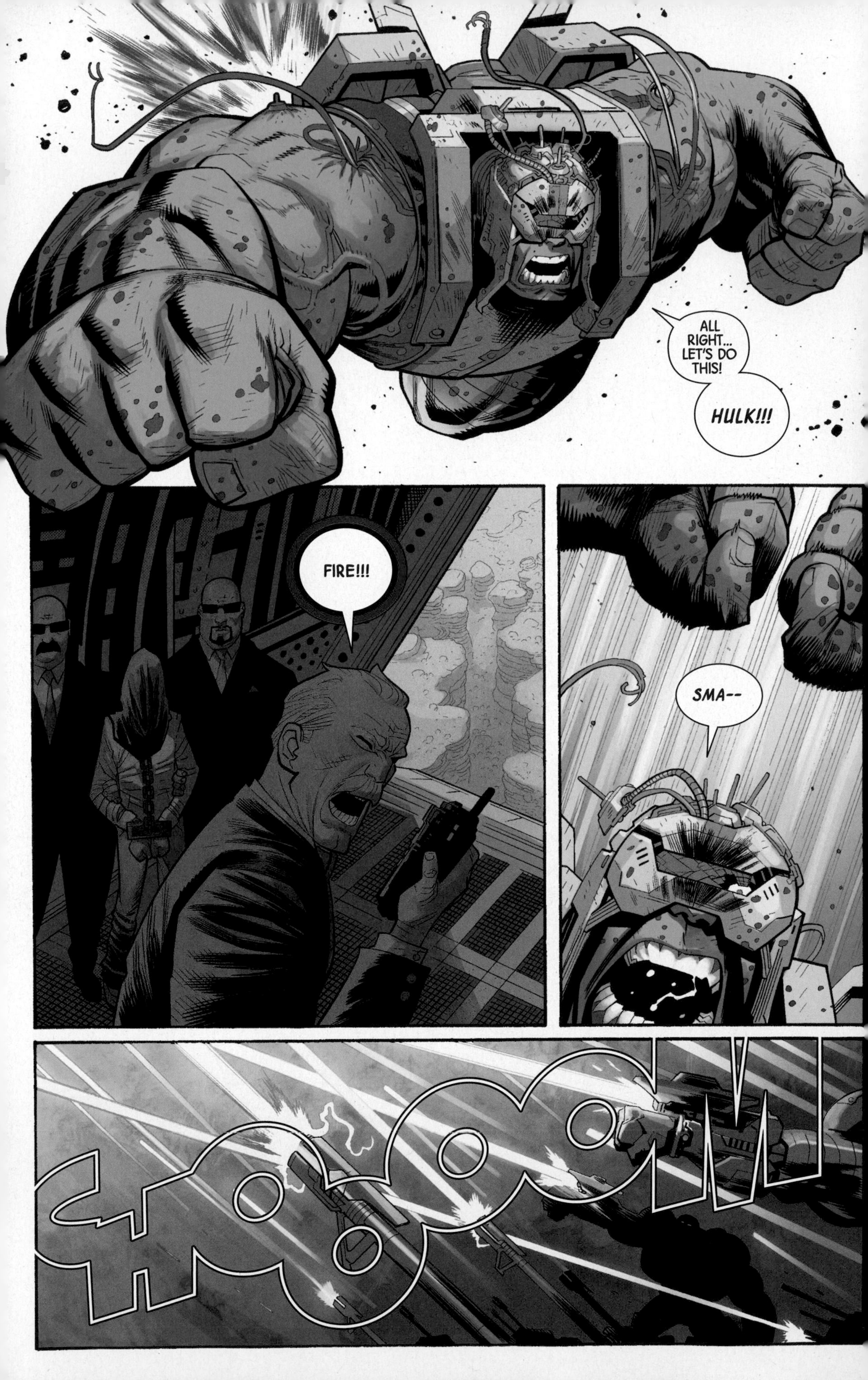
ALL RIGHT... LET'S DO THIS!
HULK!!!
FIRE!!!
SMA--

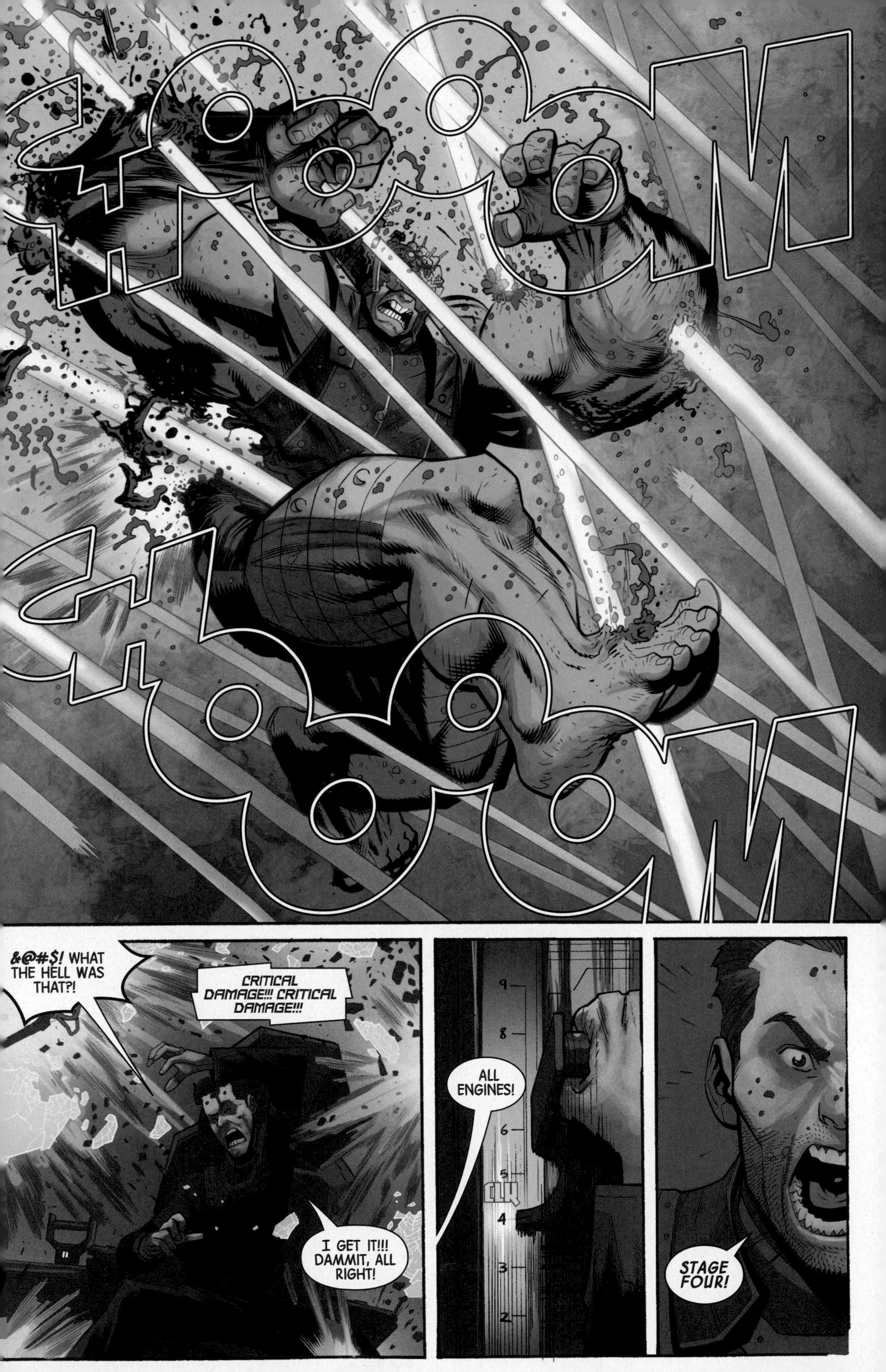

WHOOOOM
WHOOOOM
&@#$! WHAT THE HELL WAS THAT?!
CRITICAL DAMAGE!!! CRITICAL DAMAGE!!!
I GET IT!!! DAMMIT, ALL RIGHT!
ALL ENGINES!
CLIK
STAGE FOUR!

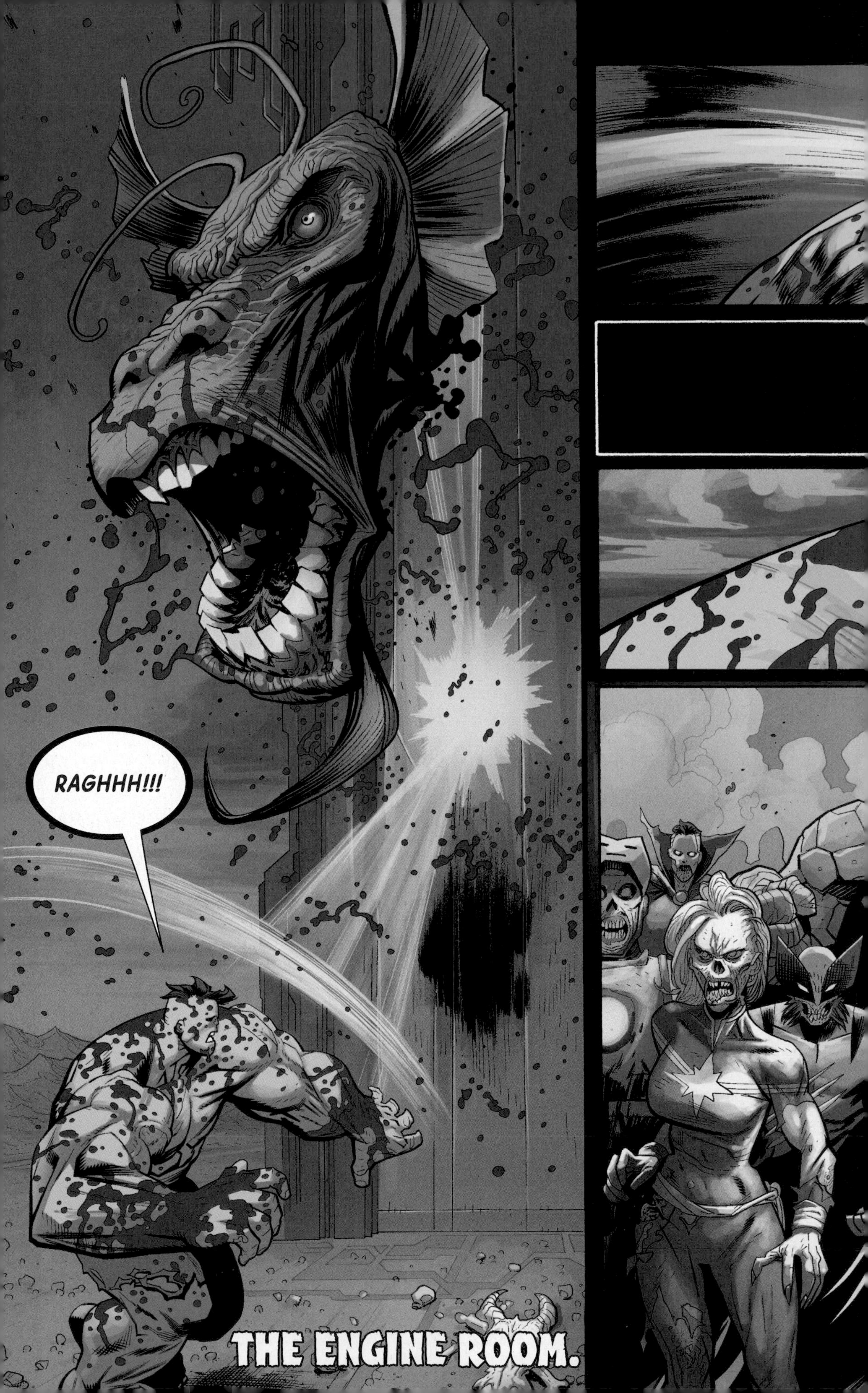
RAGHHH!!!
THE ENGINE ROOM.

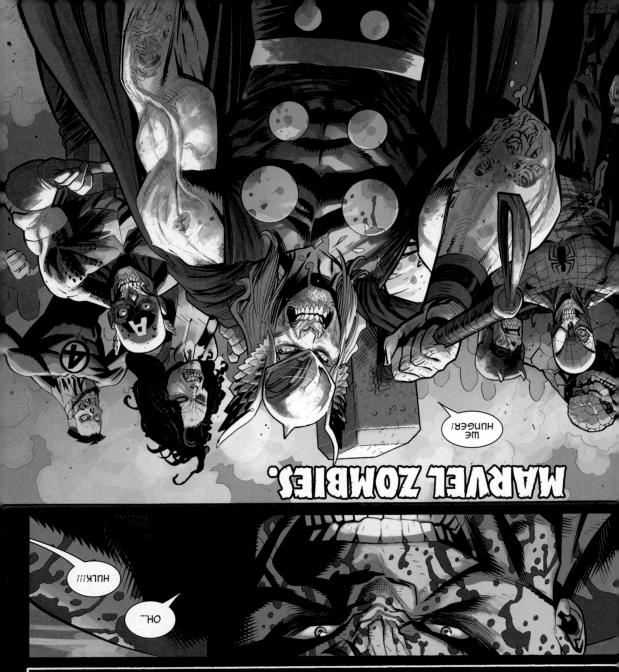

MARVEL ZOMBIES.

WE HUNGER!

OH...

HULK!!!

STAGE FOUR:

DAMMIT, BANNER...

WHAT...?

AGH!

ONK

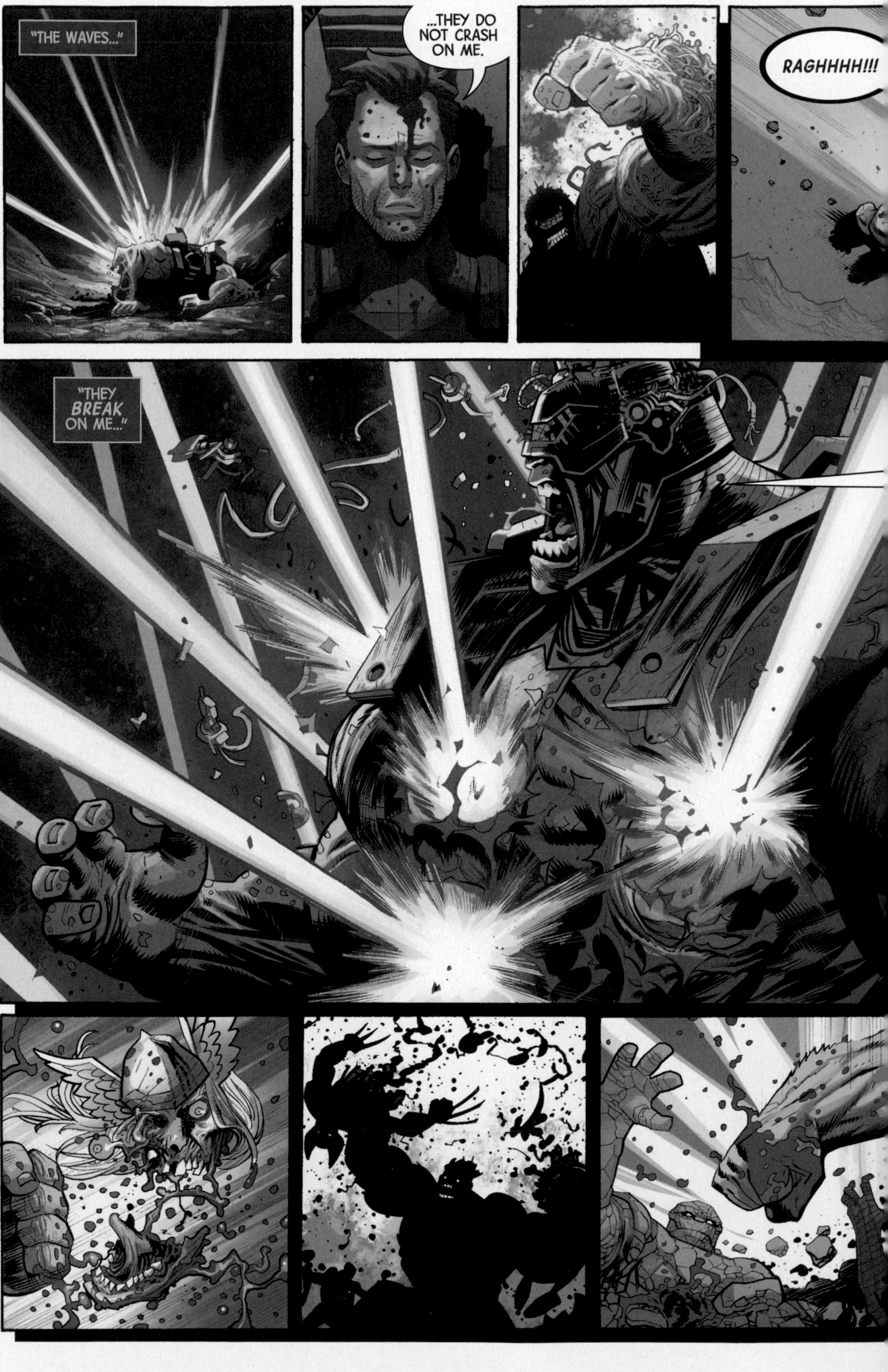
"THE WAVES..."
...THEY DO NOT CRASH ON ME.
RAGHHHH!!!
"THEY BREAK ON ME..."

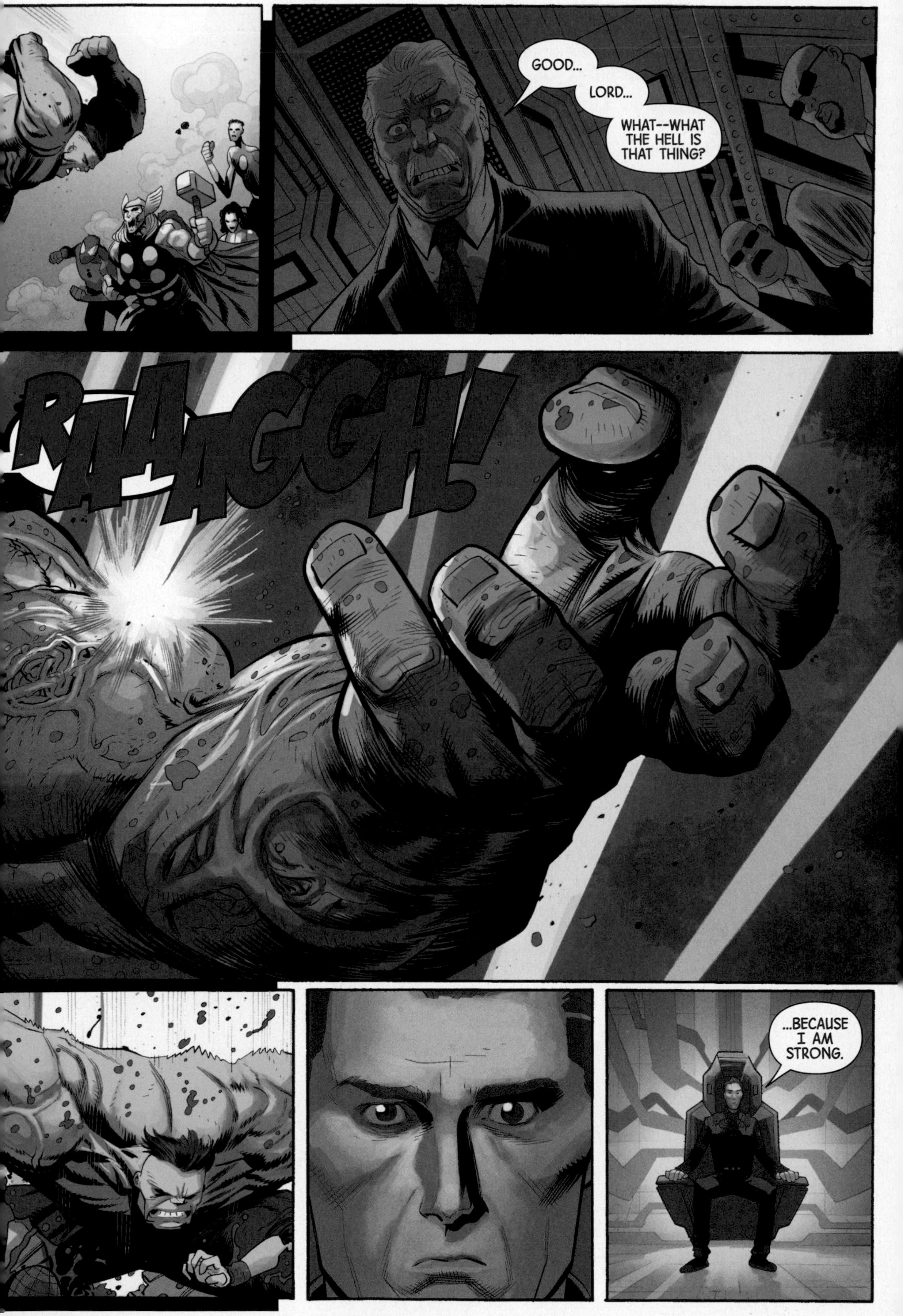
GOOD...
LORD...
WHAT--WHAT THE HELL IS THAT THING?
RAAAGGH!
...BECAUSE I AM STRONG.

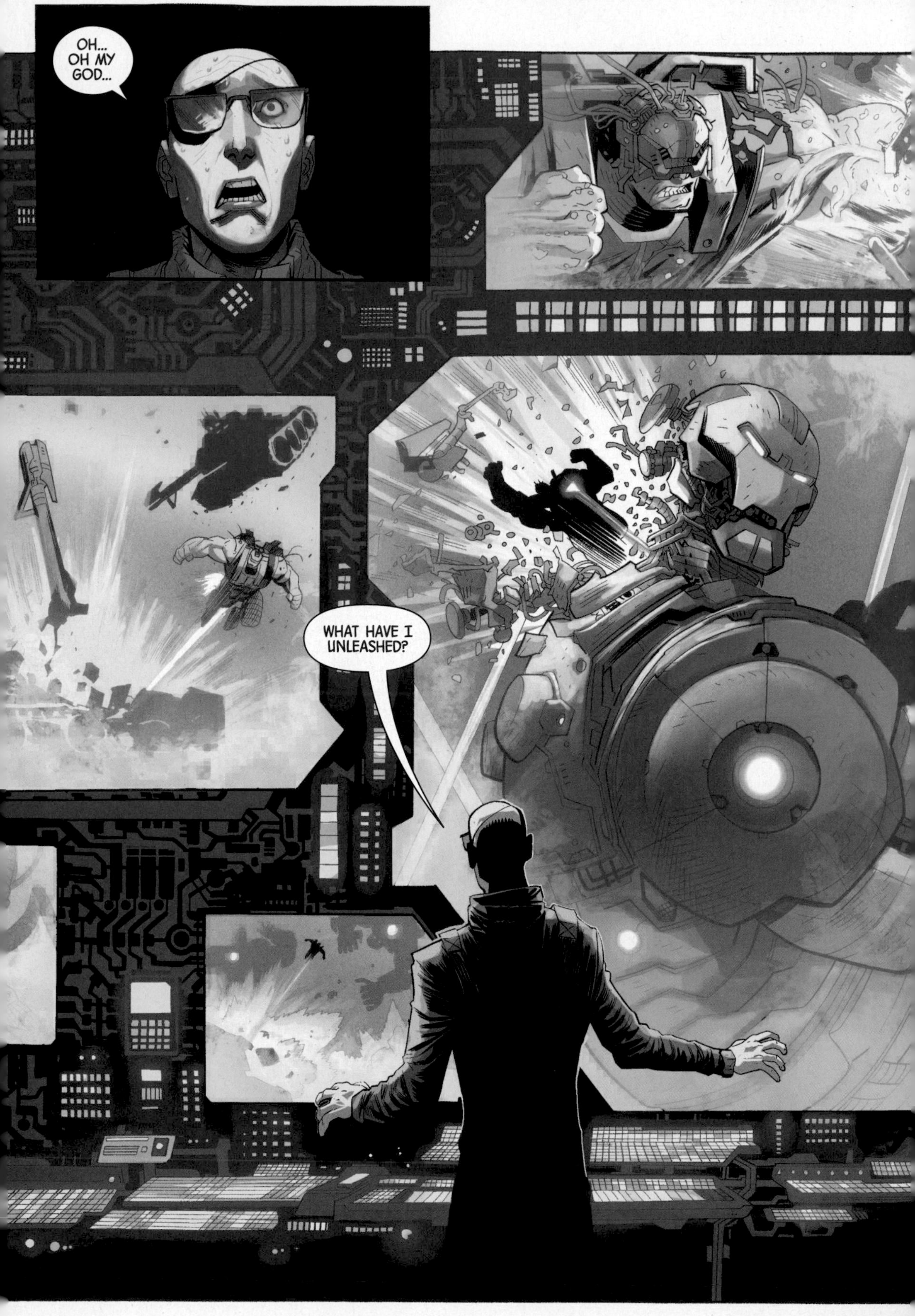
OH... OH MY GOD...
WHAT HAVE I UNLEASHED?

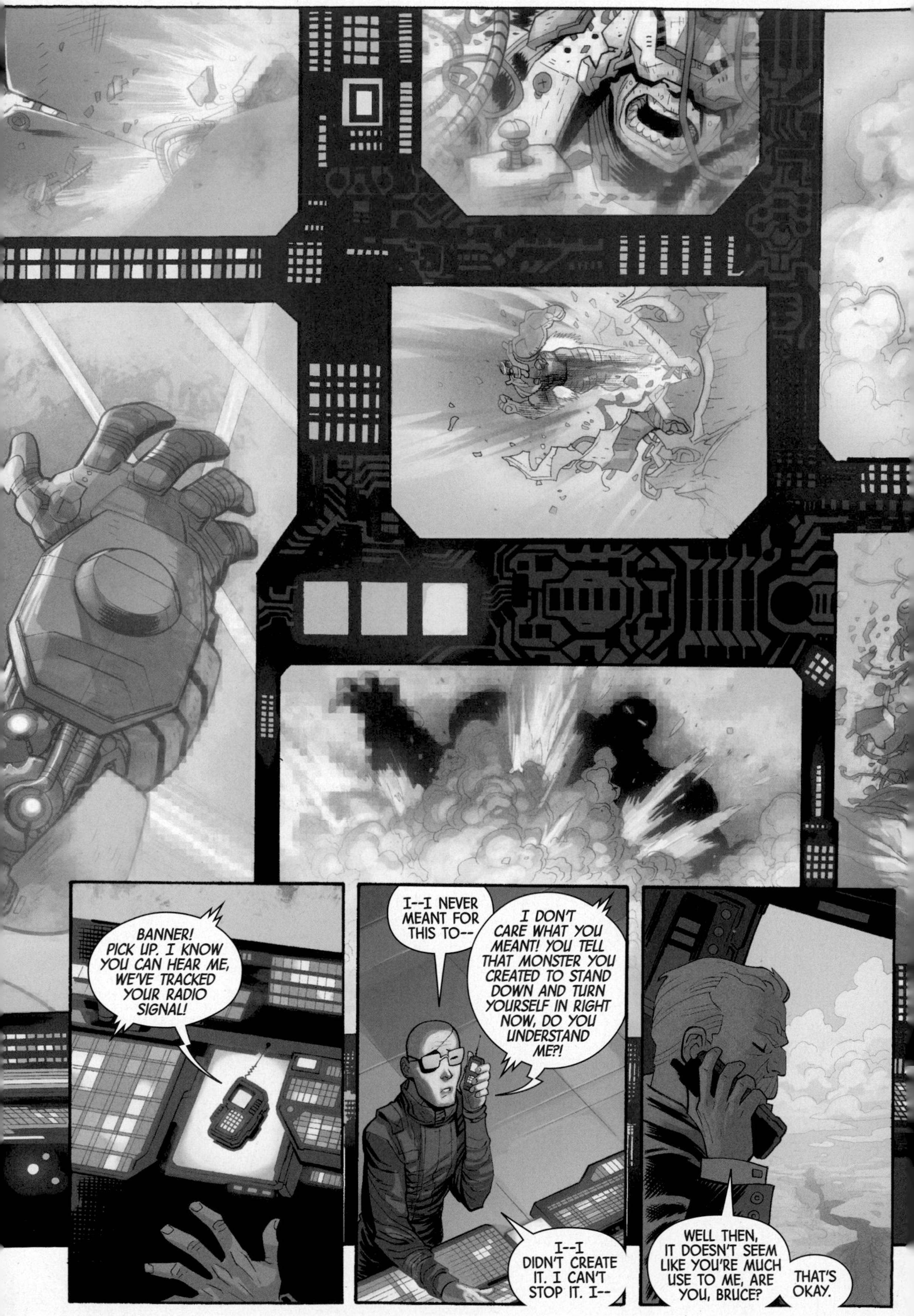
BANNER! PICK UP. I KNOW YOU CAN HEAR ME, WE'VE TRACKED YOUR RADIO SIGNAL!
I--I NEVER MEANT FOR THIS TO--
I DON'T CARE WHAT YOU MEANT! YOU TELL THAT MONSTER YOU CREATED TO STAND DOWN AND TURN YOURSELF IN RIGHT NOW, DO YOU UNDERSTAND ME?!
I--I DIDN'T CREATE IT. I CAN'T STOP IT. I--
WELL THEN, IT DOESN'T SEEM LIKE YOU'RE MUCH USE TO ME, ARE YOU, BRUCE?
THAT'S OKAY.

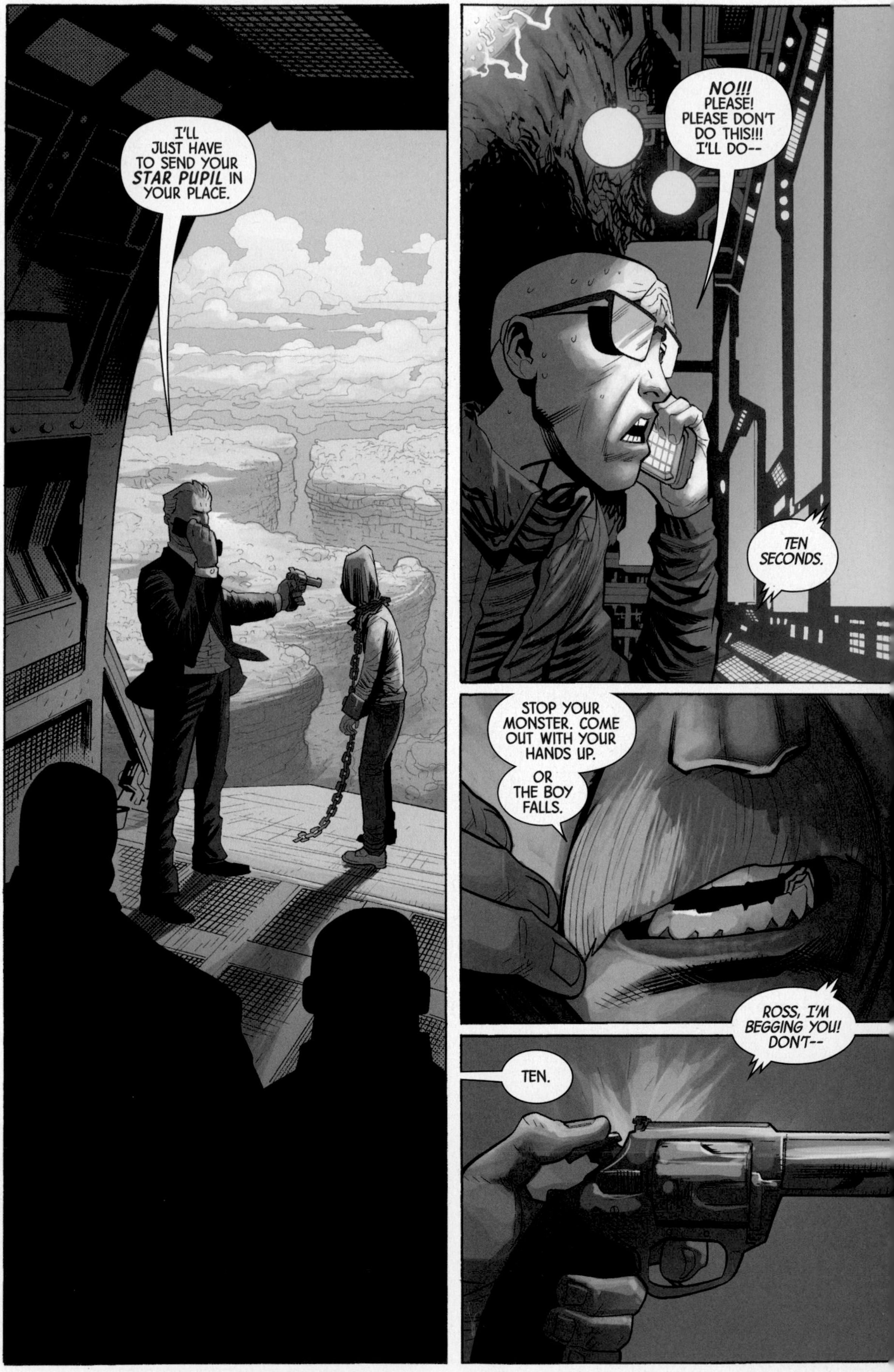
I'LL JUST HAVE TO SEND YOUR *STAR PUPIL* IN YOUR PLACE.
NO!!! PLEASE! PLEASE DON'T DO THIS!!! I'LL DO--
TEN SECONDS.
STOP YOUR MONSTER. COME OUT WITH YOUR HANDS UP.
OR THE BOY FALLS.
ROSS, I'M BEGGING YOU! DON'T--
TEN.

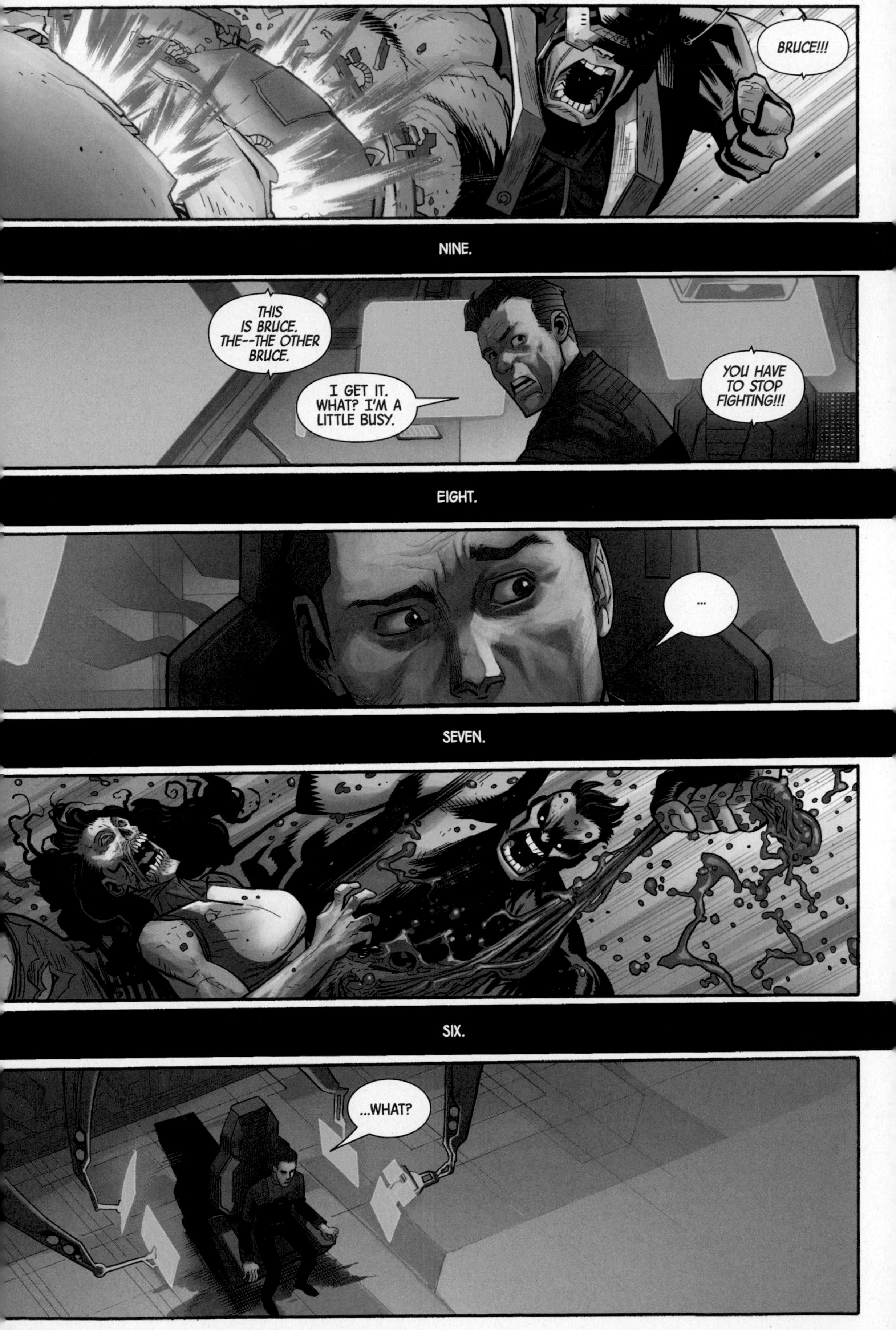
BRUCE!!!
NINE.
THIS IS BRUCE. THE--THE OTHER BRUCE.
I GET IT. WHAT? I'M A LITTLE BUSY.
YOU HAVE TO STOP FIGHTING!!!
EIGHT.
...
SEVEN.
SIX.
...WHAT?

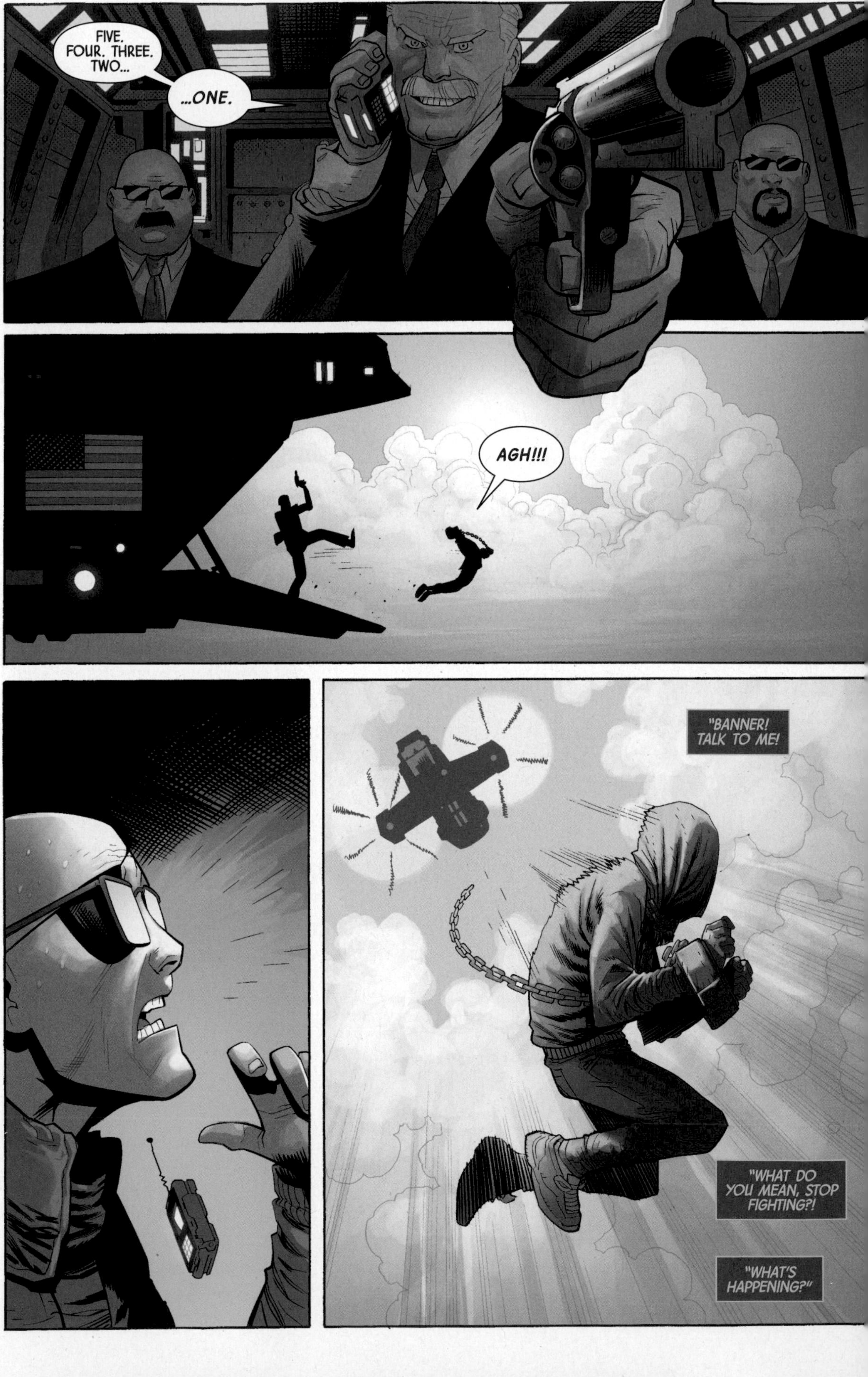
FIVE. FOUR. THREE. TWO...
...ONE.
AGH!!!
"BANNER! TALK TO ME!
"WHAT DO YOU MEAN, STOP FIGHTING?!
"WHAT'S HAPPENING?"

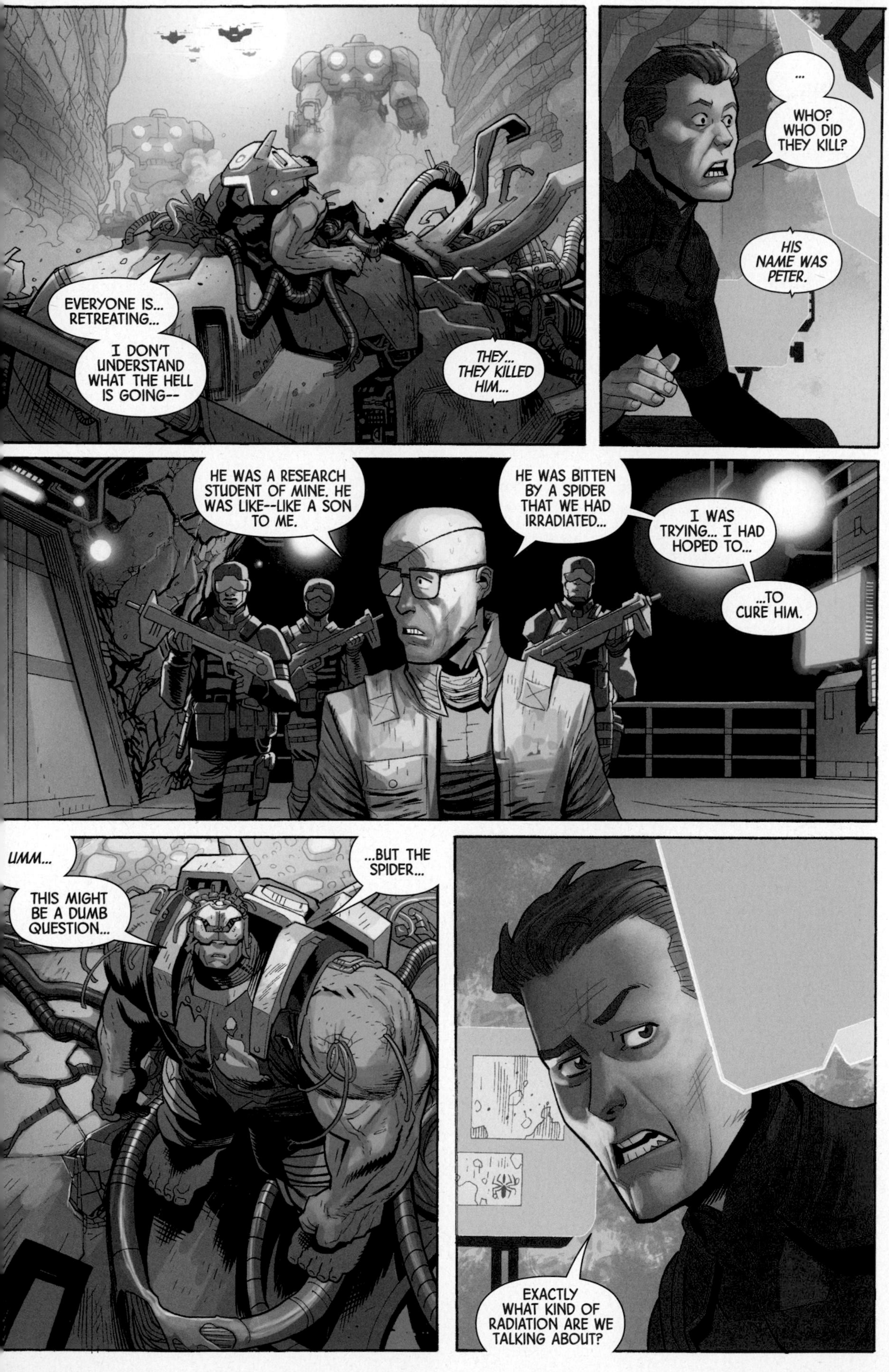
EVERYONE IS... RETREATING...
I DON'T UNDERSTAND WHAT THE HELL IS GOING--
THEY... THEY KILLED HIM...
...
WHO? WHO DID THEY KILL?
HIS NAME WAS PETER.
HE WAS A RESEARCH STUDENT OF MINE. HE WAS LIKE--LIKE A SON TO ME.
HE WAS BITTEN BY A SPIDER THAT WE HAD IRRADIATED...
I WAS TRYING... I HAD HOPED TO...
...TO CURE HIM.
UMM...
THIS MIGHT BE A DUMB QUESTION...
...BUT THE SPIDER...
EXACTLY WHAT KIND OF RADIATION ARE WE TALKING ABOUT?

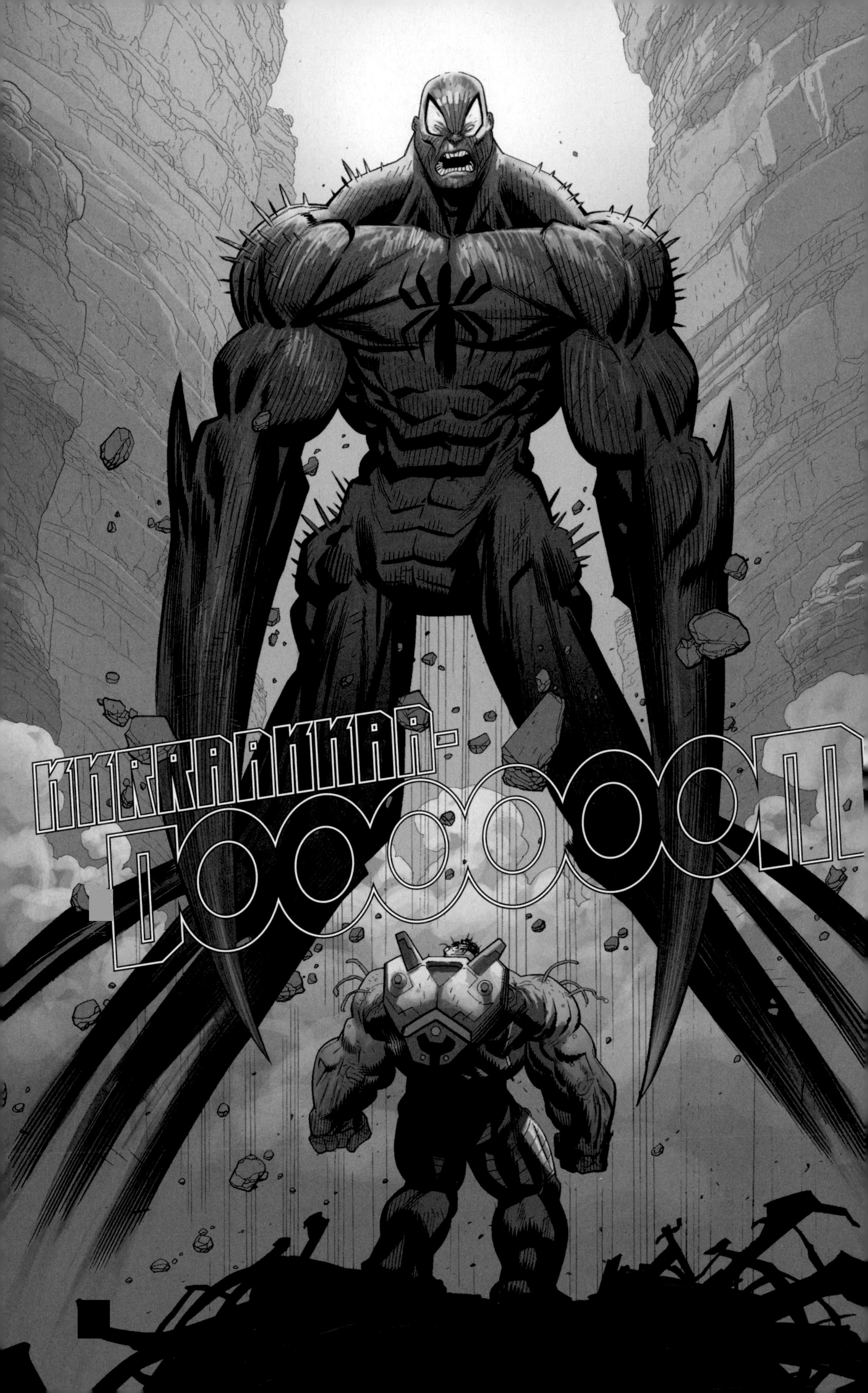
KKRRAKKAR-DOOOOOOM

#2 VARIANT BY
ADAM KUBERT & ALEJANDRO SÁNCHEZ

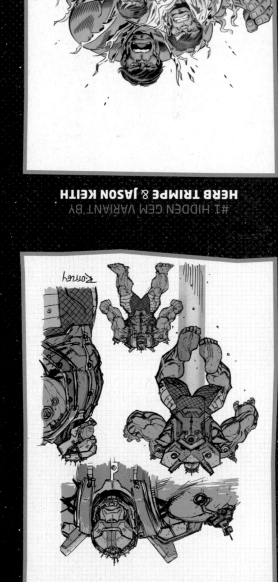

#1 HIDDEN GEM VARIANT BY
HERB TRIMPE & JASON KEITH

#1 2ND-PRINTING
CHARACTER SKETCH VARIANT BY
RYAN OTTLEY

#1 DESIGN VARIANT BY
RYAN OTTLEY

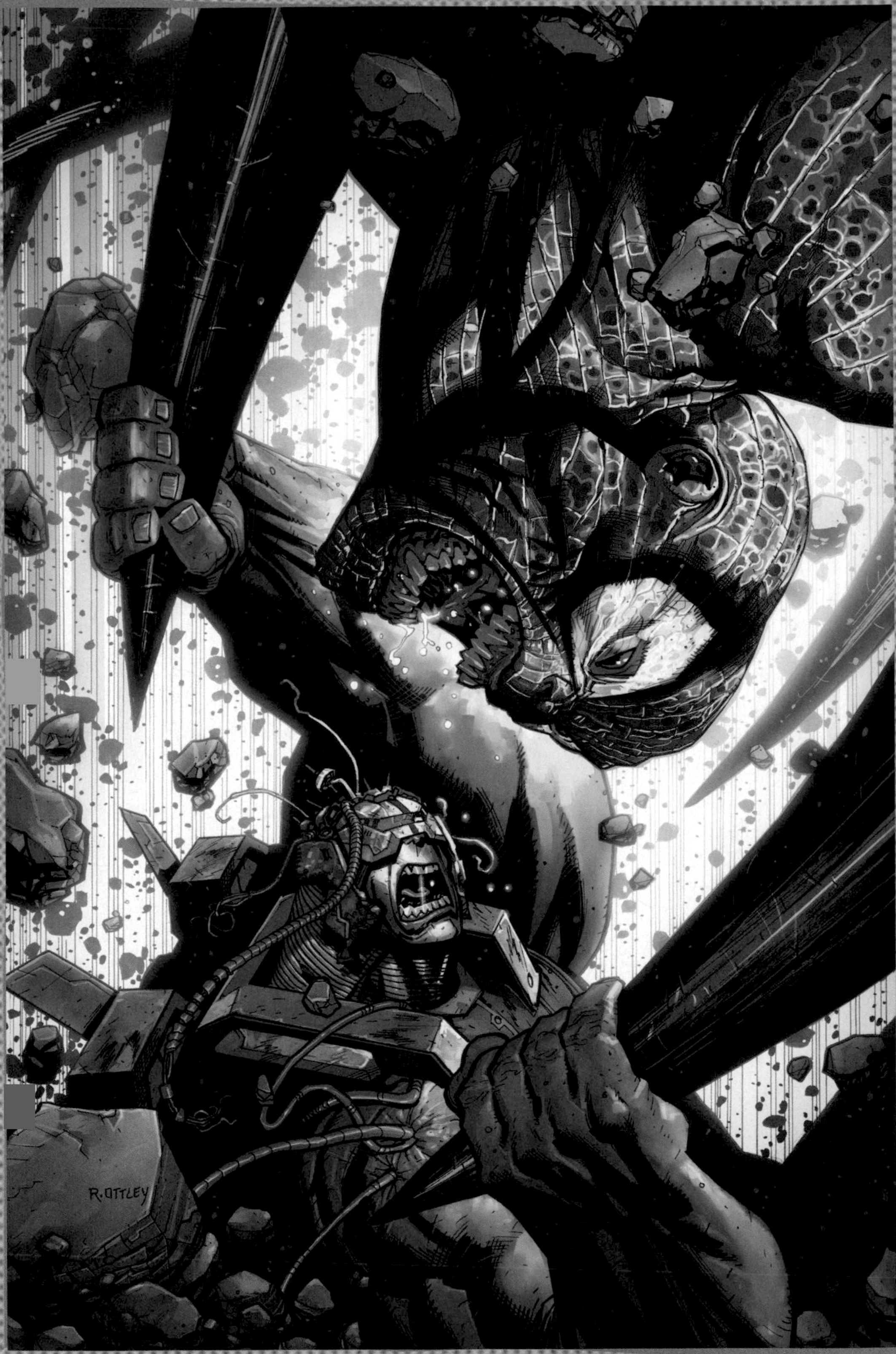
R.OTTLEY

HULK
NUMBER 5

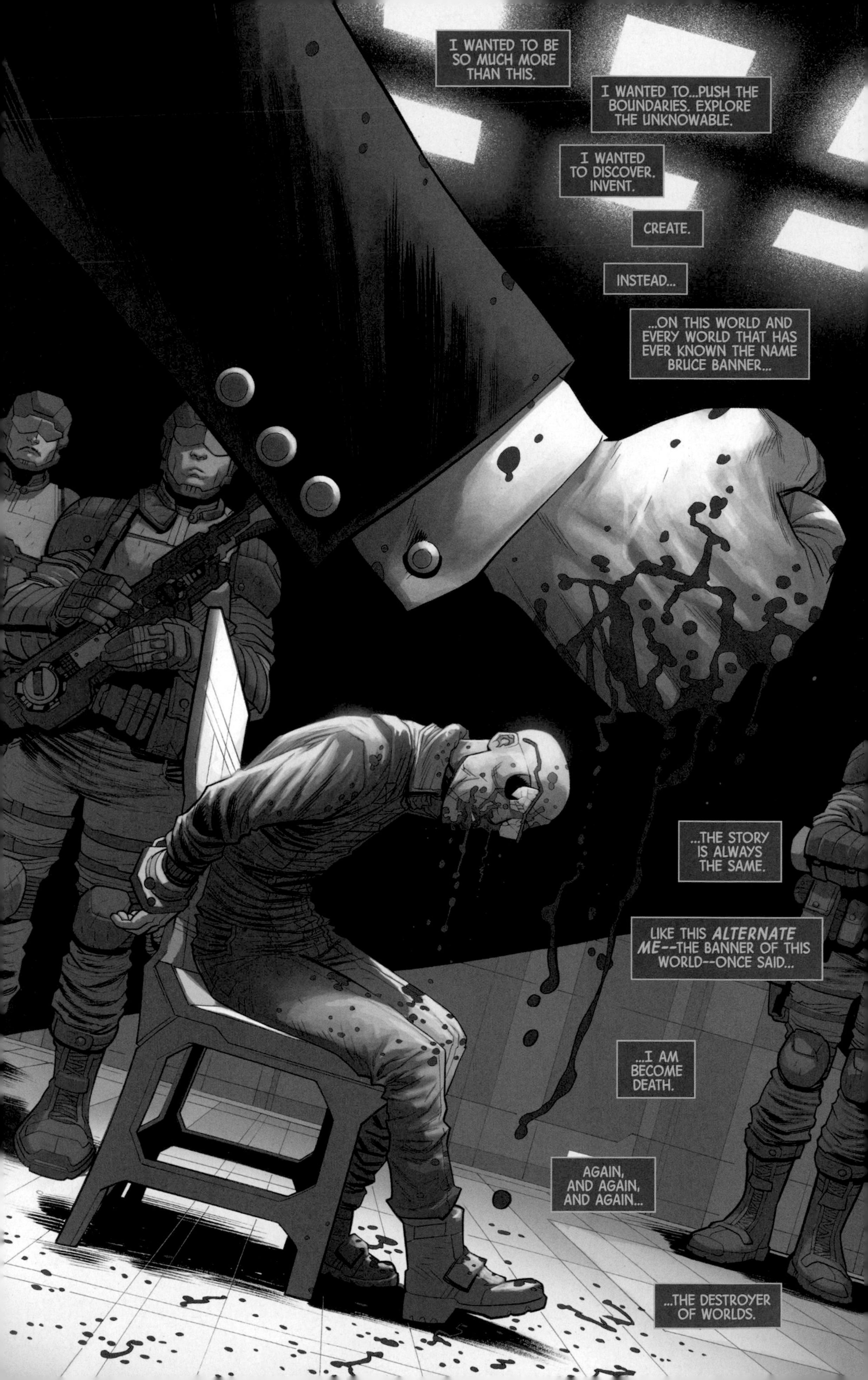
I WANTED TO BE SO MUCH MORE THAN THIS.
I WANTED TO...PUSH THE BOUNDARIES. EXPLORE THE UNKNOWABLE.
I WANTED TO DISCOVER. INVENT.
CREATE.
INSTEAD...
...ON THIS WORLD AND EVERY WORLD THAT HAS EVER KNOWN THE NAME BRUCE BANNER...
...THE STORY IS ALWAYS THE SAME.
LIKE THIS *ALTERNATE ME*--THE BANNER OF THIS WORLD--ONCE SAID...
...I AM BECOME DEATH.
AGAIN, AND AGAIN, AND AGAIN...
...THE DESTROYER OF WORLDS.

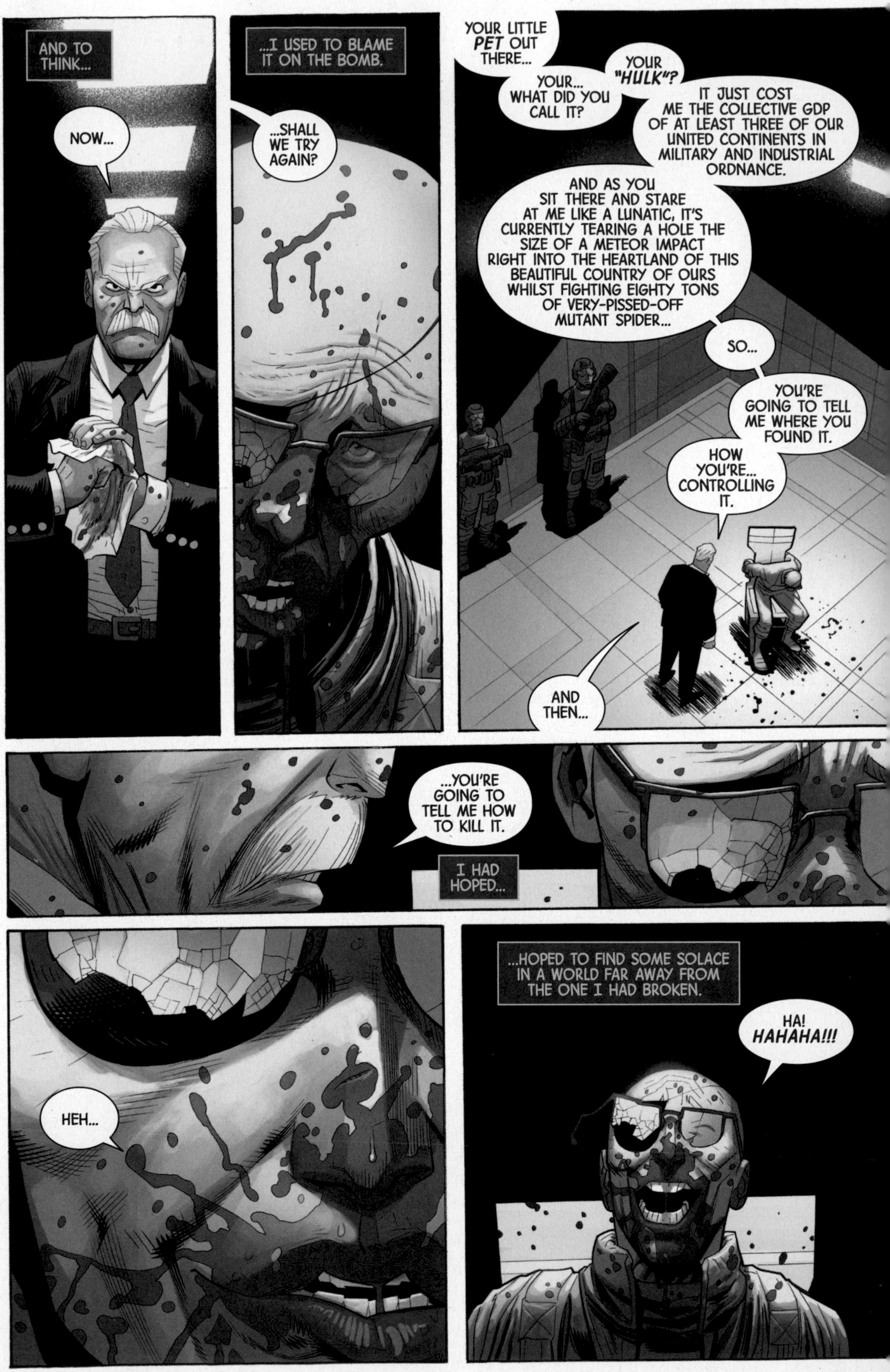
AND TO THINK...
NOW...
...I USED TO BLAME IT ON THE BOMB.
...SHALL WE TRY AGAIN?
YOUR LITTLE PET OUT THERE...
YOUR... WHAT DID YOU CALL IT?
YOUR "HULK"?
IT JUST COST ME THE COLLECTIVE GDP OF AT LEAST THREE OF OUR UNITED CONTINENTS IN MILITARY AND INDUSTRIAL ORDNANCE.
AND AS YOU SIT THERE AND STARE AT ME LIKE A LUNATIC, IT'S CURRENTLY TEARING A HOLE THE SIZE OF A METEOR IMPACT RIGHT INTO THE HEARTLAND OF THIS BEAUTIFUL COUNTRY OF OURS WHILST FIGHTING EIGHTY TONS OF VERY-PISSED-OFF MUTANT SPIDER...
SO...
YOU'RE GOING TO TELL ME WHERE YOU FOUND IT.
HOW YOU'RE... CONTROLLING IT.
AND THEN...
...YOU'RE GOING TO TELL ME HOW TO KILL IT.
I HAD HOPED...
HEH...
...HOPED TO FIND SOME SOLACE IN A WORLD FAR AWAY FROM THE ONE I HAD BROKEN.
HA! HAHAHA!!!

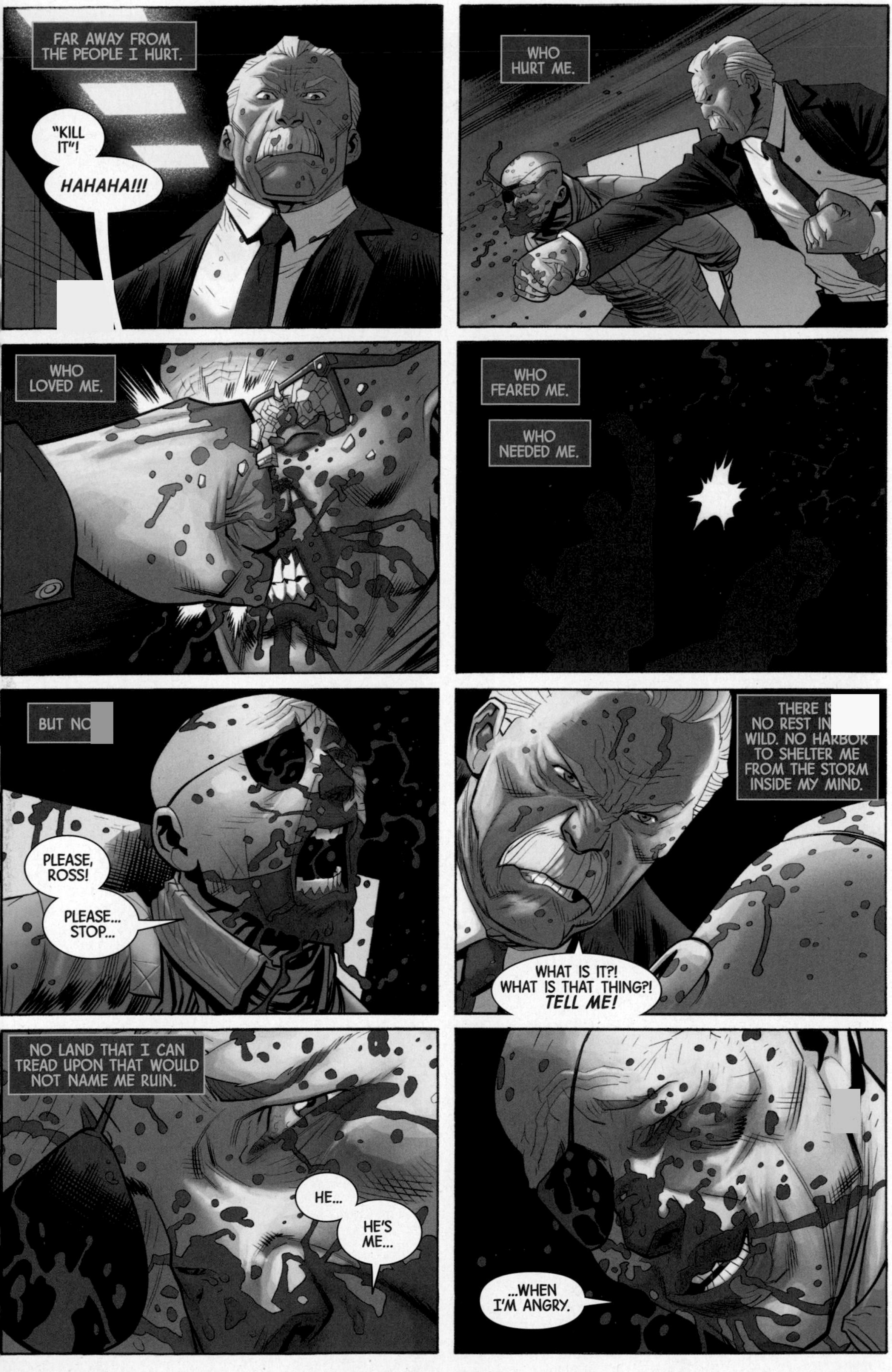
FAR AWAY FROM THE PEOPLE I HURT.
"KILL IT"!
HAHAHA!!!
WHO HURT ME.
WHO LOVED ME.
WHO FEARED ME.
WHO NEEDED ME.
BUT NO
PLEASE, ROSS!
PLEASE... STOP...
THERE I
NO REST IN
WILD. NO HARBOR
TO SHELTER ME
FROM THE STORM
INSIDE MY MIND.
WHAT IS IT?! WHAT IS THAT THING?! TELL ME!
NO LAND THAT I CAN TREAD UPON THAT WOULD NOT NAME ME RUIN.
HE...
HE'S ME...
...WHEN I'M ANGRY.

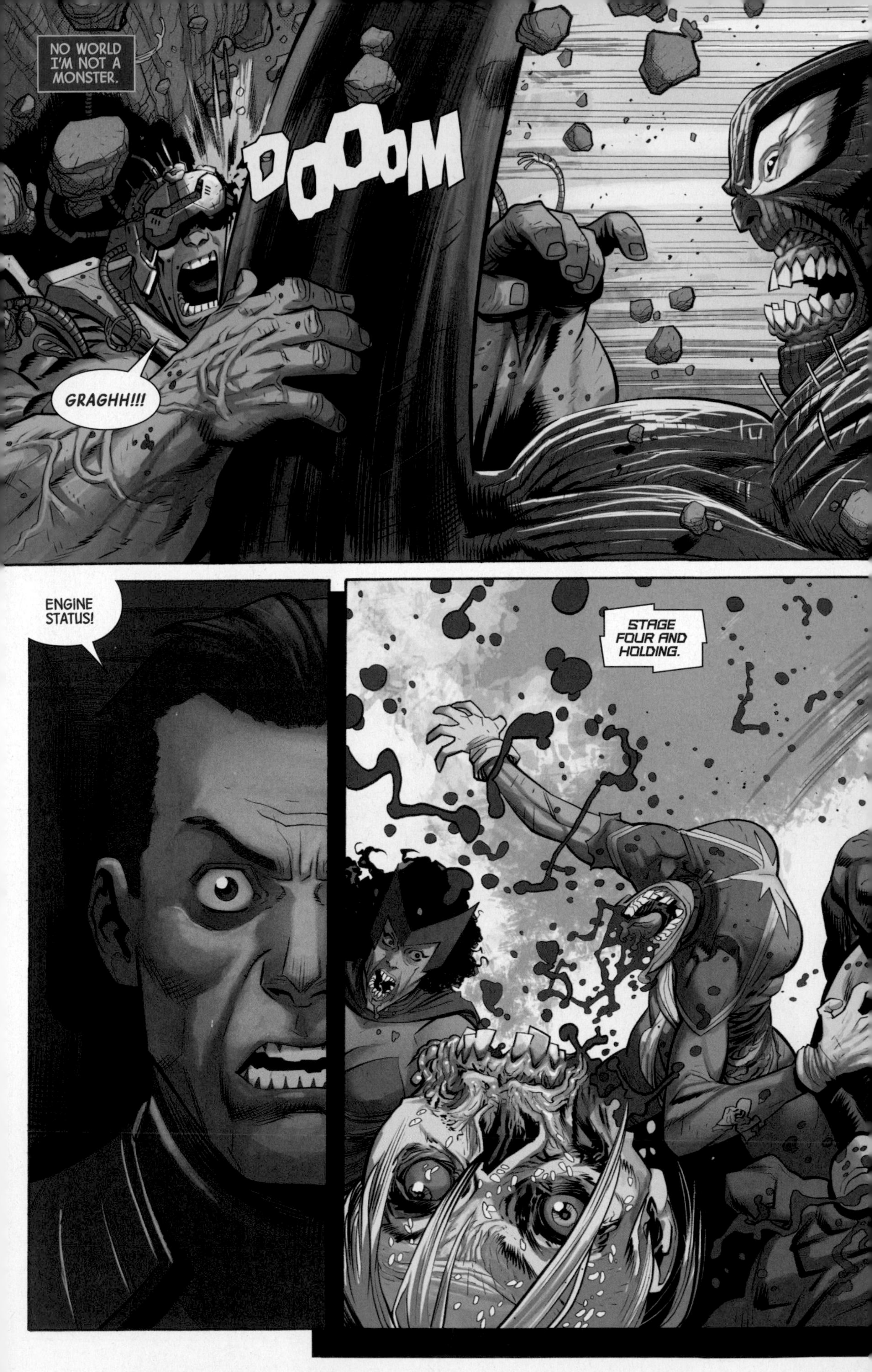
NO WORLD I'M NOT A MONSTER.
DOOOOM
GRAGHH!!!
ENGINE STATUS!
STAGE FOUR AND HOLDING.

OKAY.
DEEP BREATH, BIG GUY.

THIS IS GOING TO GET WORSE BEFORE IT GETS BETTER.

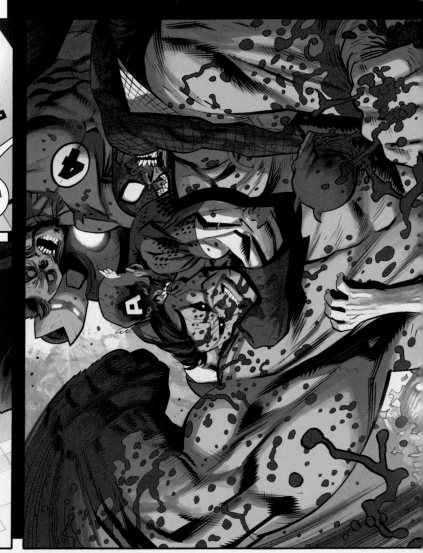

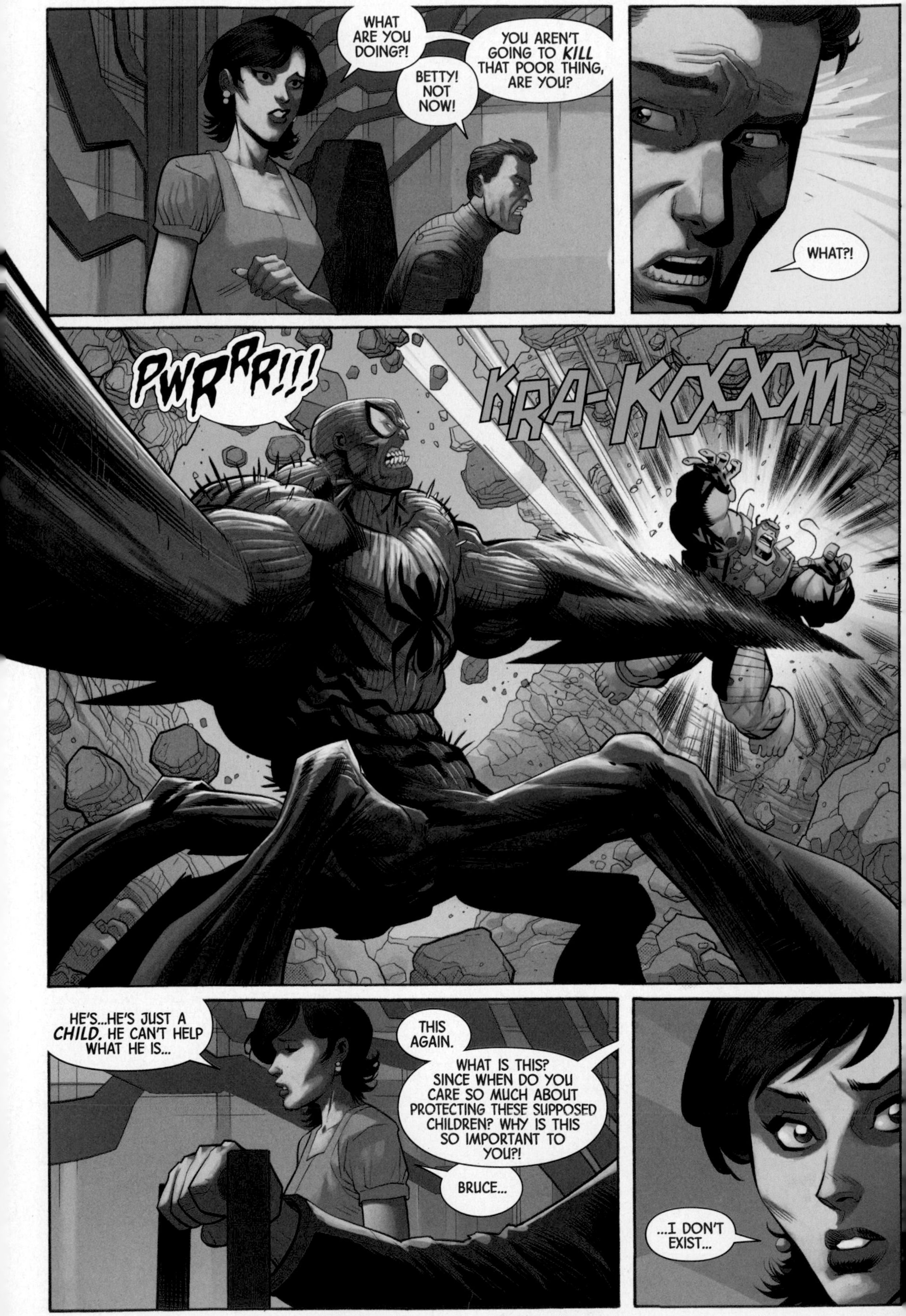
WHAT ARE YOU DOING?!
BETTY! NOT NOW!
YOU AREN'T GOING TO *KILL* THAT POOR THING, ARE YOU?
WHAT?!
PWRRR!!!
KRA-KOOOM
HE'S...HE'S JUST A *CHILD.* HE CAN'T HELP WHAT HE IS...
THIS AGAIN.
WHAT IS THIS? SINCE WHEN DO YOU CARE SO MUCH ABOUT PROTECTING THESE SUPPOSED CHILDREN? WHY IS THIS SO IMPORTANT TO YOU?!
BRUCE...
...I DON'T EXIST...

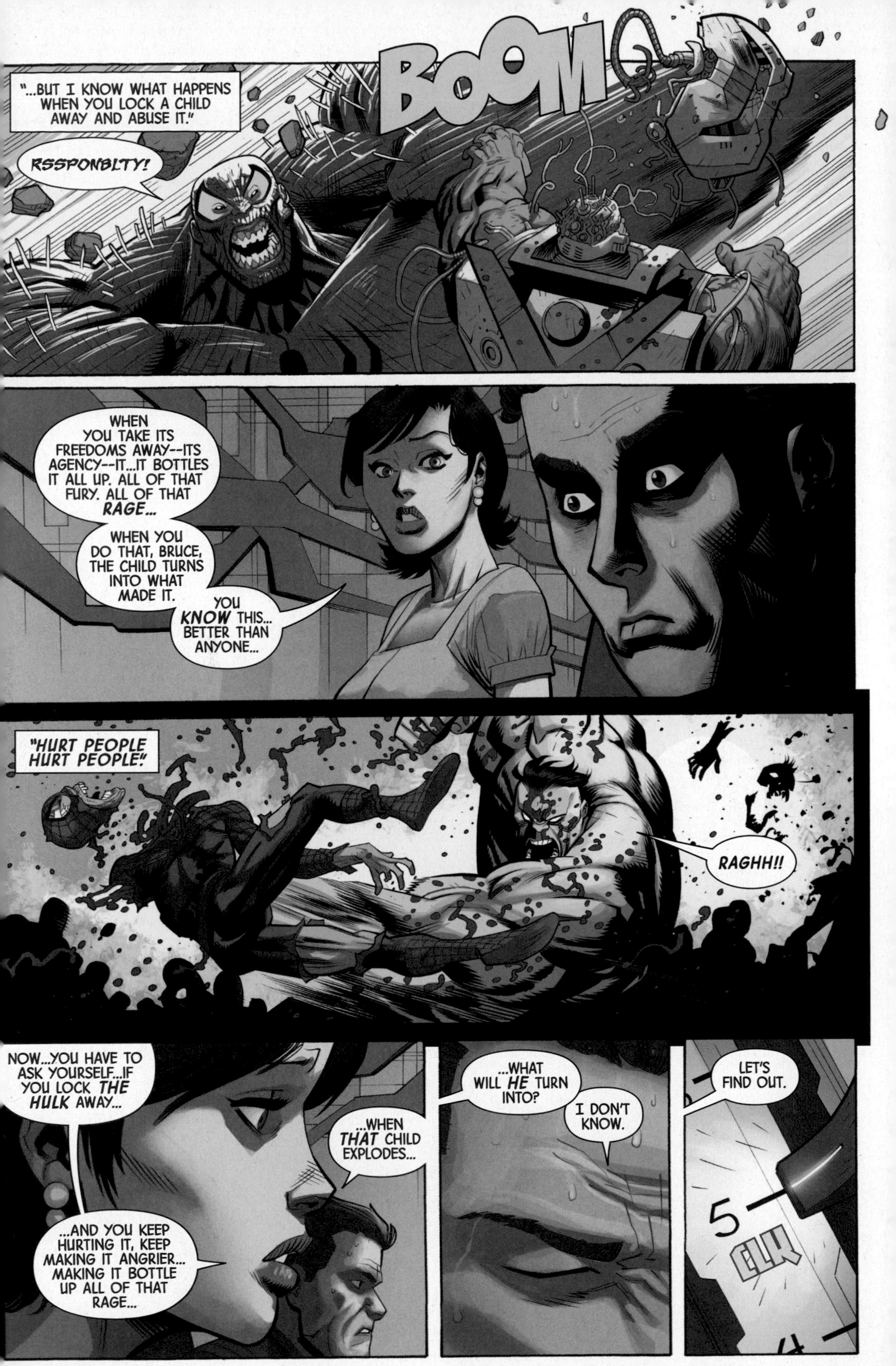
"...BUT I KNOW WHAT HAPPENS WHEN YOU LOCK A CHILD AWAY AND ABUSE IT."
BOOM
RSSPONBLTY!
WHEN YOU TAKE ITS FREEDOMS AWAY--ITS AGENCY--IT...IT BOTTLES IT ALL UP. ALL OF THAT FURY. ALL OF THAT RAGE...
WHEN YOU DO THAT, BRUCE, THE CHILD TURNS INTO WHAT MADE IT.
YOU KNOW THIS... BETTER THAN ANYONE...
"HURT PEOPLE HURT PEOPLE."
RAGHH!!
NOW...YOU HAVE TO ASK YOURSELF...IF YOU LOCK THE HULK AWAY...
...AND YOU KEEP HURTING IT, KEEP MAKING IT ANGRIER... MAKING IT BOTTLE UP ALL OF THAT RAGE...
...WHEN THAT CHILD EXPLODES...
...WHAT WILL HE TURN INTO?
I DON'T KNOW.
LET'S FIND OUT.
5
CLK

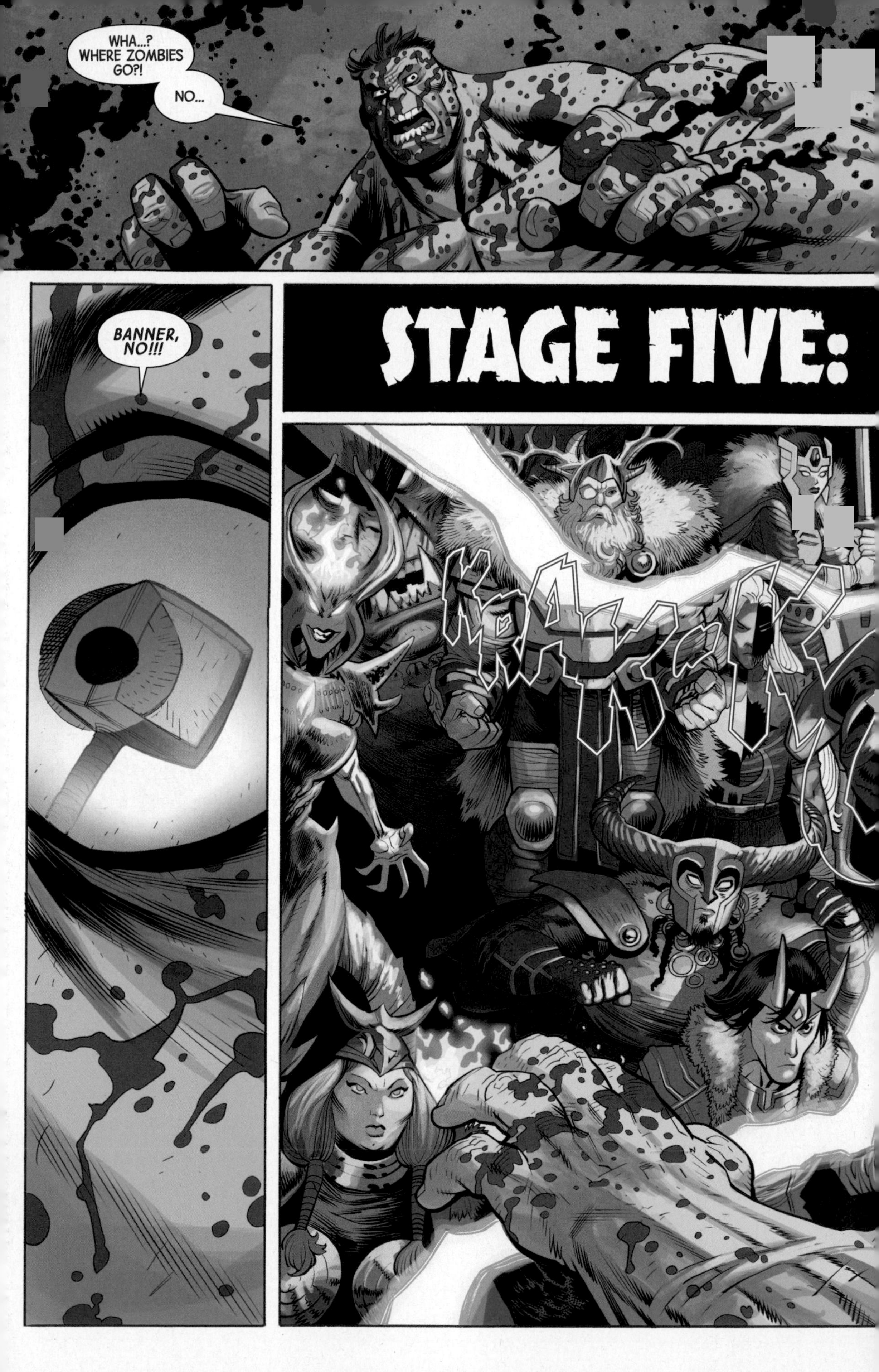
WHA...? WHERE ZOMBIES GO?!
NO...
BANNER, NO!!!
STAGE FIVE:

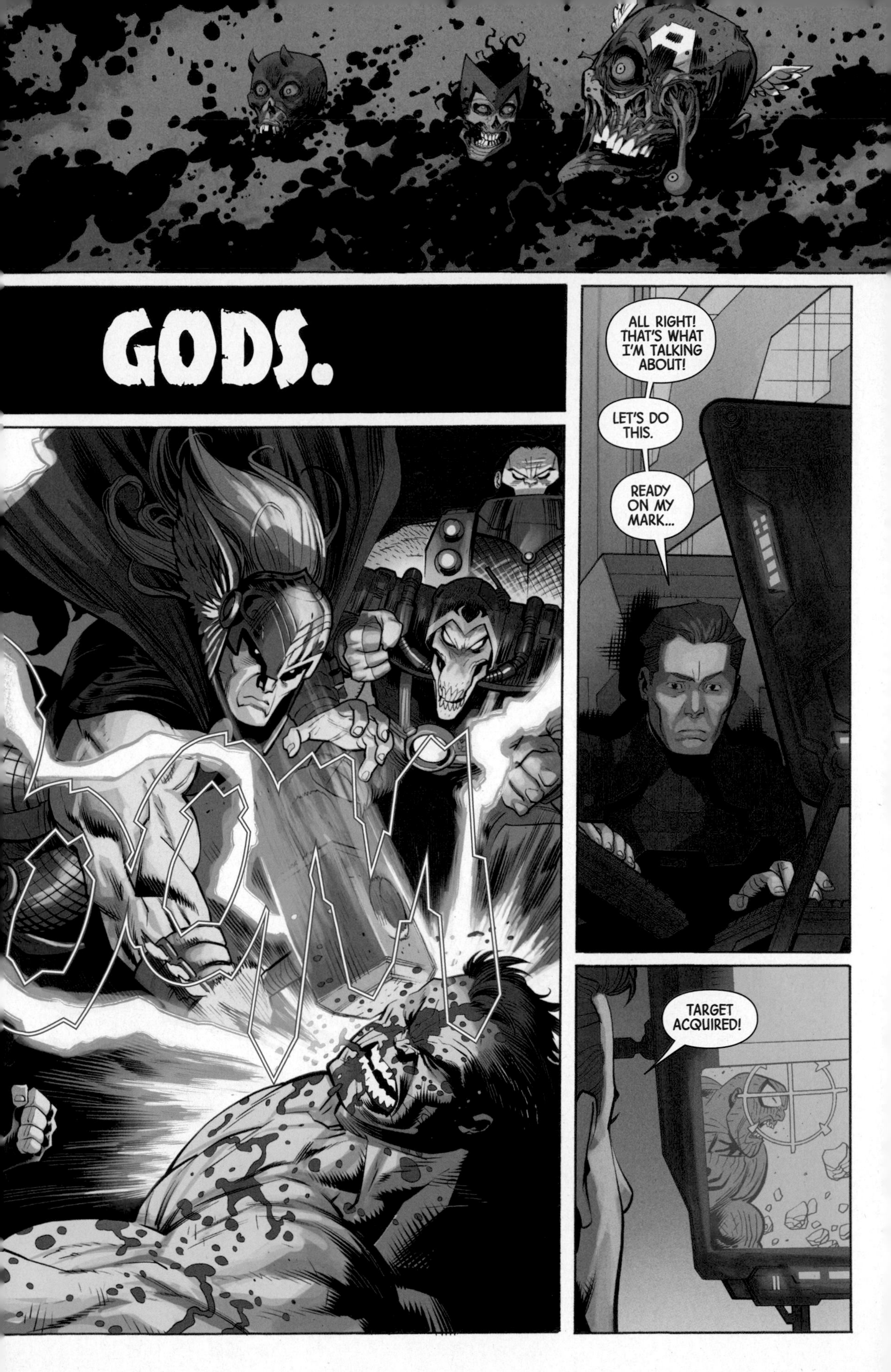
GODS.
DOOM
ALL RIGHT! THAT'S WHAT I'M TALKING ABOUT!
LET'S DO THIS.
READY ON MY MARK...
TARGET ACQUIRED!

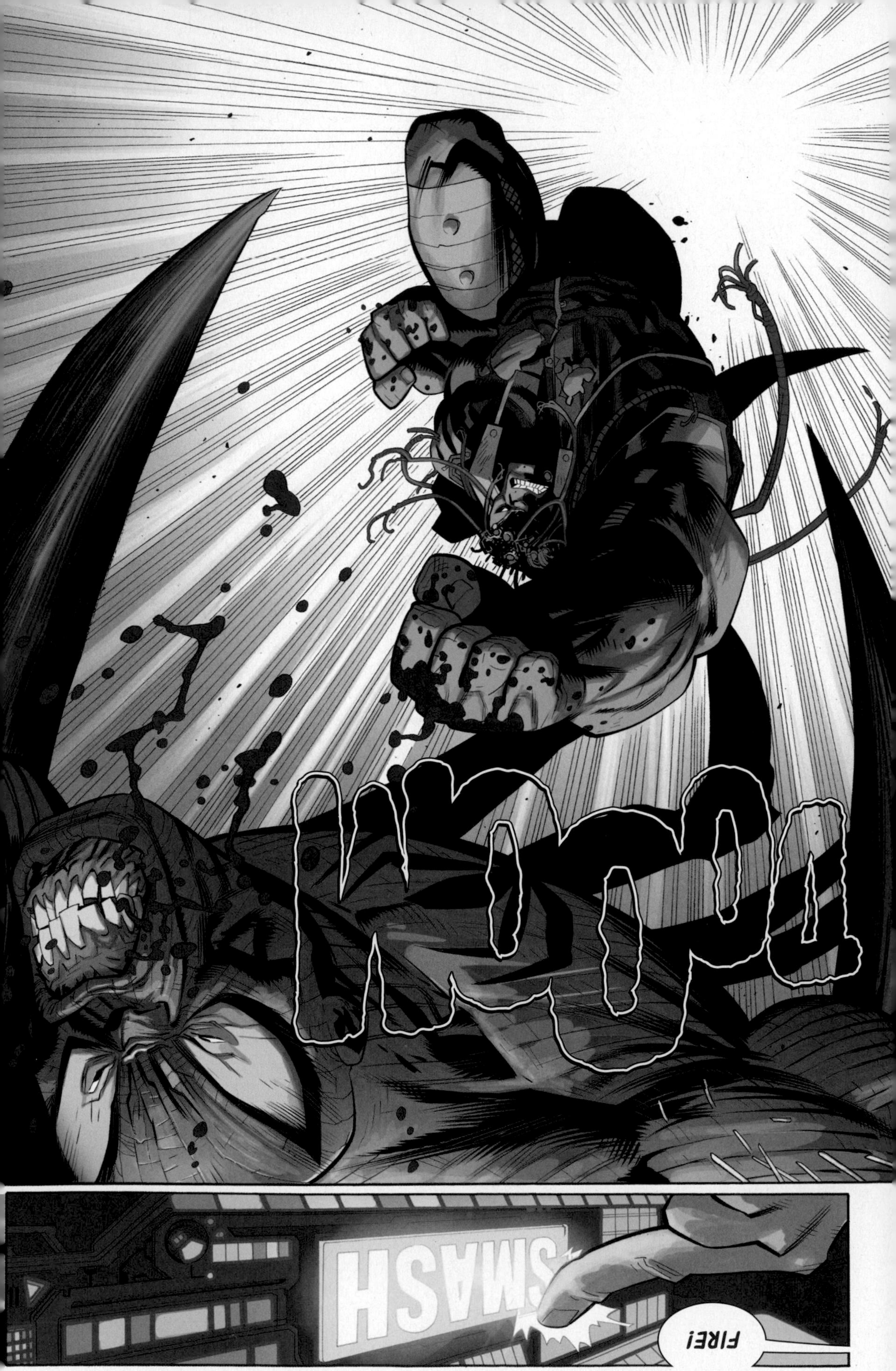
SMASH
FIRE!

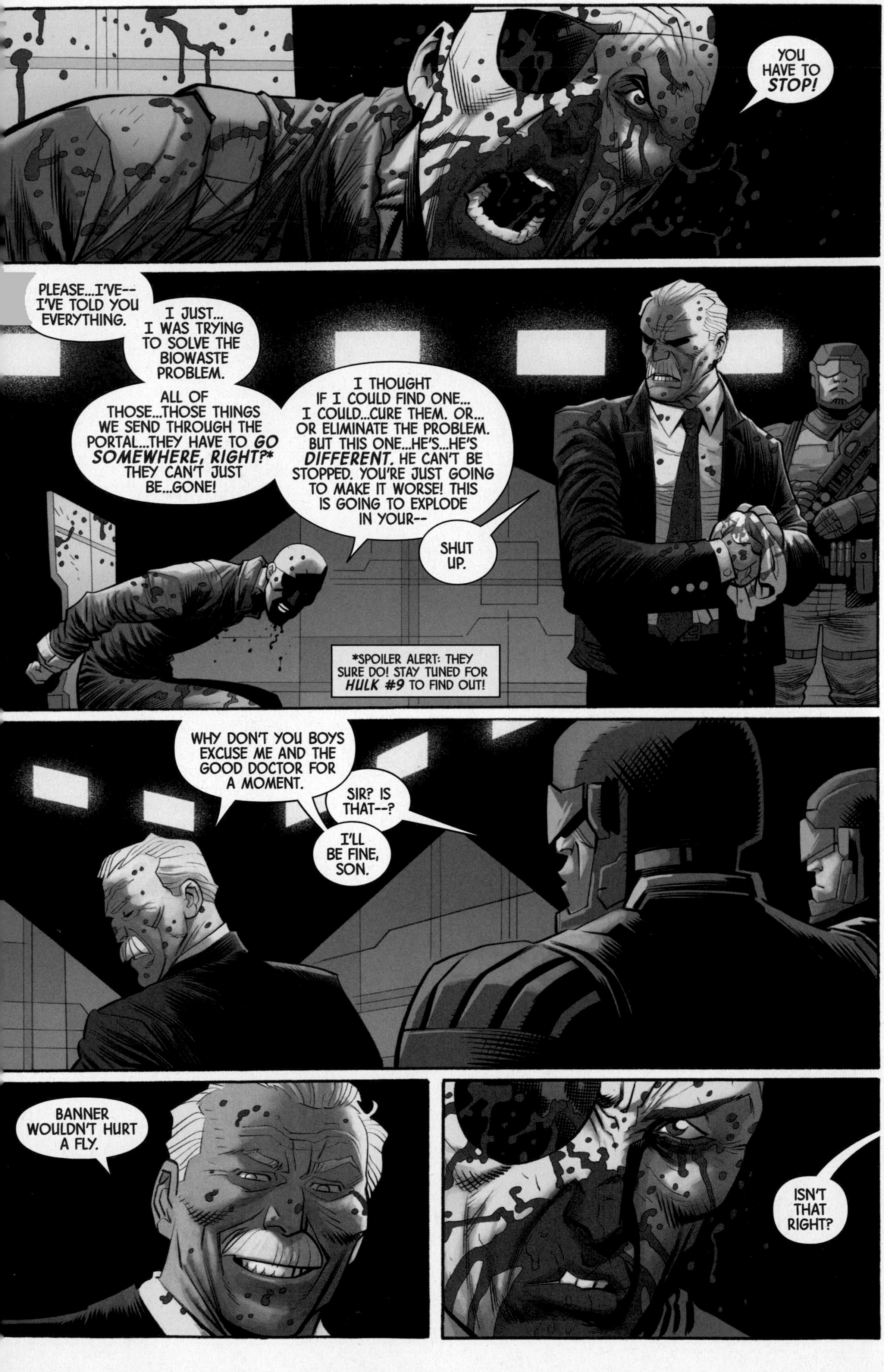
YOU HAVE TO *STOP!*
PLEASE...I'VE-- I'VE TOLD YOU EVERYTHING.
I JUST... I WAS TRYING TO SOLVE THE BIOWASTE PROBLEM.
ALL OF THOSE...THOSE THINGS WE SEND THROUGH THE PORTAL...THEY HAVE TO *GO SOMEWHERE, RIGHT?** THEY CAN'T JUST BE...GONE!
I THOUGHT IF I COULD FIND ONE... I COULD...CURE THEM. OR... OR ELIMINATE THE PROBLEM. BUT THIS ONE...HE'S...HE'S *DIFFERENT.* HE CAN'T BE STOPPED. YOU'RE JUST GOING TO MAKE IT WORSE! THIS IS GOING TO EXPLODE IN YOUR--
SHUT UP.
*SPOILER ALERT: THEY SURE DO! STAY TUNED FOR *HULK #9* TO FIND OUT!
WHY DON'T YOU BOYS EXCUSE ME AND THE GOOD DOCTOR FOR A MOMENT.
SIR? IS THAT--?
I'LL BE FINE, SON.
BANNER WOULDN'T HURT A FLY.
ISN'T THAT RIGHT?

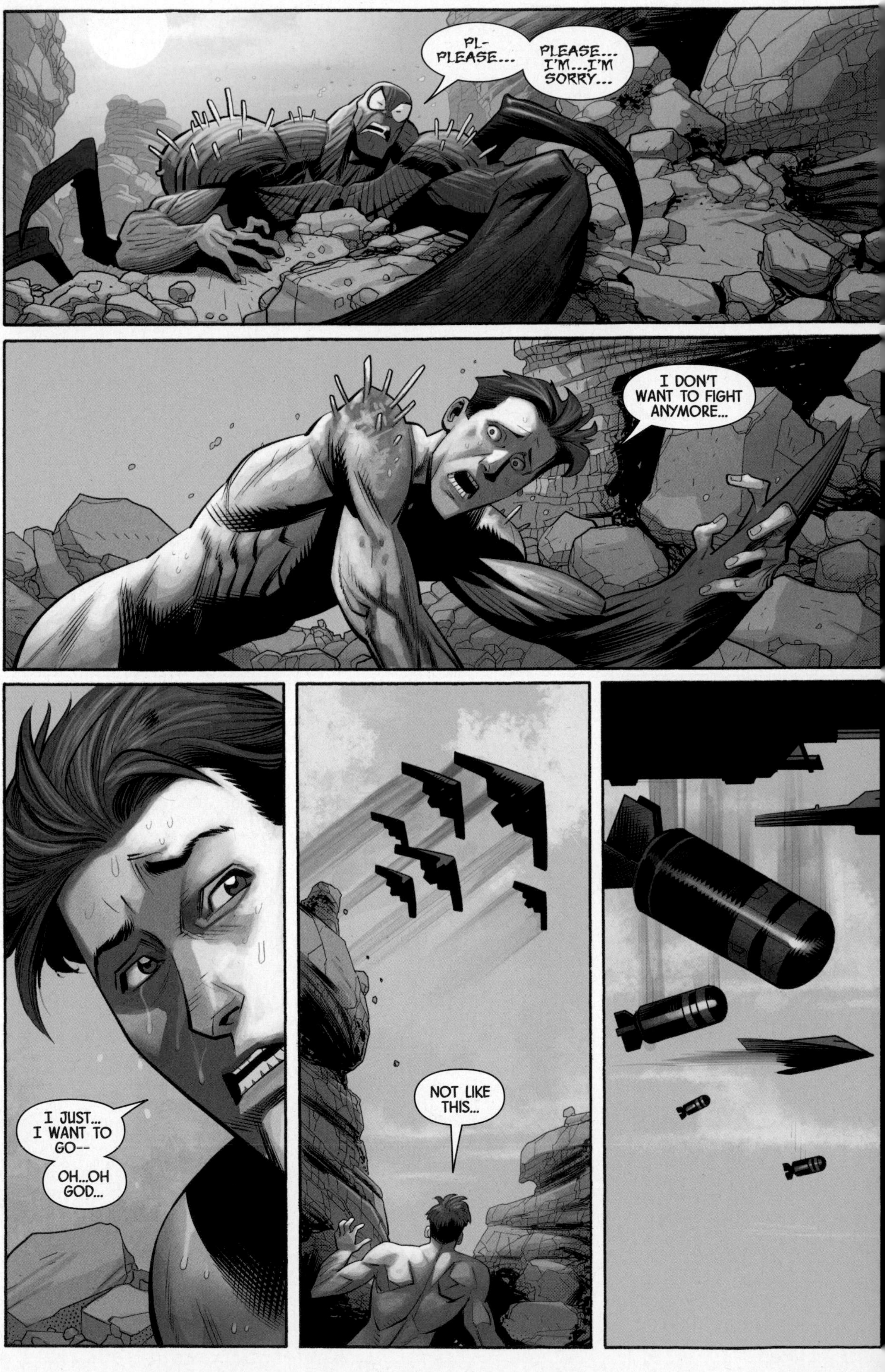
PL-
PLEASE...
PLEASE... I'M...I'M SORRY...
I DON'T WANT TO FIGHT ANYMORE...
I JUST... I WANT TO GO--
OH...OH GOD...
NOT LIKE THIS...

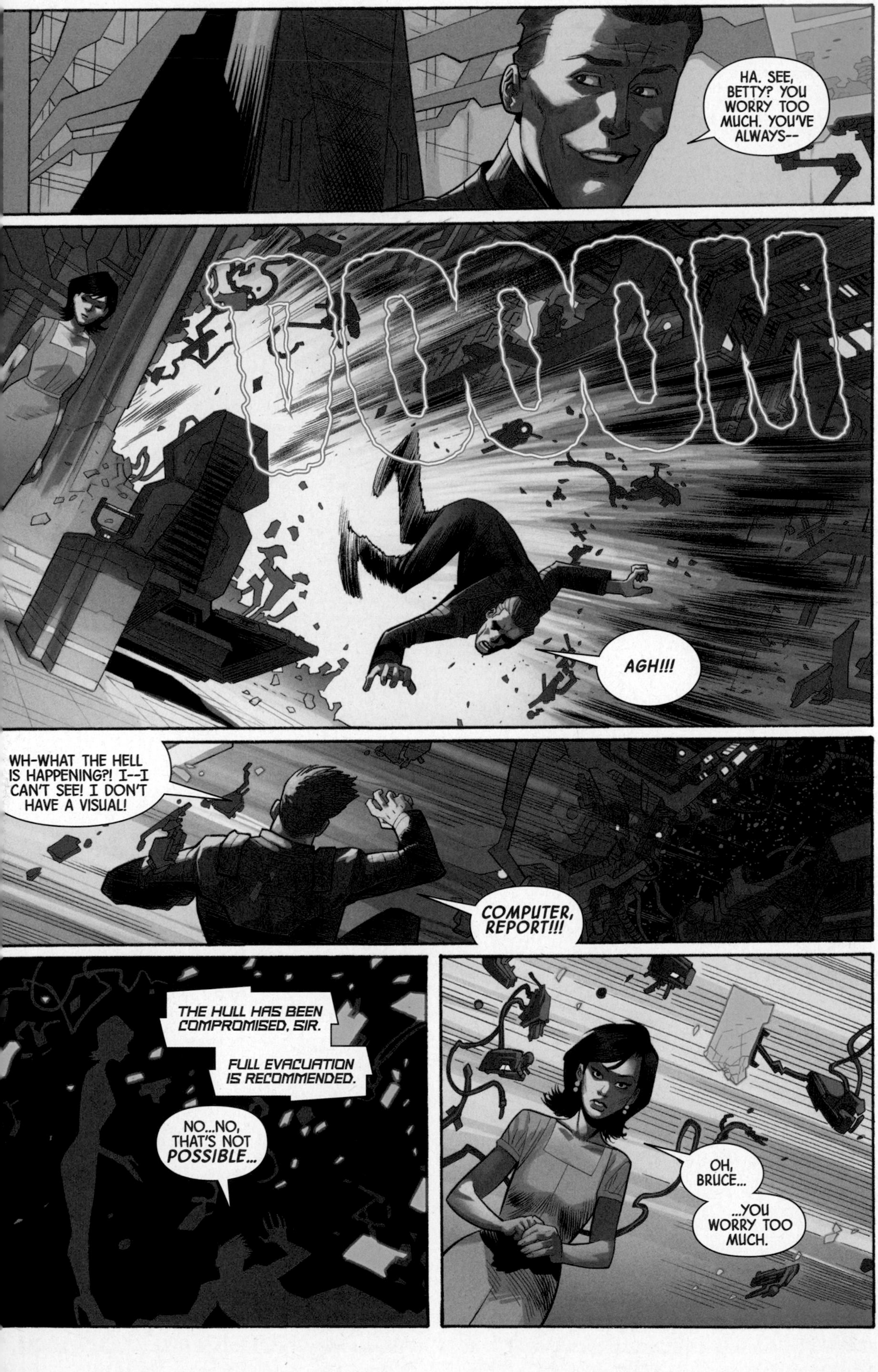
HA. SEE, BETTY? YOU WORRY TOO MUCH. YOU'VE ALWAYS--
DOOOM
AGH!!!
WH-WHAT THE HELL IS HAPPENING?! I--I CAN'T SEE! I DON'T HAVE A VISUAL!
COMPUTER, REPORT!!!
THE HULL HAS BEEN COMPROMISED, SIR.
FULL EVACUATION IS RECOMMENDED.
NO...NO, THAT'S NOT POSSIBLE...
OH, BRUCE...
...YOU WORRY TOO MUCH.

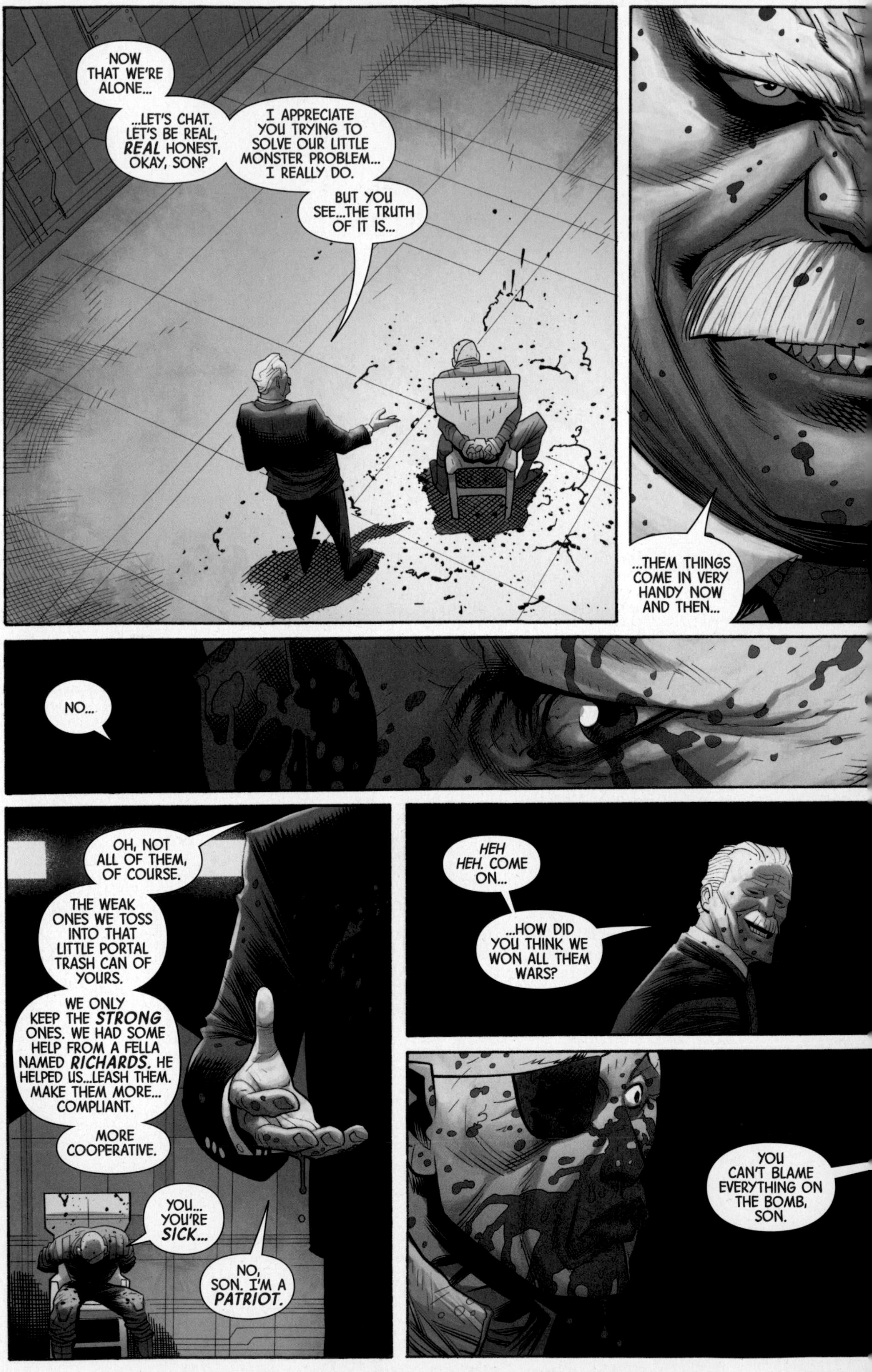
NOW THAT WE'RE ALONE...
...LET'S CHAT. LET'S BE REAL, *REAL* HONEST, OKAY, SON?
I APPRECIATE YOU TRYING TO SOLVE OUR LITTLE MONSTER PROBLEM... I REALLY DO.
BUT YOU SEE...THE TRUTH OF IT IS...
...THEM THINGS COME IN VERY HANDY NOW AND THEN...
NO...
OH, NOT ALL OF THEM, OF COURSE.
THE WEAK ONES WE TOSS INTO THAT LITTLE PORTAL TRASH CAN OF YOURS.
WE ONLY KEEP THE *STRONG* ONES. WE HAD SOME HELP FROM A FELLA NAMED *RICHARDS.* HE HELPED US...LEASH THEM. MAKE THEM MORE... COMPLIANT.
MORE COOPERATIVE.
YOU... YOU'RE *SICK*...
NO, SON. I'M A *PATRIOT.*
HEH HEH. COME ON...
...HOW DID YOU THINK WE WON ALL THEM WARS?
YOU CAN'T BLAME EVERYTHING ON THE BOMB, SON.

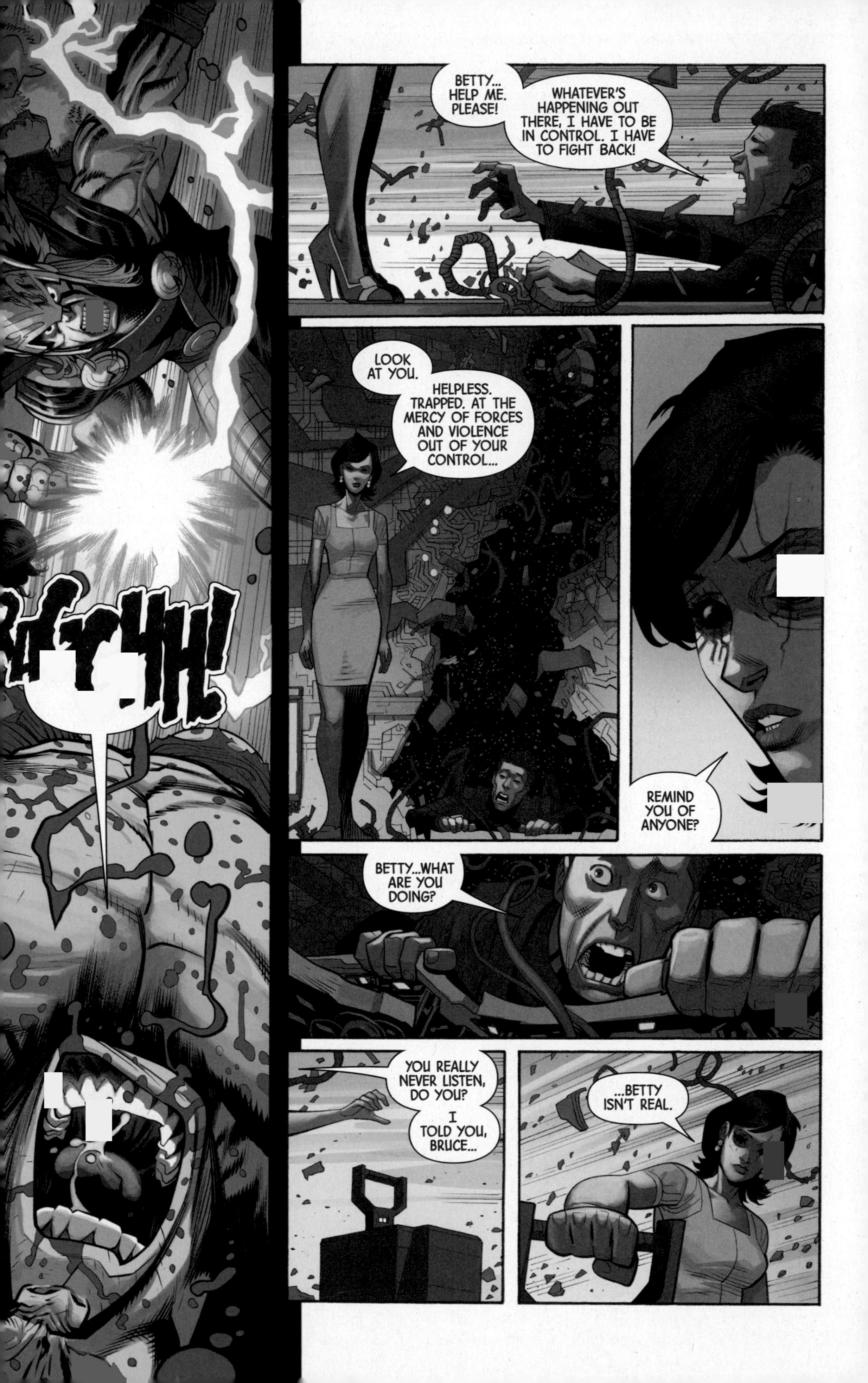
BETTY... HELP ME. PLEASE!
WHATEVER'S HAPPENING OUT THERE, I HAVE TO BE IN CONTROL. I HAVE TO FIGHT BACK!
LOOK AT YOU.
HELPLESS. TRAPPED. AT THE MERCY OF FORCES AND VIOLENCE OUT OF YOUR CONTROL...
REMIND YOU OF ANYONE?
BETTY...WHAT ARE YOU DOING?
YOU REALLY NEVER LISTEN, DO YOU?
I TOLD YOU, BRUCE...
...BETTY ISN'T REAL.

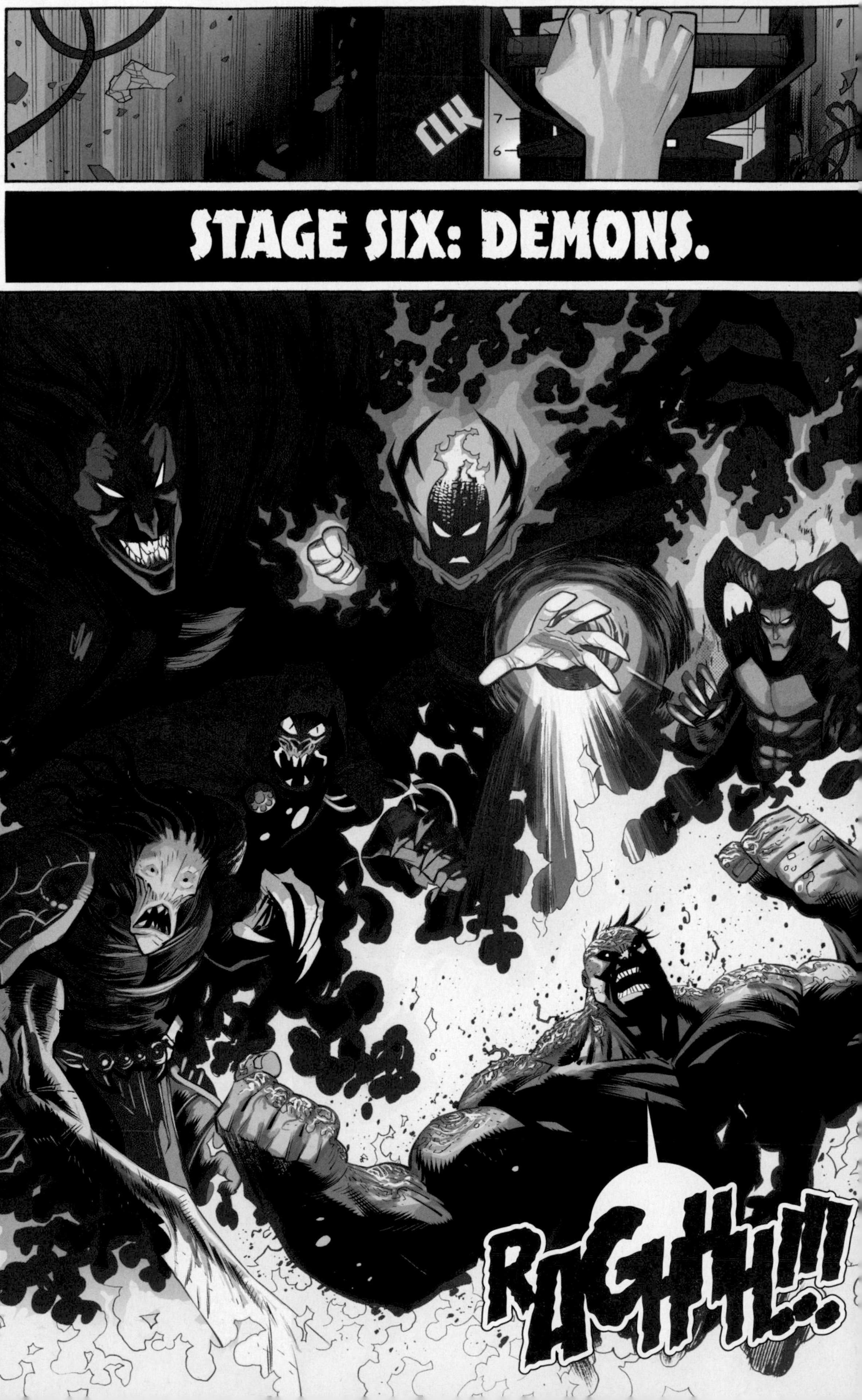
CLK
7
6
STAGE SIX: DEMONS.
RAGHH!!!

YOU--YOU'RE A MONSTER! YOU CAN'T DO THIS!
OH, I ALREADY HAVE.
YOUR LITTLE EXPERIMENT IS OVER.
PSSHHH
NO. NO, YOU...
YOU CAN'T JUST USE THEM LIKE THAT!
THOSE ARE PEOPLE!!!
RRRRRR
OH, GROW UP.
THOSE AREN'T PEOPLE ANYMORE, BRUCE...

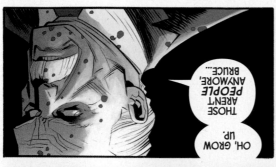

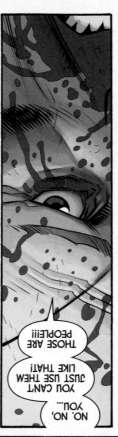

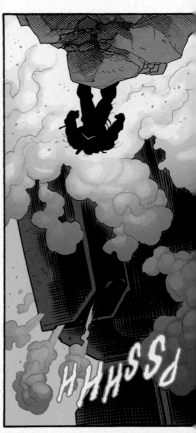

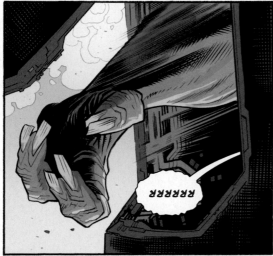

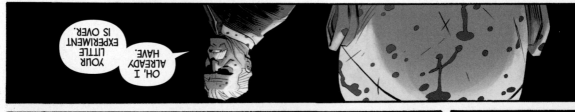

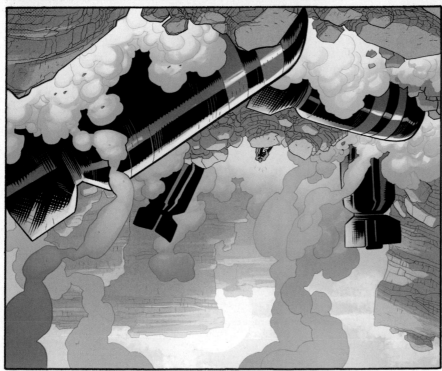

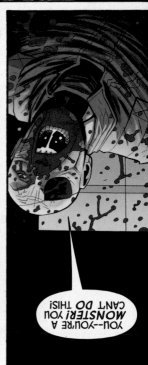

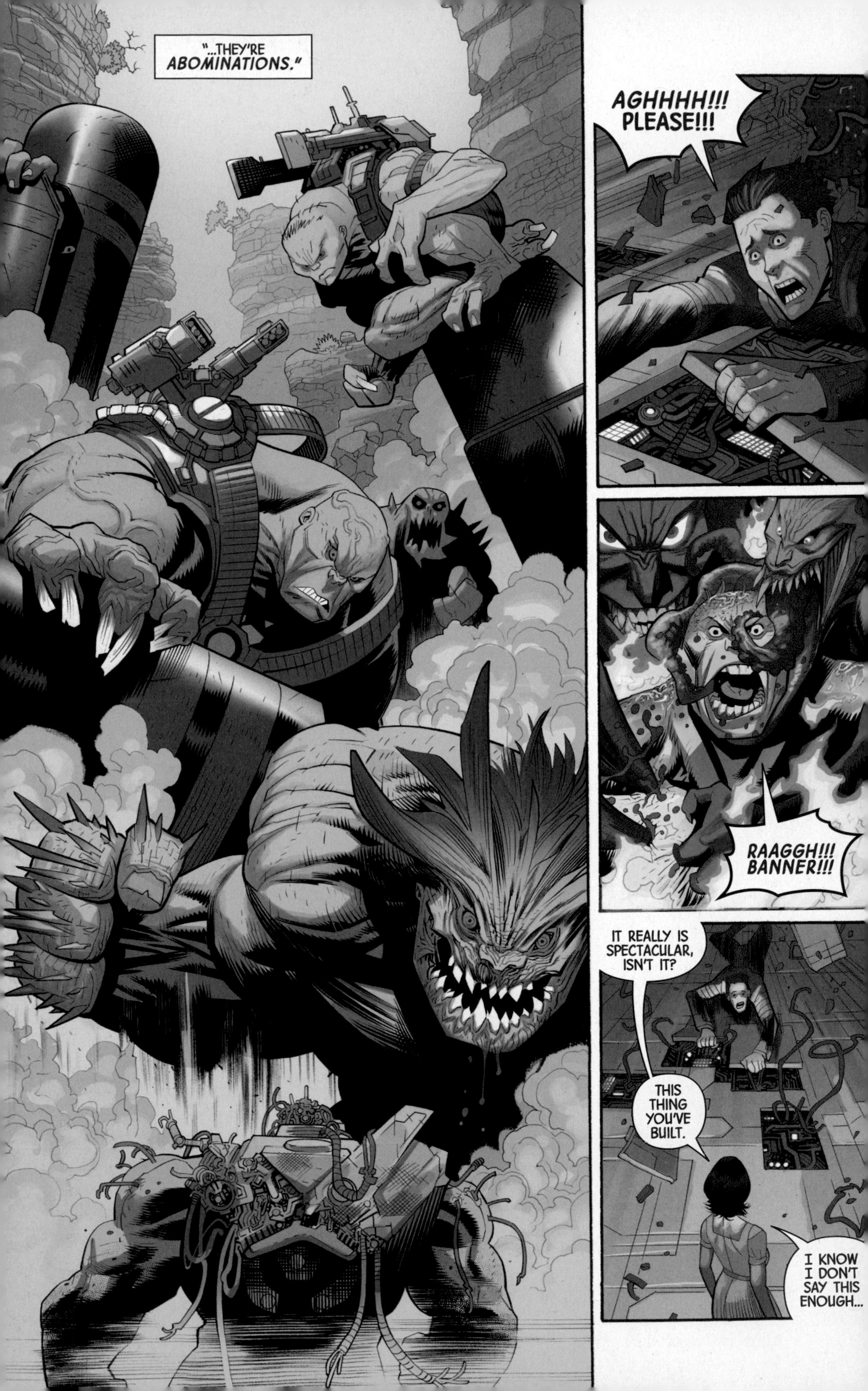
"...THEY'RE ABOMINATIONS."
AGHHHH!!! PLEASE!!!
RAAGGH!!! BANNER!!!
IT REALLY IS SPECTACULAR, ISN'T IT?
THIS THING YOU'VE BUILT.
I KNOW I DON'T SAY THIS ENOUGH...

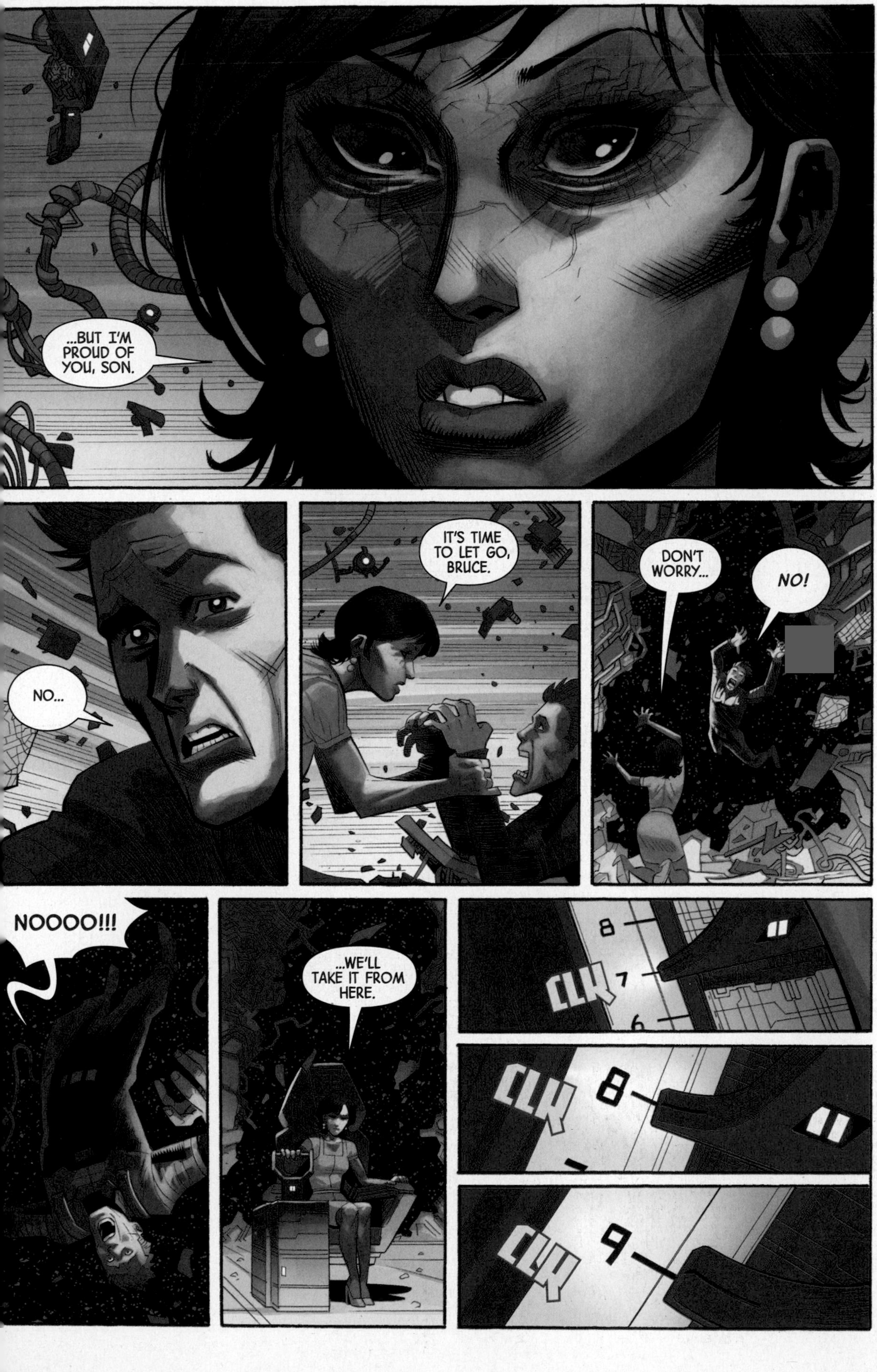
...BUT I'M PROUD OF YOU, SON.
NO...
IT'S TIME TO LET GO, BRUCE.
DON'T WORRY...
NO!
NOOOO!!!
...WE'LL TAKE IT FROM HERE.
8
7
6
CLK
8
CLK
9
CLK

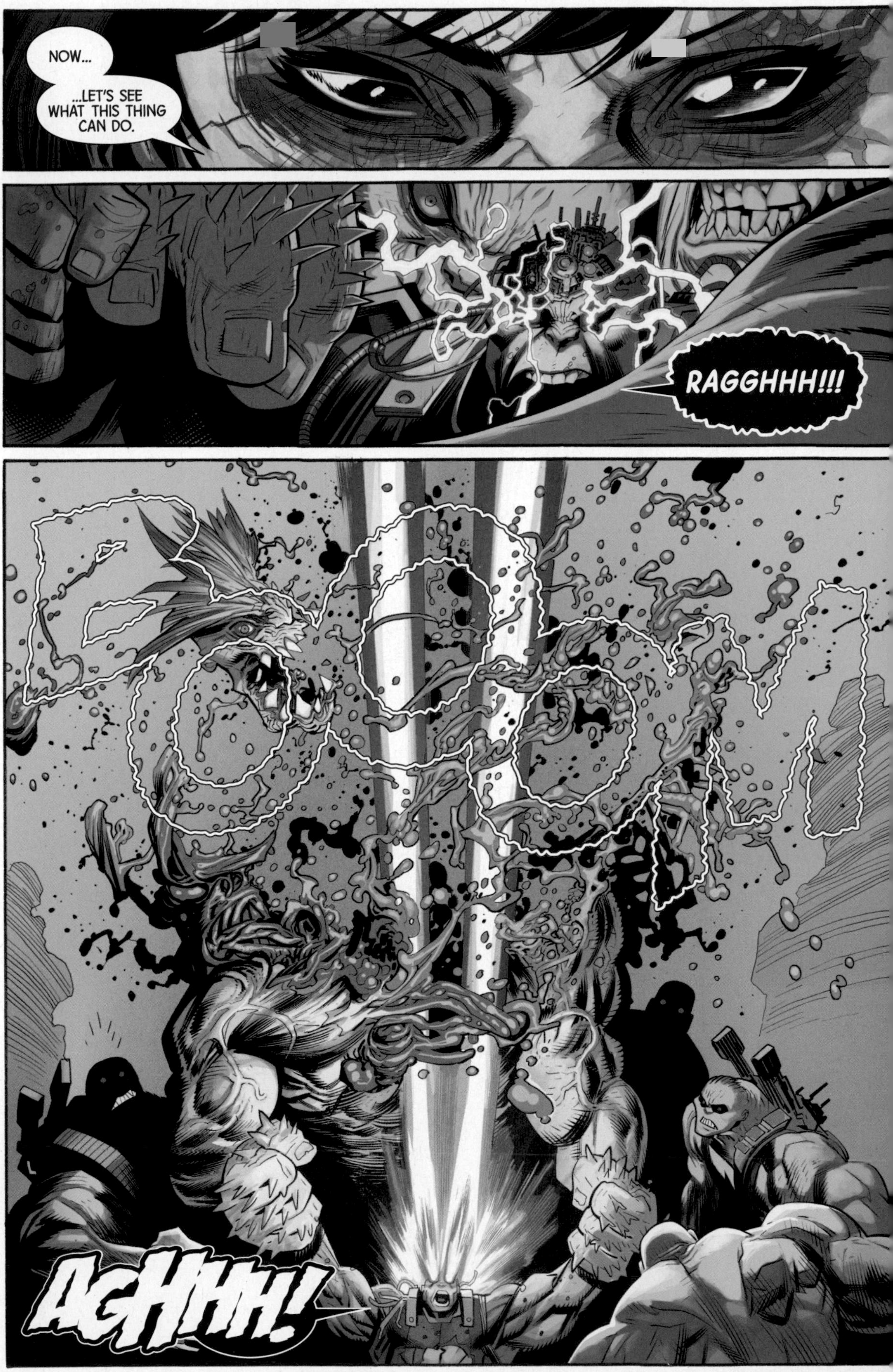
NOW...
...LET'S SEE WHAT THIS THING CAN DO.
RAGGHHH!!!
BOOOOM
AGHHH!

#3 VARIANT BY
TRADD MOORE & HEATHER MOORE

#3 CLASSIC HOMAGE VARIANT BY
DAVID NAKAYAMA

#2 DEVIL'S REIGN VARIANT BY
PETE WOODS

#3 HEADSHOT SKETCH VARIANT BY
JIM CHEUNG

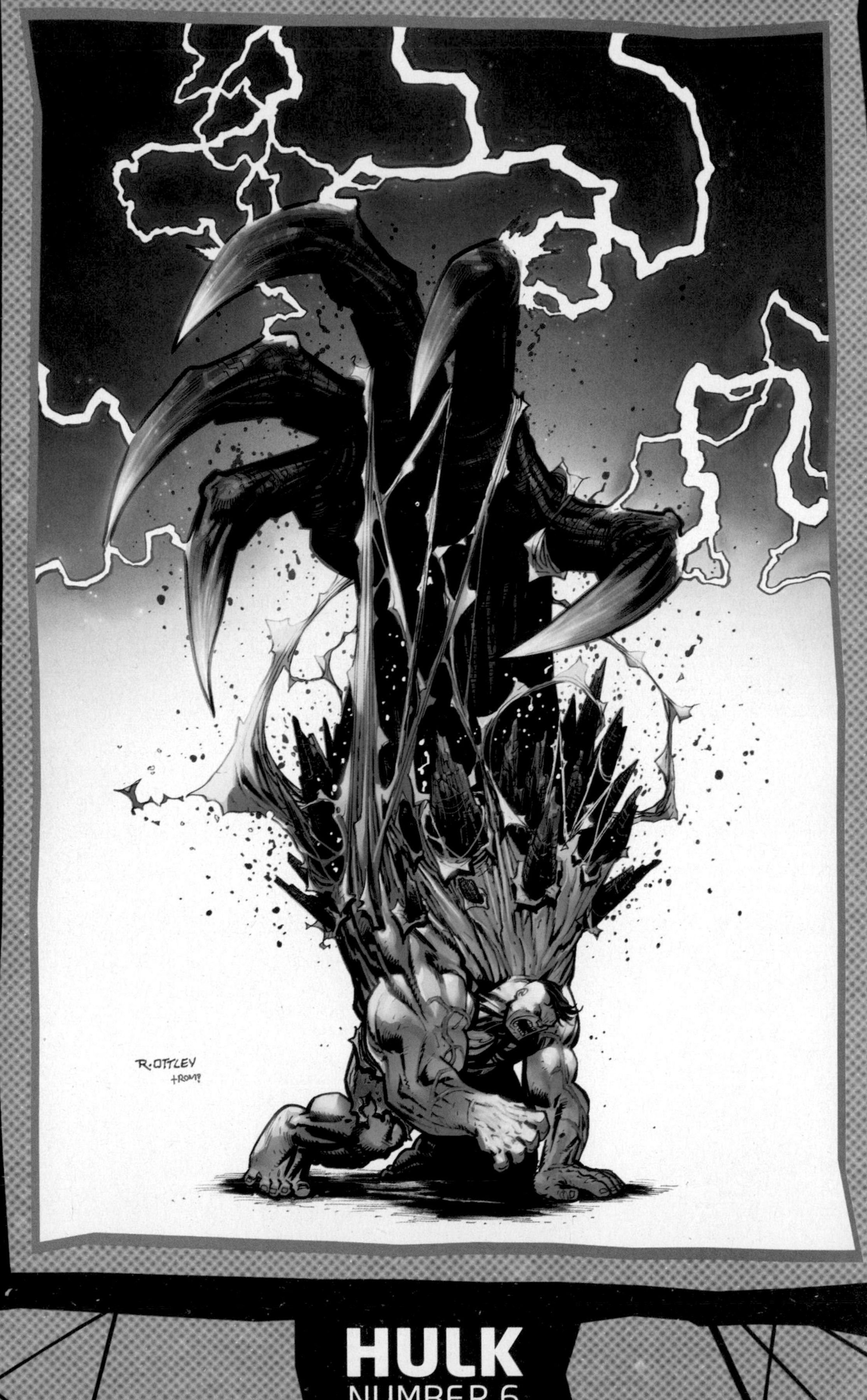
R.OTTLEY
+ROMP

HULK
NUMBER 6

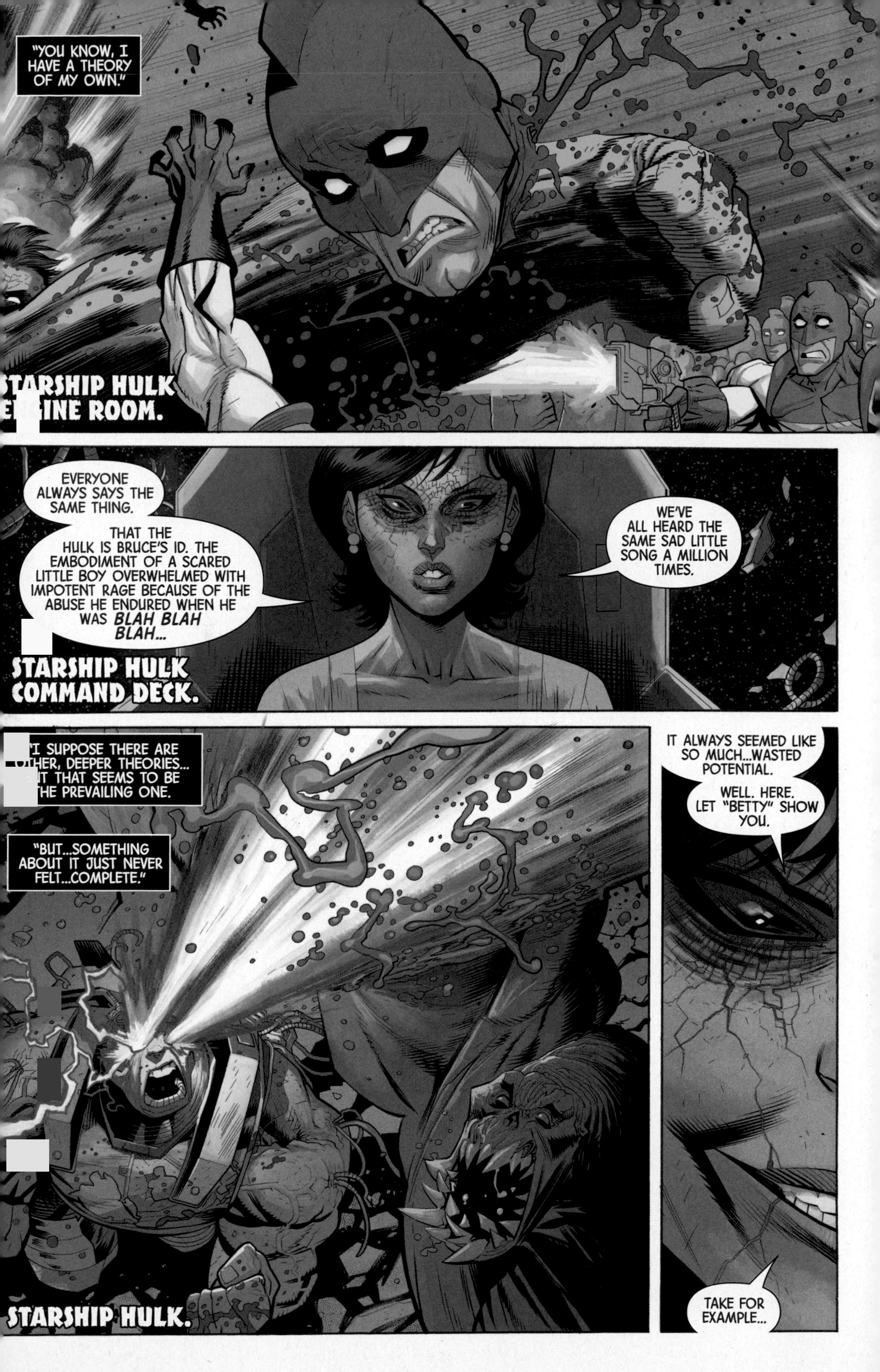
"YOU KNOW, I HAVE A THEORY OF MY OWN."
TARSHIP HULK
INE ROOM.
EVERYONE ALWAYS SAYS THE SAME THING.
THAT THE HULK IS BRUCE'S ID. THE EMBODIMENT OF A SCARED LITTLE BOY OVERWHELMED WITH IMPOTENT RAGE BECAUSE OF THE ABUSE HE ENDURED WHEN HE WAS *BLAH BLAH BLAH*...
WE'VE ALL HEARD THE SAME SAD LITTLE SONG A MILLION TIMES.
STARSHIP HULK COMMAND DECK.
I SUPPOSE THERE ARE
HER, DEEPER THEORIES...
IT THAT SEEMS TO BE
HE PREVAILING ONE.
"BUT...SOMETHING ABOUT IT JUST NEVER FELT...COMPLETE."
STARSHIP HULK.
IT ALWAYS SEEMED LIKE SO MUCH...WASTED POTENTIAL.
WELL. HERE. LET "BETTY" SHOW YOU.
TAKE FOR EXAMPLE...

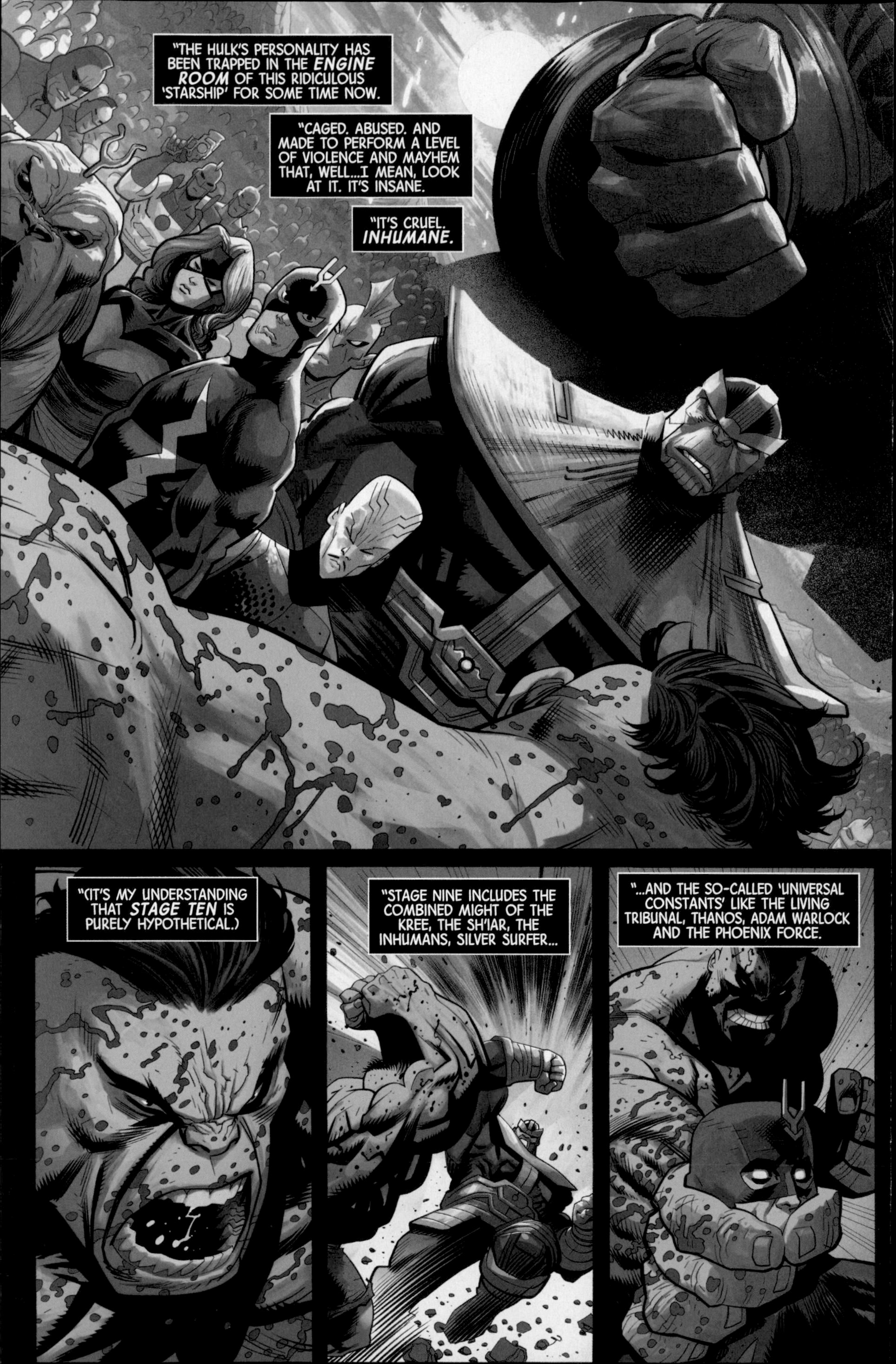
"THE HULK'S PERSONALITY HAS BEEN TRAPPED IN THE ***ENGINE ROOM*** OF THIS RIDICULOUS 'STARSHIP' FOR SOME TIME NOW.
"CAGED. ABUSED. AND MADE TO PERFORM A LEVEL OF VIOLENCE AND MAYHEM THAT, WELL...I MEAN, LOOK AT IT. IT'S INSANE.
"IT'S CRUEL. ***INHUMANE.***
"(IT'S MY UNDERSTANDING THAT ***STAGE TEN*** IS PURELY HYPOTHETICAL.)
"STAGE NINE INCLUDES THE COMBINED MIGHT OF THE KREE, THE SH'IAR, THE INHUMANS, SILVER SURFER...
"...AND THE SO-CALLED 'UNIVERSAL CONSTANTS' LIKE THE LIVING TRIBUNAL, THANOS, ADAM WARLOCK AND THE PHOENIX FORCE.

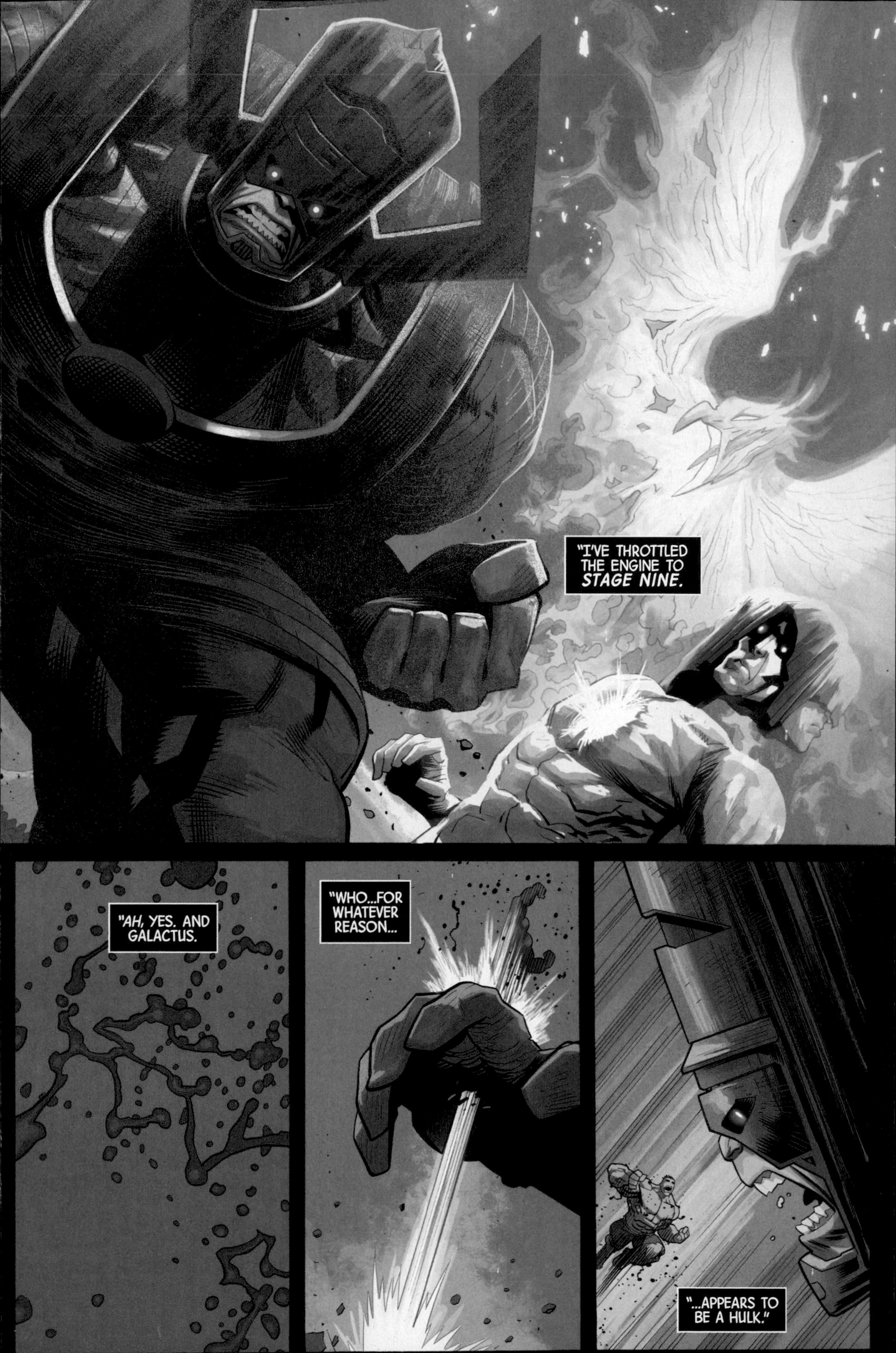
"I'VE THROTTLED THE ENGINE TO *STAGE NINE.*
"*AH*, YES. AND GALACTUS.
"WHO...FOR WHATEVER REASON...
"...APPEARS TO BE A HULK."

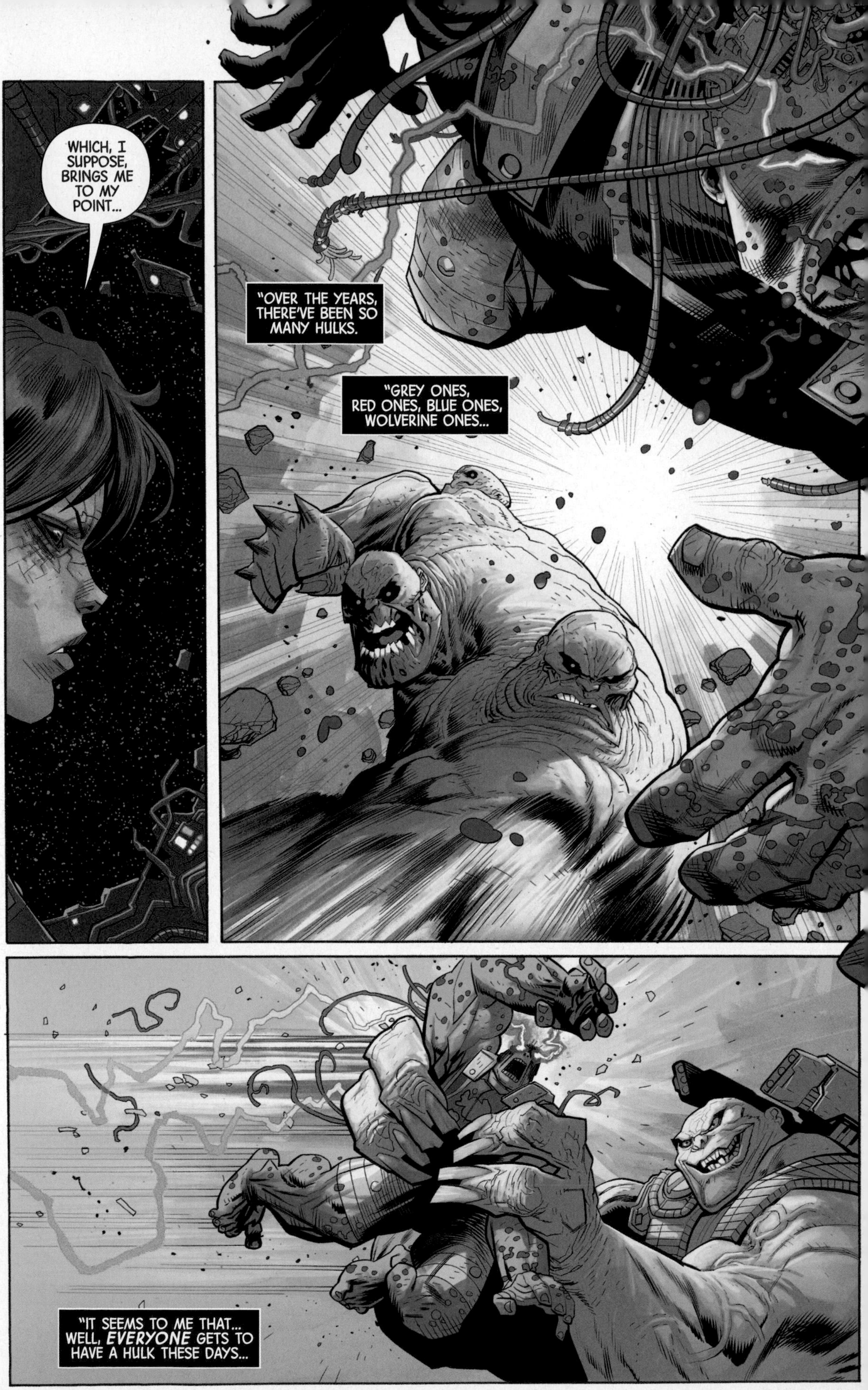
WHICH, I SUPPOSE, BRINGS ME TO MY POINT...
"OVER THE YEARS, THERE'VE BEEN SO MANY HULKS.
"GREY ONES, RED ONES, BLUE ONES, WOLVERINE ONES...
"IT SEEMS TO ME THAT... WELL, *EVERYONE* GETS TO HAVE A HULK THESE DAYS...

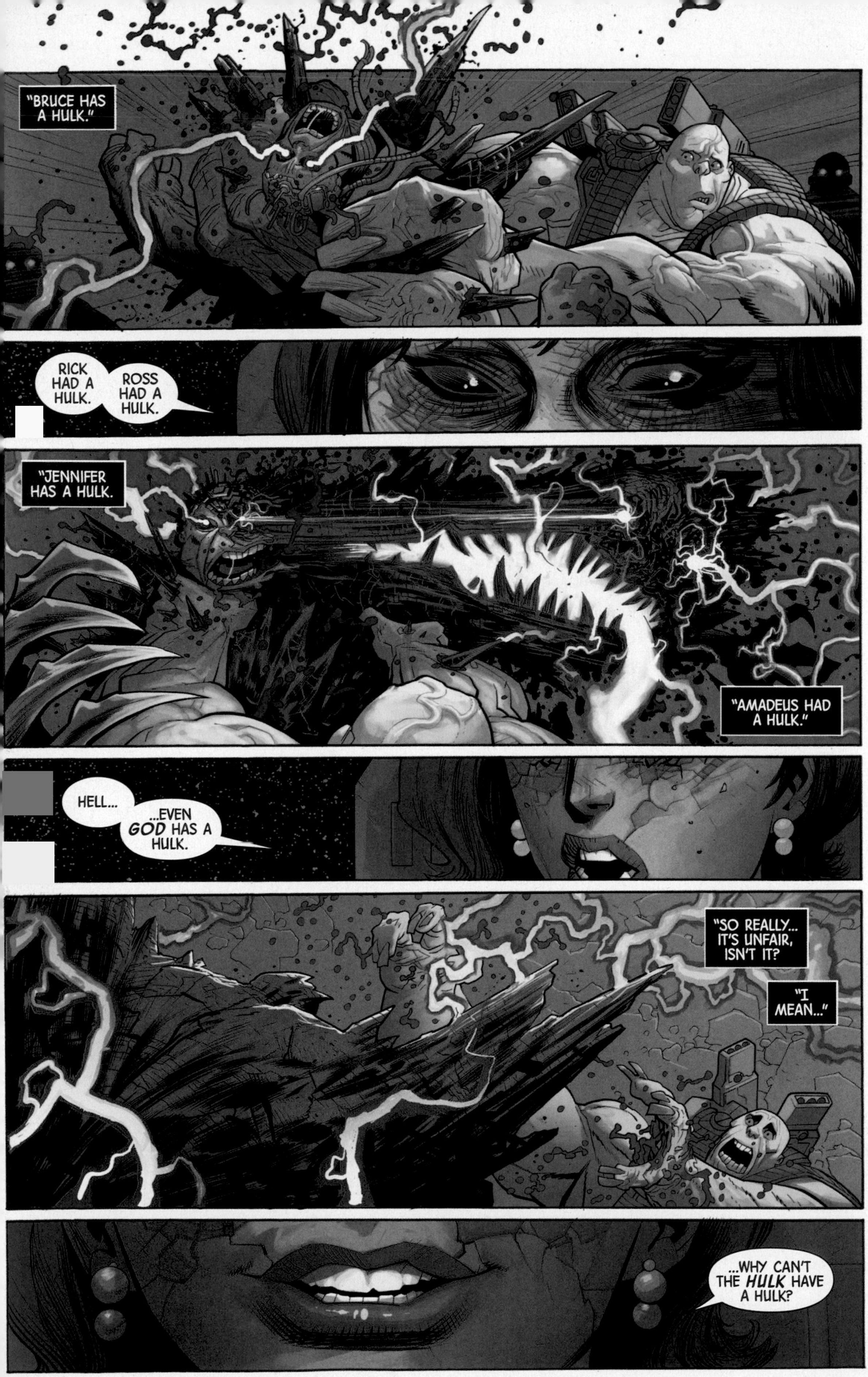
"BRUCE HAS A HULK."
RICK HAD A HULK.
ROSS HAD A HULK.
"JENNIFER HAS A HULK.
"AMADEUS HAD A HULK."
HELL...
...EVEN GOD HAS A HULK.
"SO REALLY... IT'S UNFAIR, ISN'T IT?
"I MEAN..."
...WHY CAN'T THE HULK HAVE A HULK?

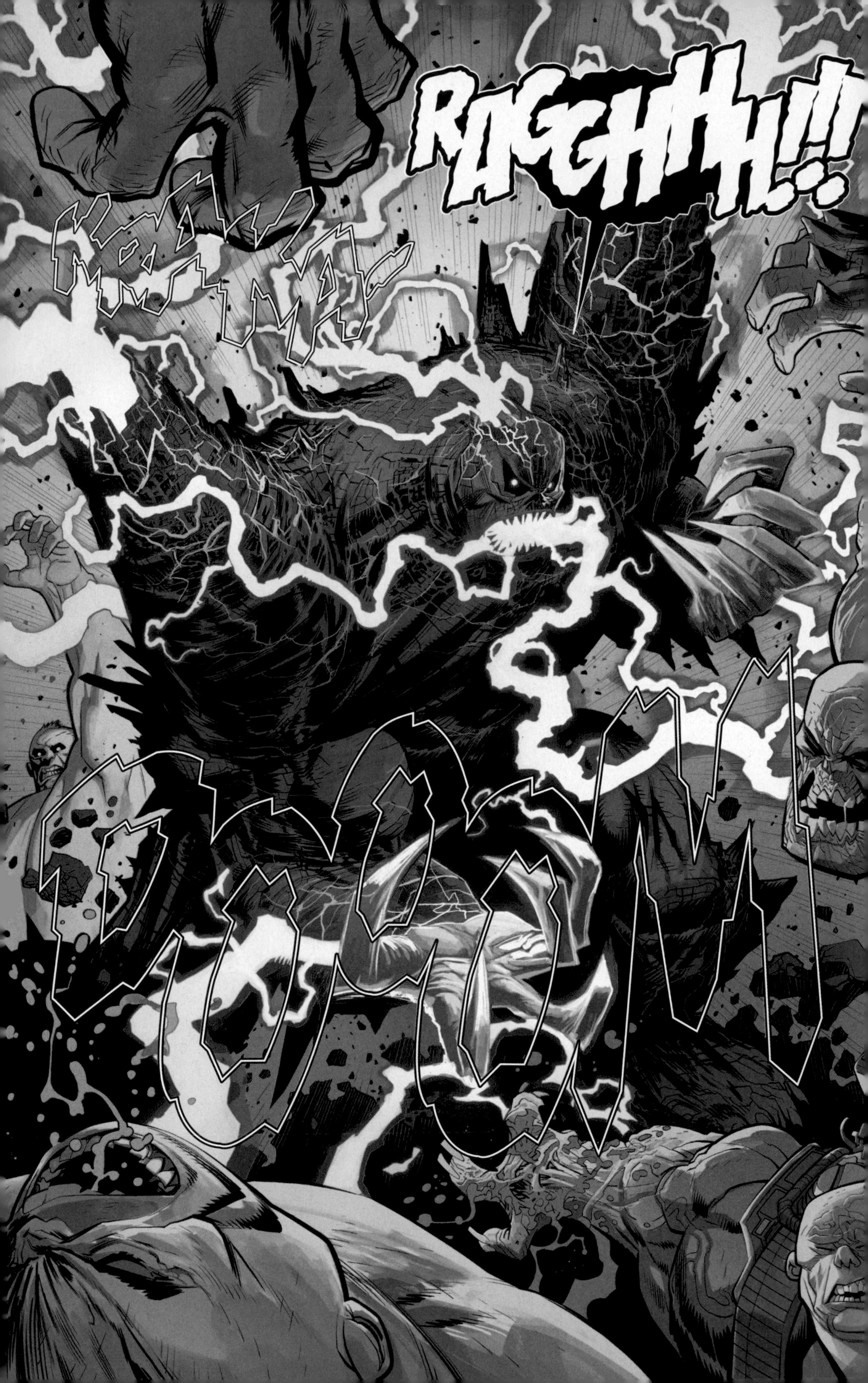
RAGHHH!!
DOOOM

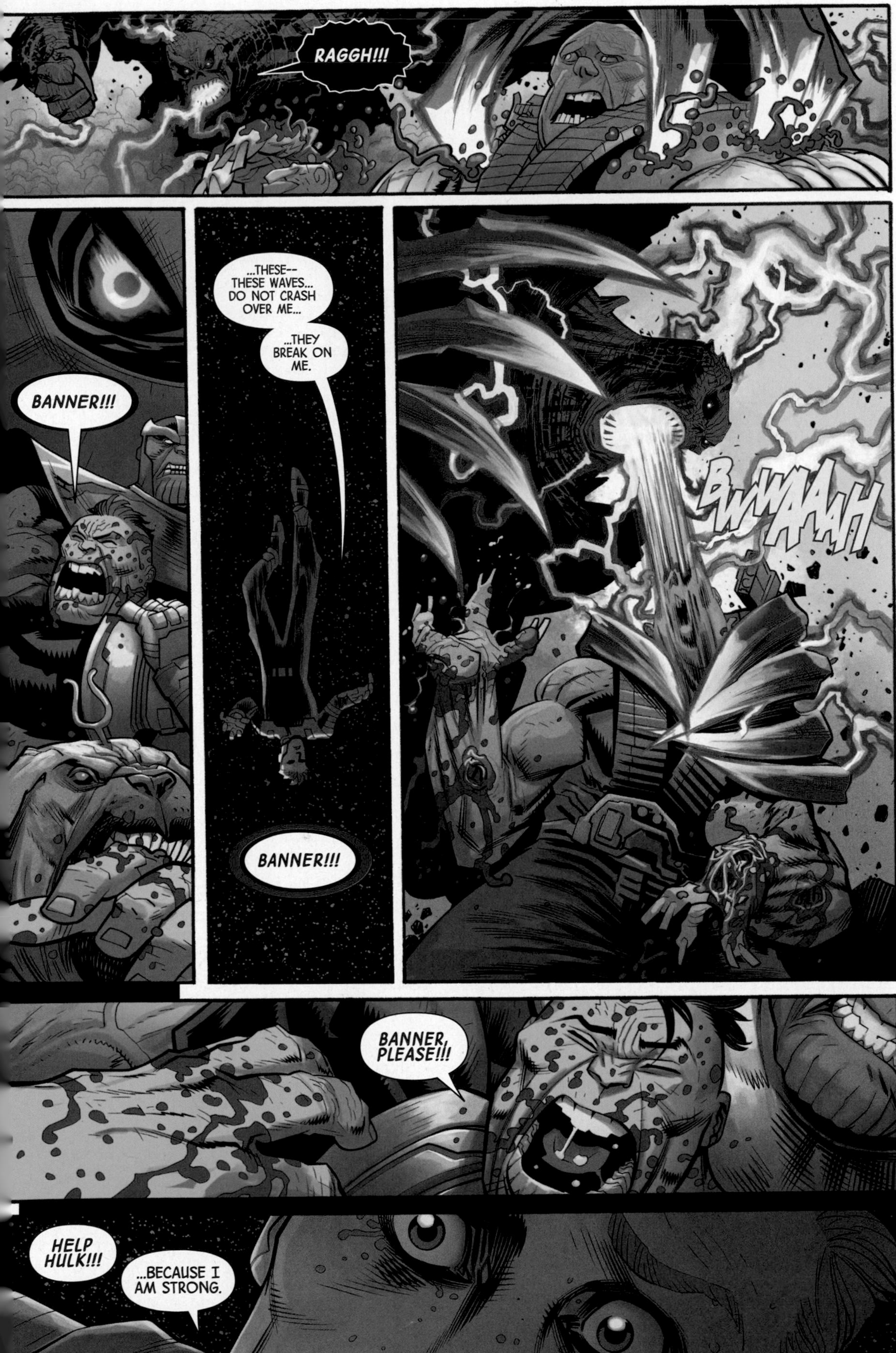
RAGGH!!!
BANNER!!!
...THESE-- THESE WAVES... DO NOT CRASH OVER ME...
...THEY BREAK ON ME.
BANNER!!!
BWAAAAH
BANNER, PLEASE!!!
HELP HULK!!!
...BECAUSE I AM STRONG.

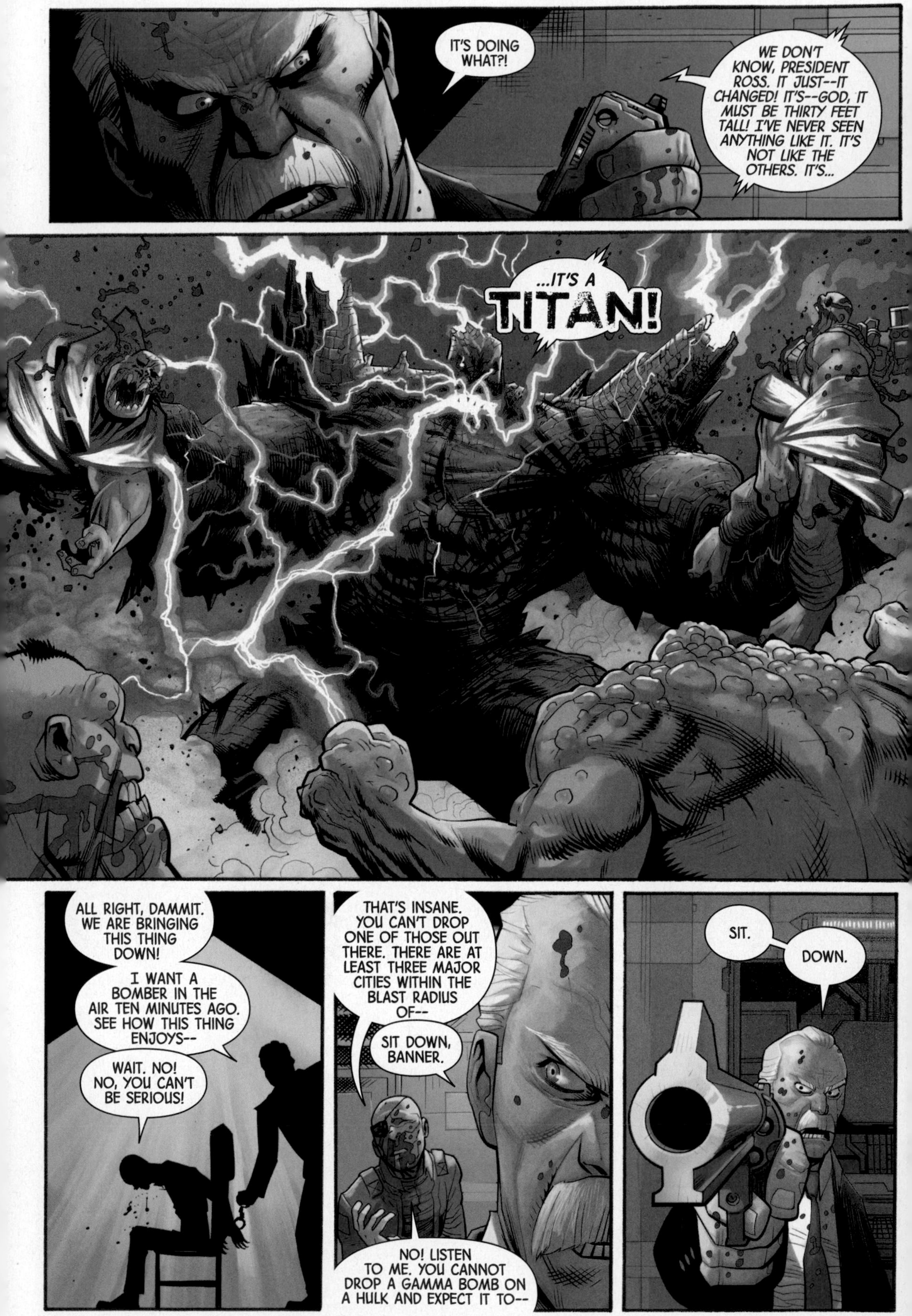
IT'S DOING WHAT?!
WE DON'T KNOW, PRESIDENT ROSS. IT JUST--IT CHANGED! IT'S--GOD, IT MUST BE THIRTY FEET TALL! I'VE NEVER SEEN ANYTHING LIKE IT. IT'S NOT LIKE THE OTHERS. IT'S...
...IT'S A TITAN!
ALL RIGHT, DAMMIT. WE ARE BRINGING THIS THING DOWN!
I WANT A BOMBER IN THE AIR TEN MINUTES AGO. SEE HOW THIS THING ENJOYS--
WAIT. NO! NO, YOU CAN'T BE SERIOUS!
THAT'S INSANE. YOU CAN'T DROP ONE OF THOSE OUT THERE. THERE ARE AT LEAST THREE MAJOR CITIES WITHIN THE BLAST RADIUS OF--
SIT DOWN, BANNER.
NO! LISTEN TO ME. YOU CANNOT DROP A GAMMA BOMB ON A HULK AND EXPECT IT TO--
SIT.
DOWN.

AGGHHH!!!

THAT WASN'T SO HARD. NOW GET ME COMMS ON THE LINE. WE'RE GOING TO NEED A HELL OF A STORY TO SELL TO THE LAMBS WHEN WE GET THIS--

THAT'S WHAT I LIKE TO HEAR.

SEE?

BIRD IS IN THE AIR, MISTER PRESIDENT. TEN MINUTES UNTIL TOUCHDOWN.

WE'RE DOING THIS TOGETHER, RIGHT, SON?

WE BOTH WILL.

PLEASE...

YOU'LL KILL THOUSANDS...

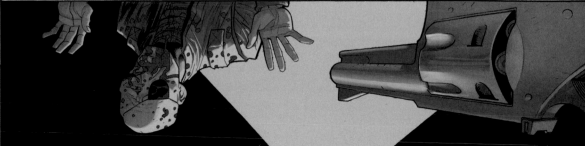

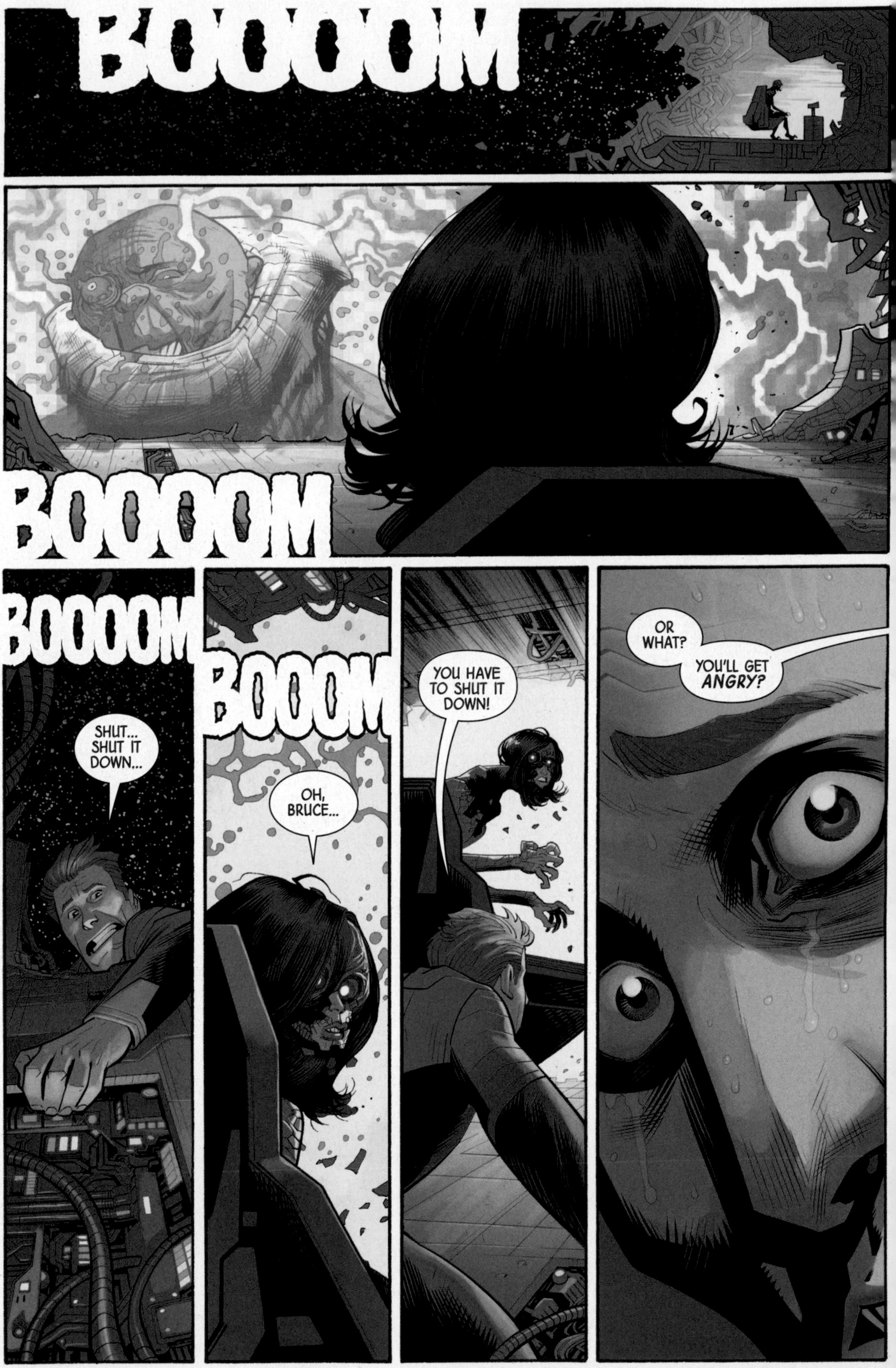
BOOOOM
BOOOOM
BOOOOM
SHUT... SHUT IT DOWN...
BOOOM
OH, BRUCE...
YOU HAVE TO SHUT IT DOWN!
OR WHAT?
YOU'LL GET *ANGRY?*

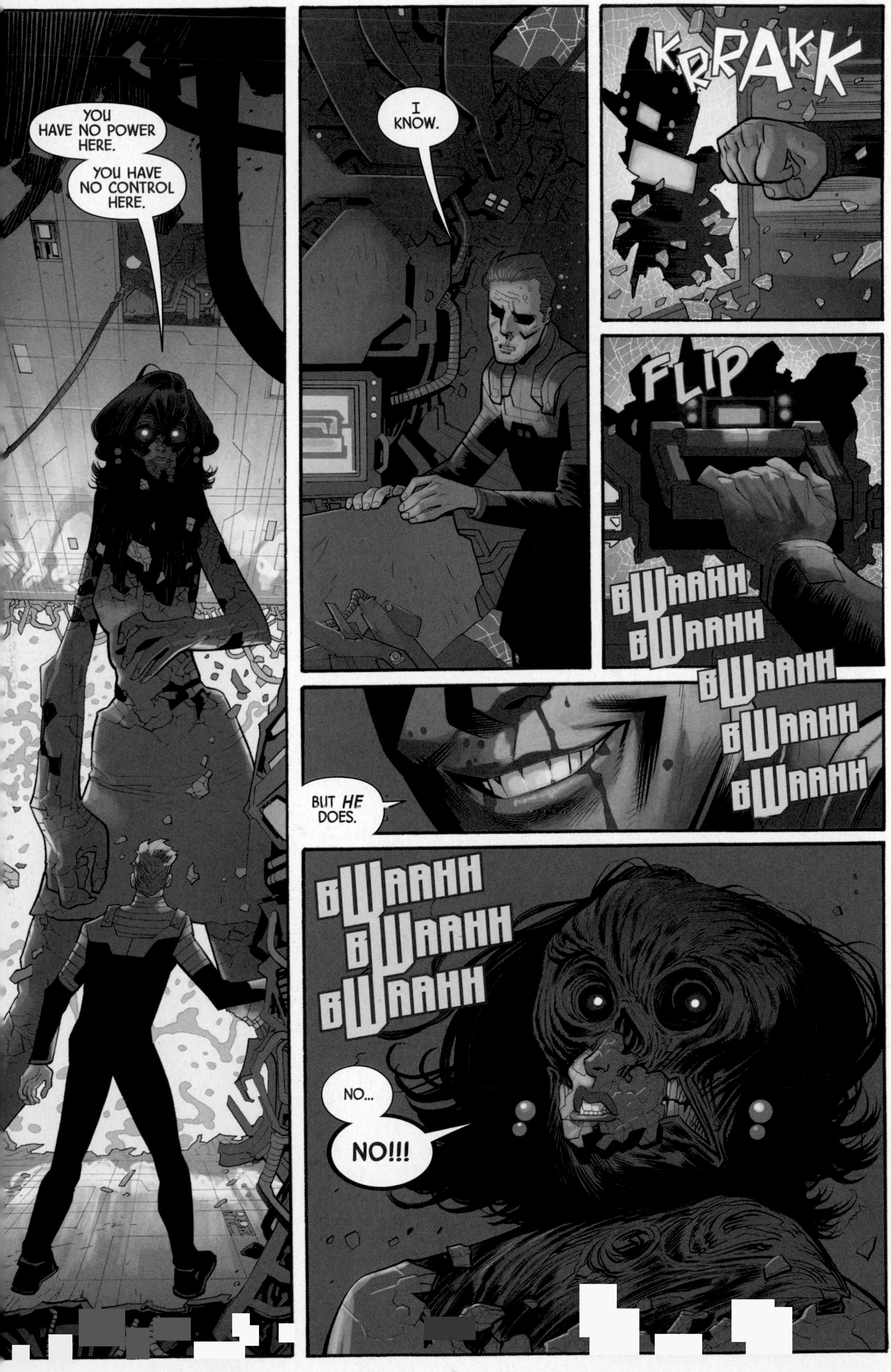
YOU HAVE NO POWER HERE.
YOU HAVE NO CONTROL HERE.
I KNOW.
KRRAKK
FLIP
BWAAHH
BWAAHH
BWAAHH
BWAAHH
BWAAHH
BUT HE DOES.
BWAAHH
BWAAHH
BWAAHH
NO...
NO!!!

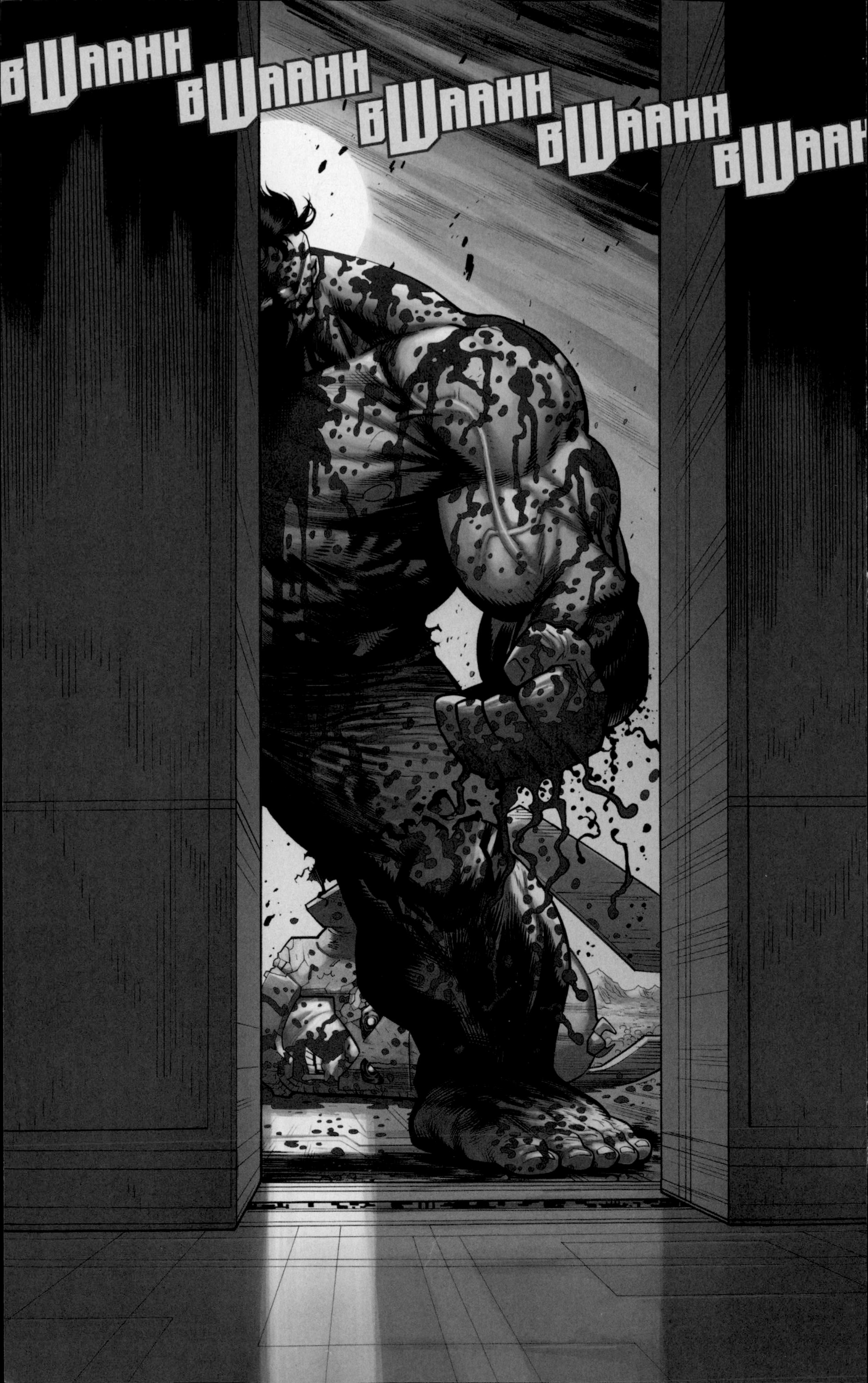
BWAAHH
BWAAHH
BWAAHH
BWAAHH
BWAA

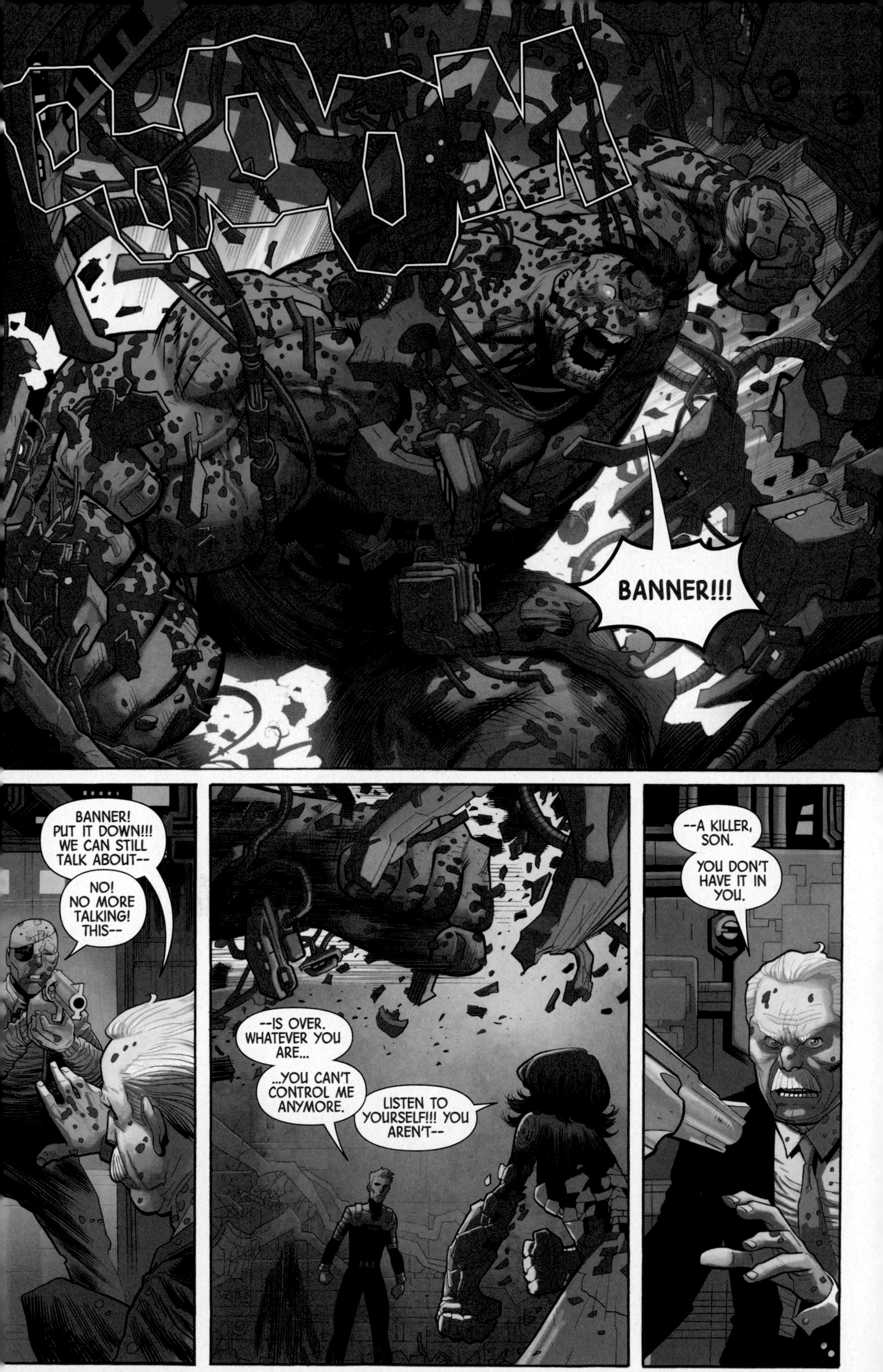
BOOOM
BANNER!!!
BANNER! PUT IT DOWN!!! WE CAN STILL TALK ABOUT--
NO! NO MORE TALKING! THIS--
--IS OVER. WHATEVER YOU ARE...
...YOU CAN'T CONTROL ME ANYMORE.
LISTEN TO YOURSELF!!! YOU AREN'T--
--A KILLER, SON.
YOU DON'T HAVE IT IN YOU.

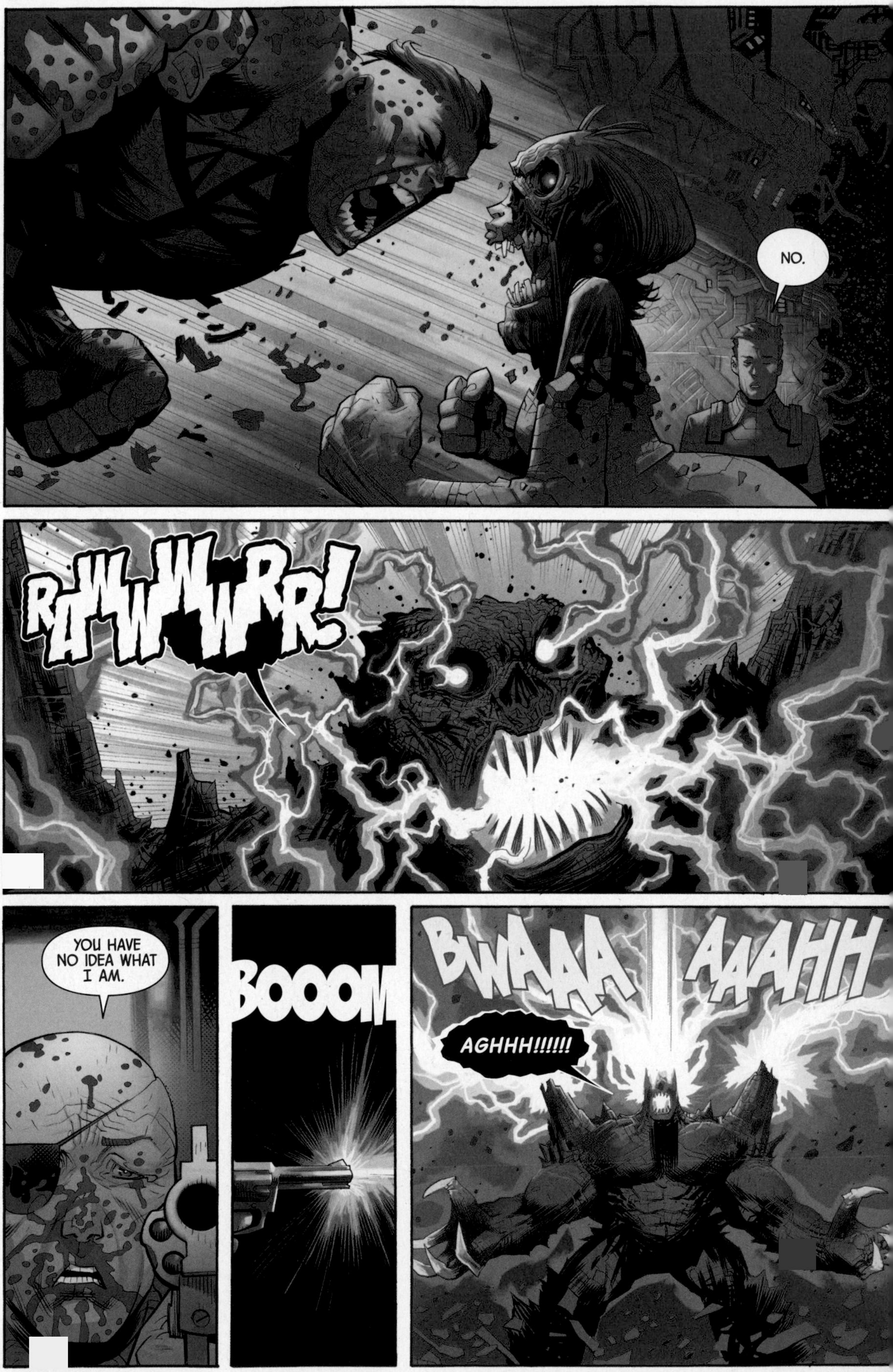
NO.
RAWWWWRR!
YOU HAVE NO IDEA WHAT I AM.
BOOOM
BWAAA AAAHH
AGHHH!!!!!!

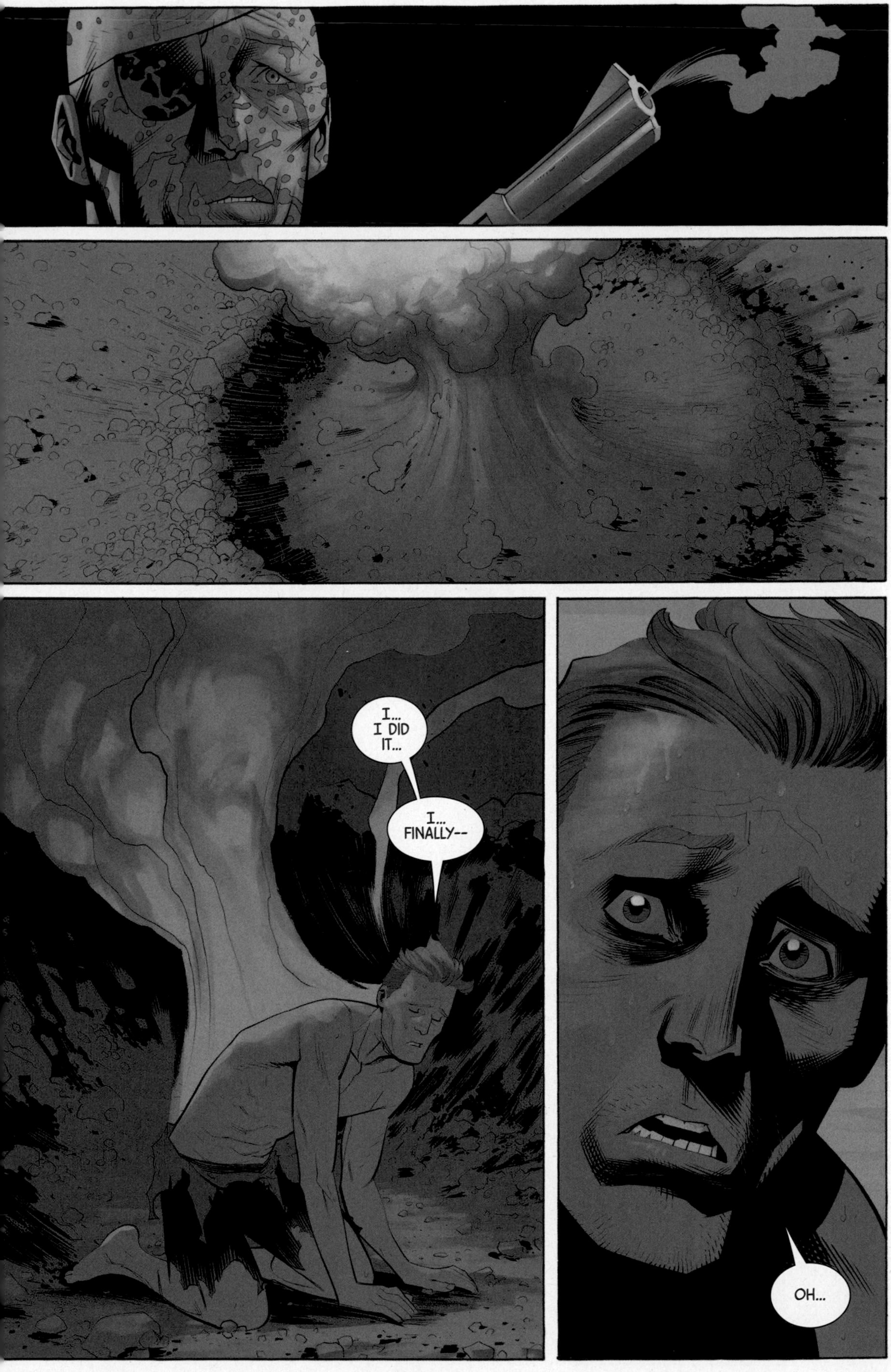
I... I DID IT...
I... FINALLY--
OH...

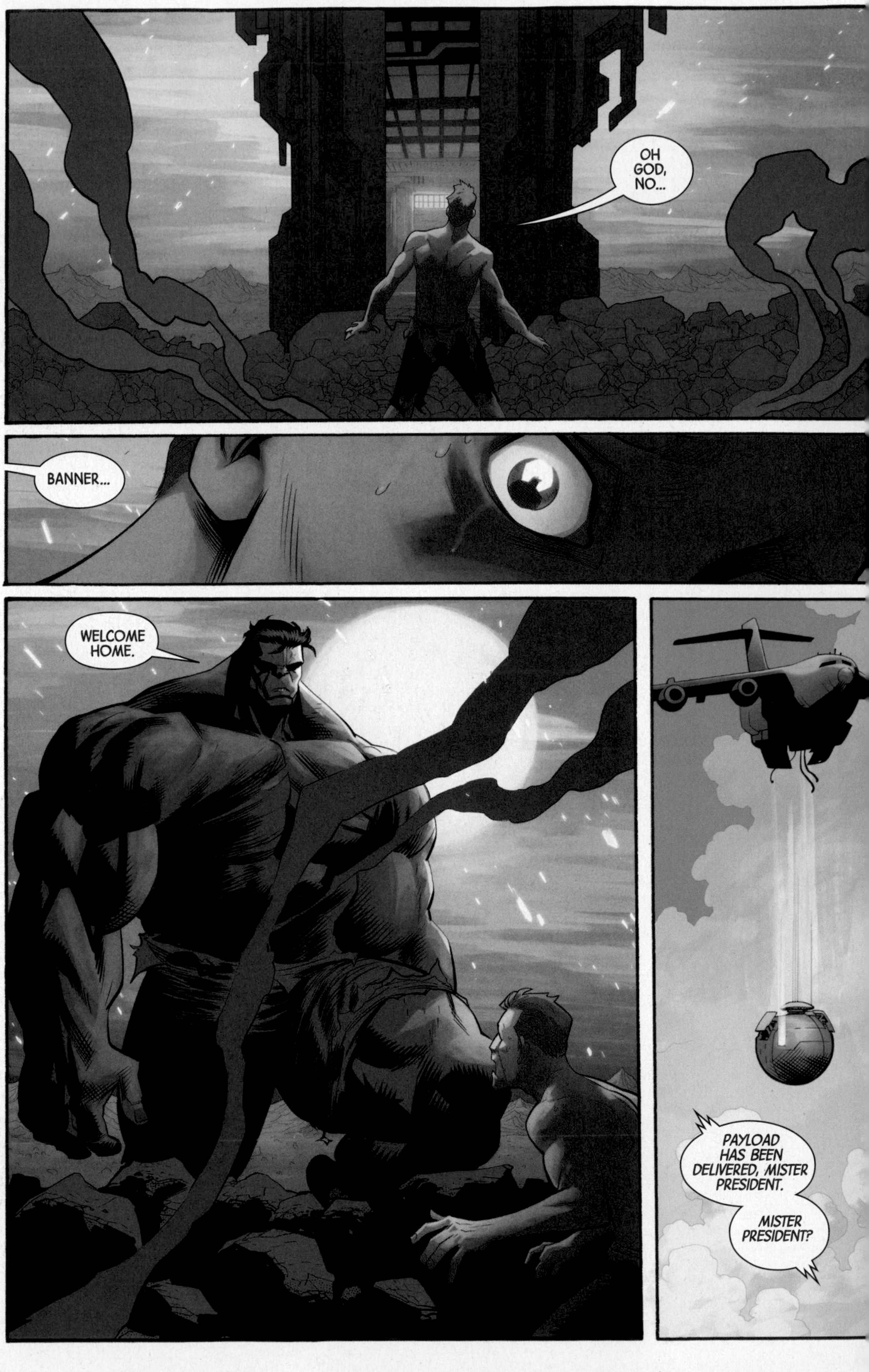
OH GOD, NO...
BANNER...
WELCOME HOME.
PAYLOAD HAS BEEN DELIVERED, MISTER PRESIDENT.
MISTER PRESIDENT?

"...YOU HAVE TO RUNiii

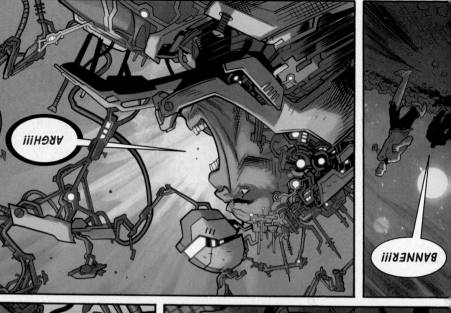

iiiHGRA

BANNERiii

BUT-- PLEASE, LISTEN TO ME...

"...BUT I'VE GAINED ACCESS TO THE SYSTEMS IN MY LABORATORY. IF YOU CAN GET THERE, I BELIEVE WE CAN WORK TOGETHER TO MINIMIZE THE DESTRUCTION.

"...BUT ROSS HAS LAUNCHED A G-BOMB TO STOP YOU. THE FALLOUT WILL KILL THOUSANDS AND I--I CAN'T STOP IT...

I DON'T KNOW IF YOU CAN HEAR ME OR NOT...

BRUCE! CAN YOU HEAR ME?

BRUCE! COME IN!

COMPUTER! INITIATE REPAIR SEQUENCE! NOWiii

BANNER!

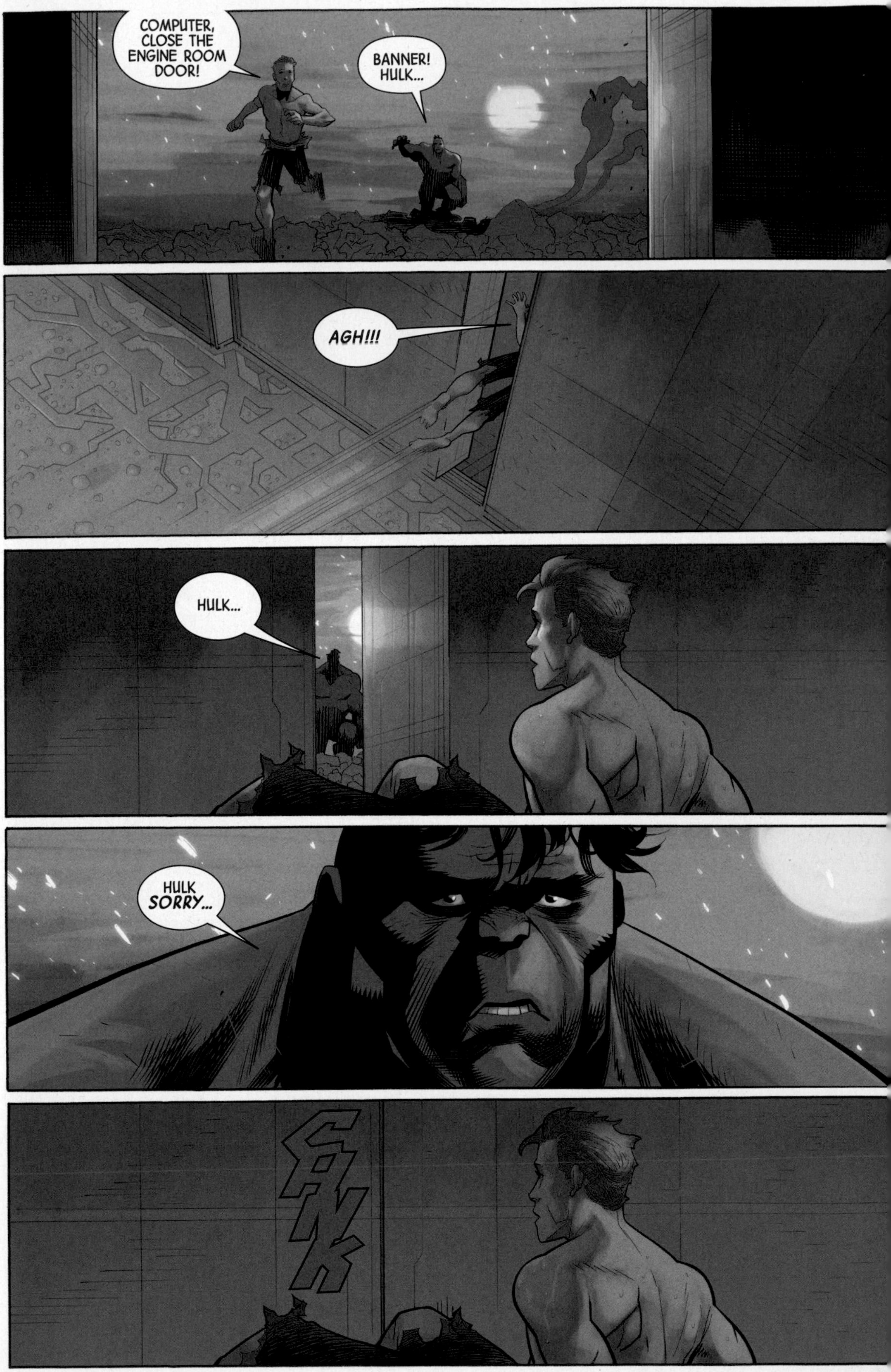
COMPUTER, CLOSE THE ENGINE ROOM DOOR!
BANNER! HULK...
AGH!!!
HULK...
HULK SORRY...
CHNK

BRUCE! COME IN! PLEASE, COME IN! WE DON'T HAVE--

I'M...I'M HERE.

I READ YOU.

WHAT CAN I DO?

OH, THANK GOD!

NOW LISTEN CLOSELY!

"I NEED YOU TO OVERLOAD THE ENERGY SIGNATURE TO THE PORTAL THAT BROUGHT YOU HERE.

"OPEN IT AS WIDE AS YOU CAN!"

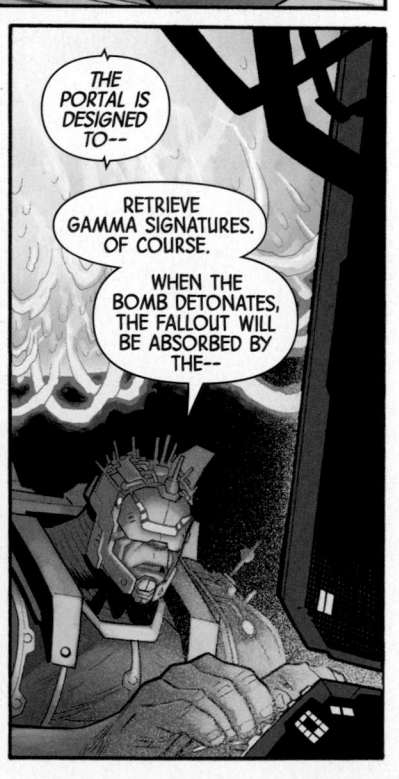

THE PORTAL IS DESIGNED TO--

RETRIEVE GAMMA SIGNATURES. OF COURSE.

WHEN THE BOMB DETONATES, THE FALLOUT WILL BE ABSORBED BY THE--

BRUCE! IT'S WORKING! THE RADIATION! IT'S BEING SIPHONED OFF AND ABSORBED...

THANK YOU. I'M SORRY IT HAD TO END LIKE THIS, BUT--

IT'S OKAY...

...THIS WAS ALWAYS GOING TO BLOW UP IN MY FACE.

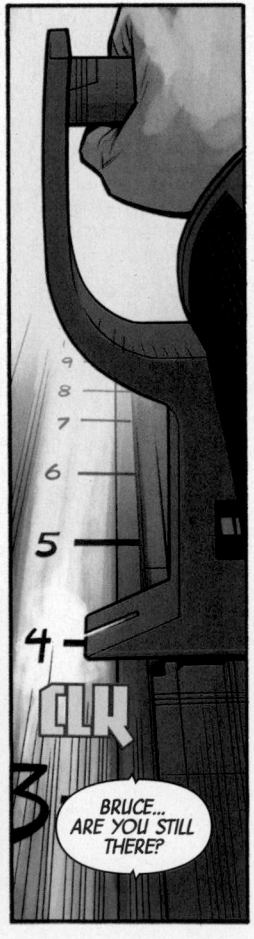

BRUCE... ARE YOU STILL THERE?

I'M NOT SURE WHERE THAT PORTAL WILL SEND YOU...

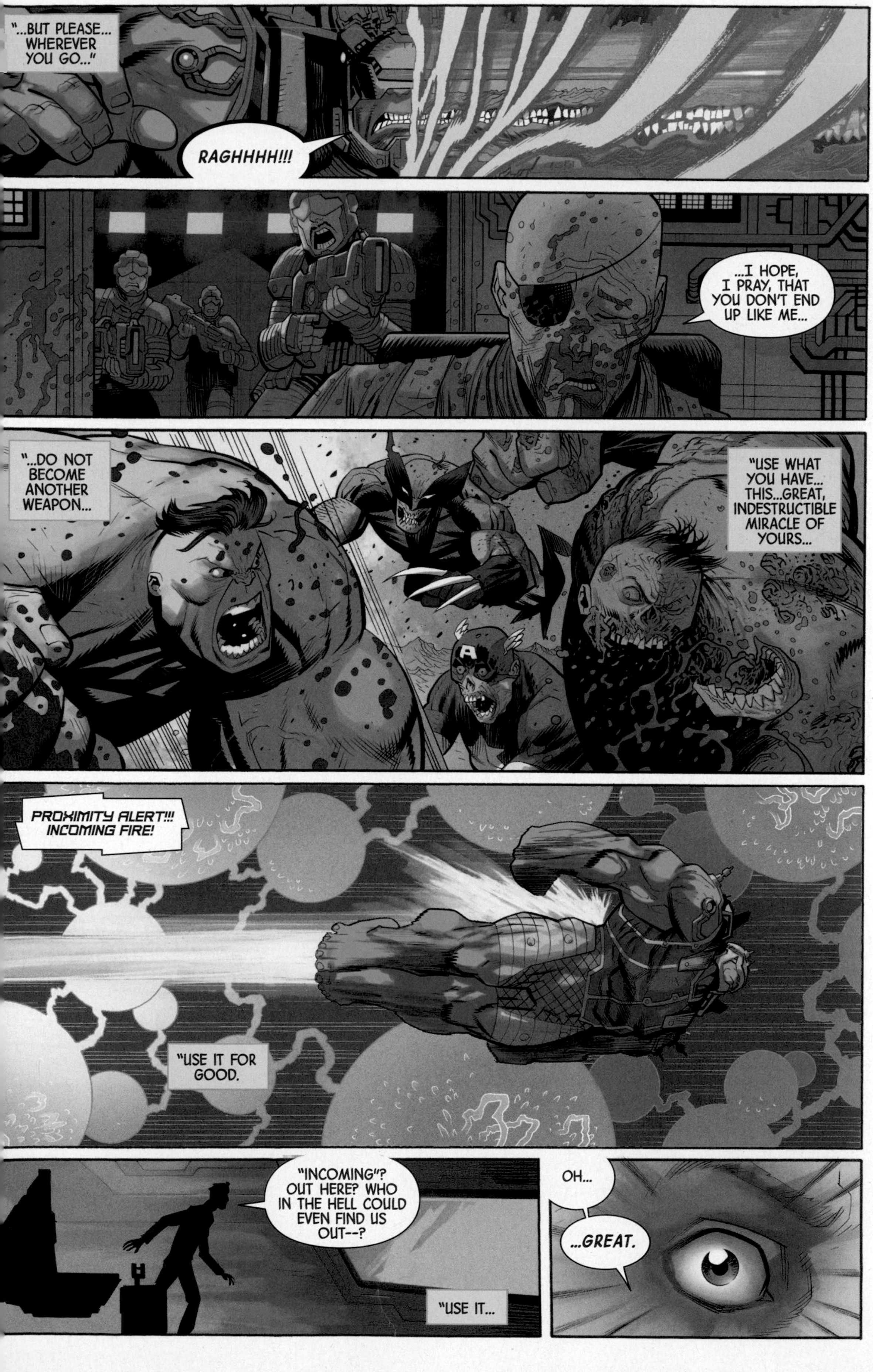

"...BUT PLEASE... WHEREVER YOU GO..."
RAGHHHH!!!
...I HOPE, I PRAY, THAT YOU DON'T END UP LIKE ME...
"...DO NOT BECOME ANOTHER WEAPON...
"USE WHAT YOU HAVE... THIS...GREAT, INDESTRUCTIBLE MIRACLE OF YOURS...
PROXIMITY ALERT!!! INCOMING FIRE!
"USE IT FOR GOOD.
"INCOMING"? OUT HERE? WHO IN THE HELL COULD EVEN FIND US OUT--?
"USE IT...
OH...
...GREAT.

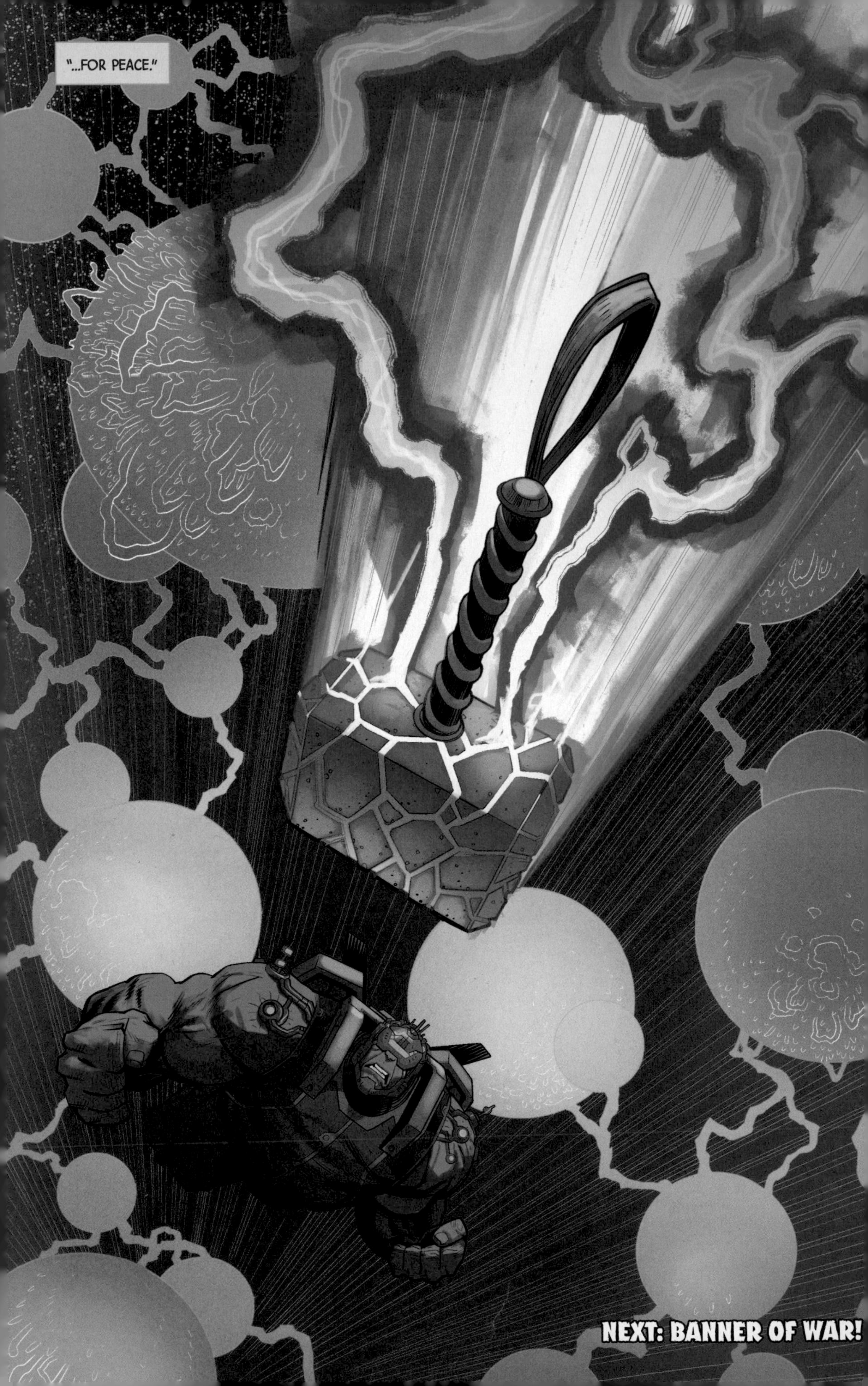
"...FOR PEACE."
NEXT: BANNER OF WAR!

#4 2ND PRINTING VARIANT BY
RYAN OTTLEY & ROMULO FAJARDO JR.

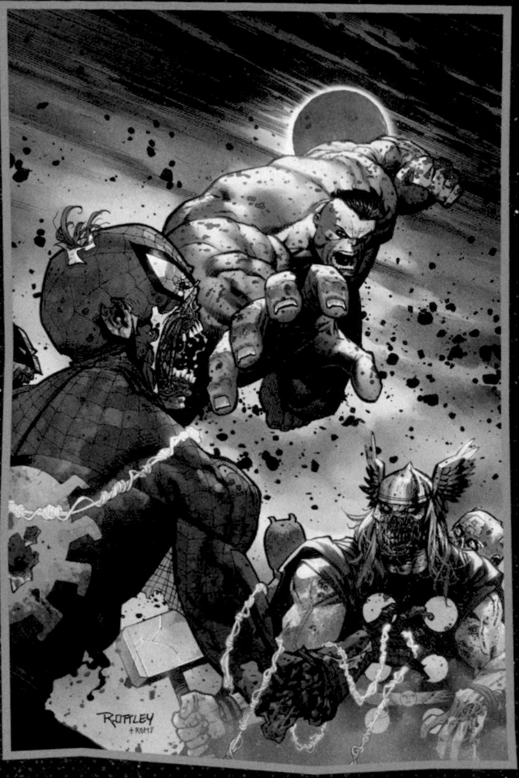
ROTTLEY
+ROMY

#4 VARIANT BY
E.M. GIST

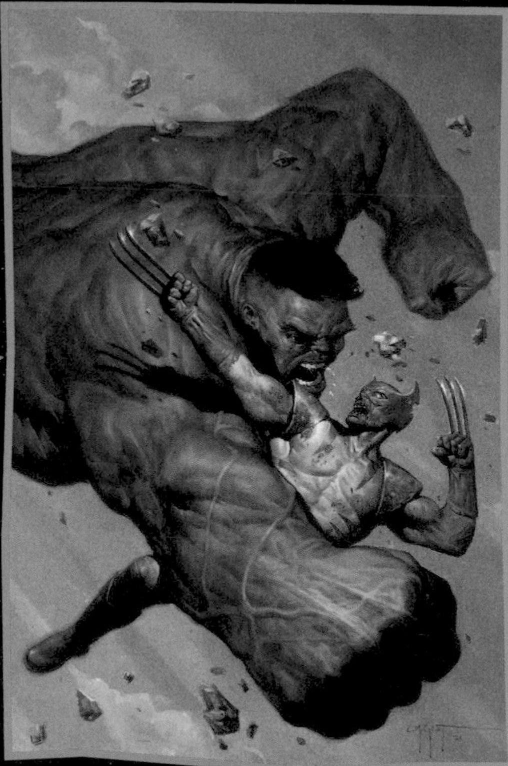

#5 VARIANT BY
JORGE FORNÉS

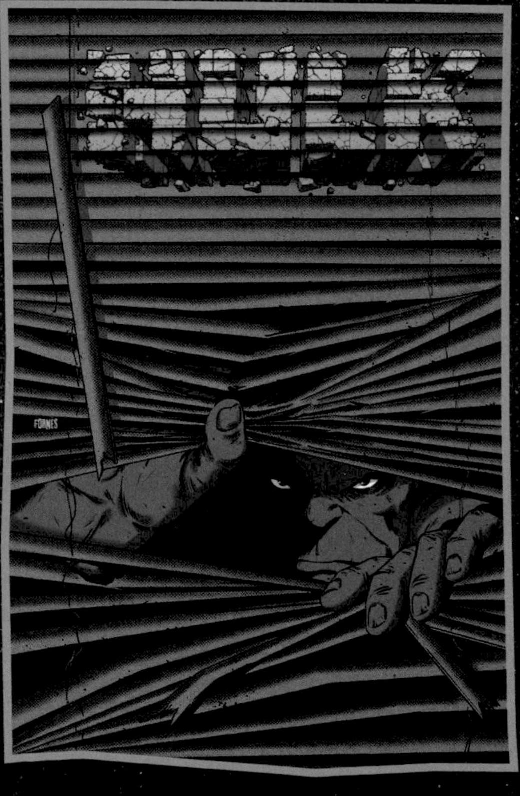
FORNES

#5 VARIANT BY
PEPE LARRAZ

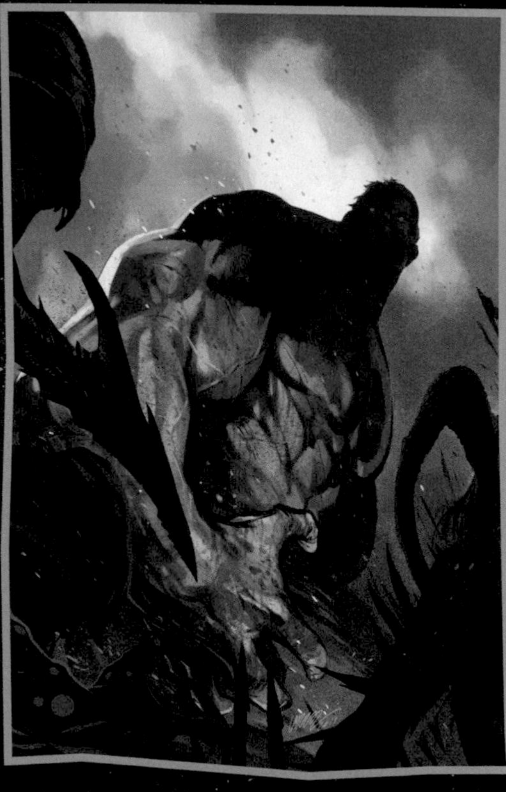

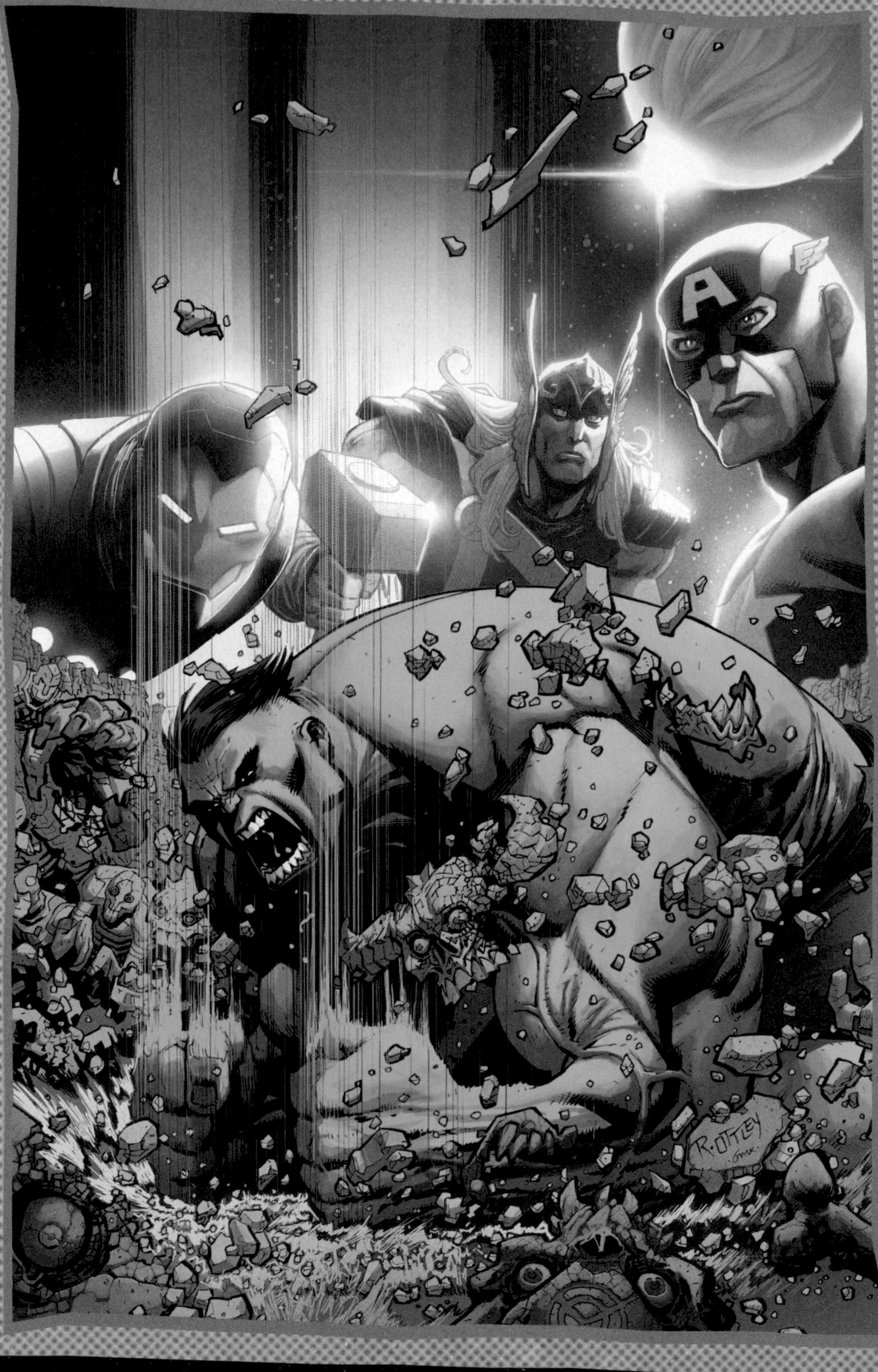
R. OTTLEY

FREE COMIC BOOK DAY 2021
(AVENGERS/HULK)

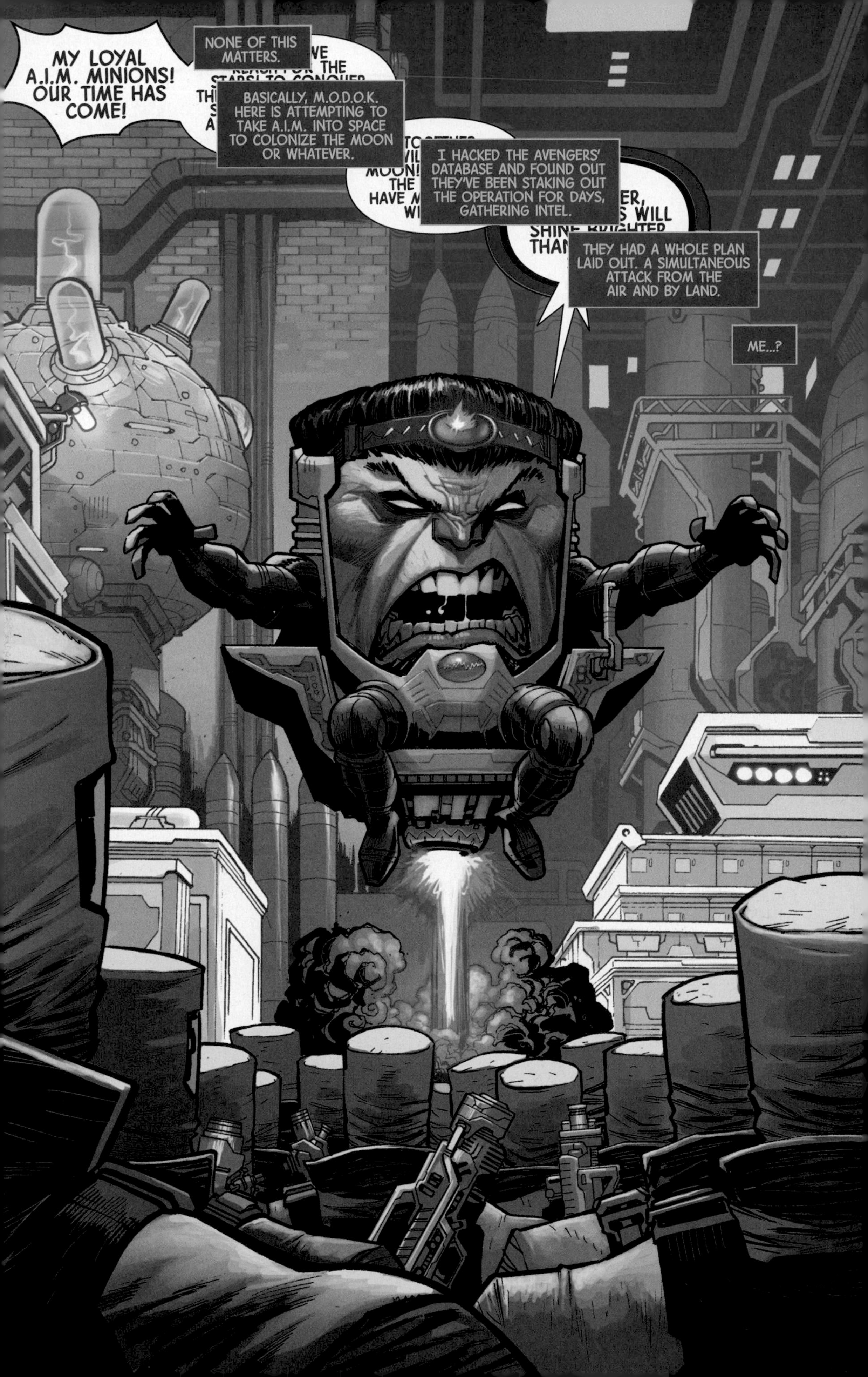
MY LOYAL A.I.M. MINIONS! OUR TIME HAS COME!
NONE OF THIS MATTERS.
BASICALLY, M.O.D.O.K. HERE IS ATTEMPTING TO TAKE A.I.M. INTO SPACE TO COLONIZE THE MOON OR WHATEVER.
I HACKED THE AVENGERS' DATABASE AND FOUND OUT THEY'VE BEEN STAKING OUT THE OPERATION FOR DAYS, GATHERING INTEL.
THEY HAD A WHOLE PLAN LAID OUT. A SIMULTANEOUS ATTACK FROM THE AIR AND BY LAND.
ME...?

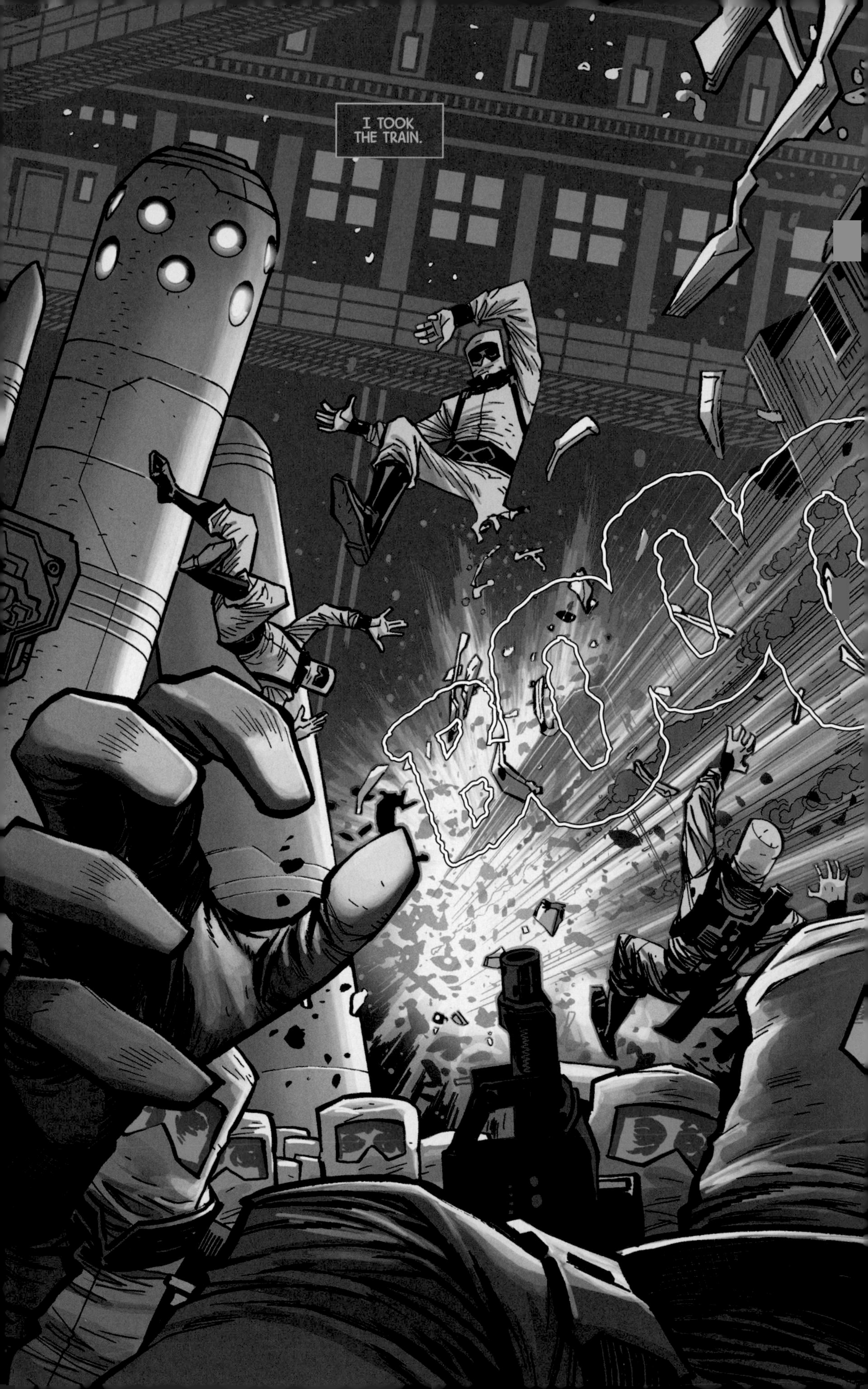
I TOOK THE TRAIN.

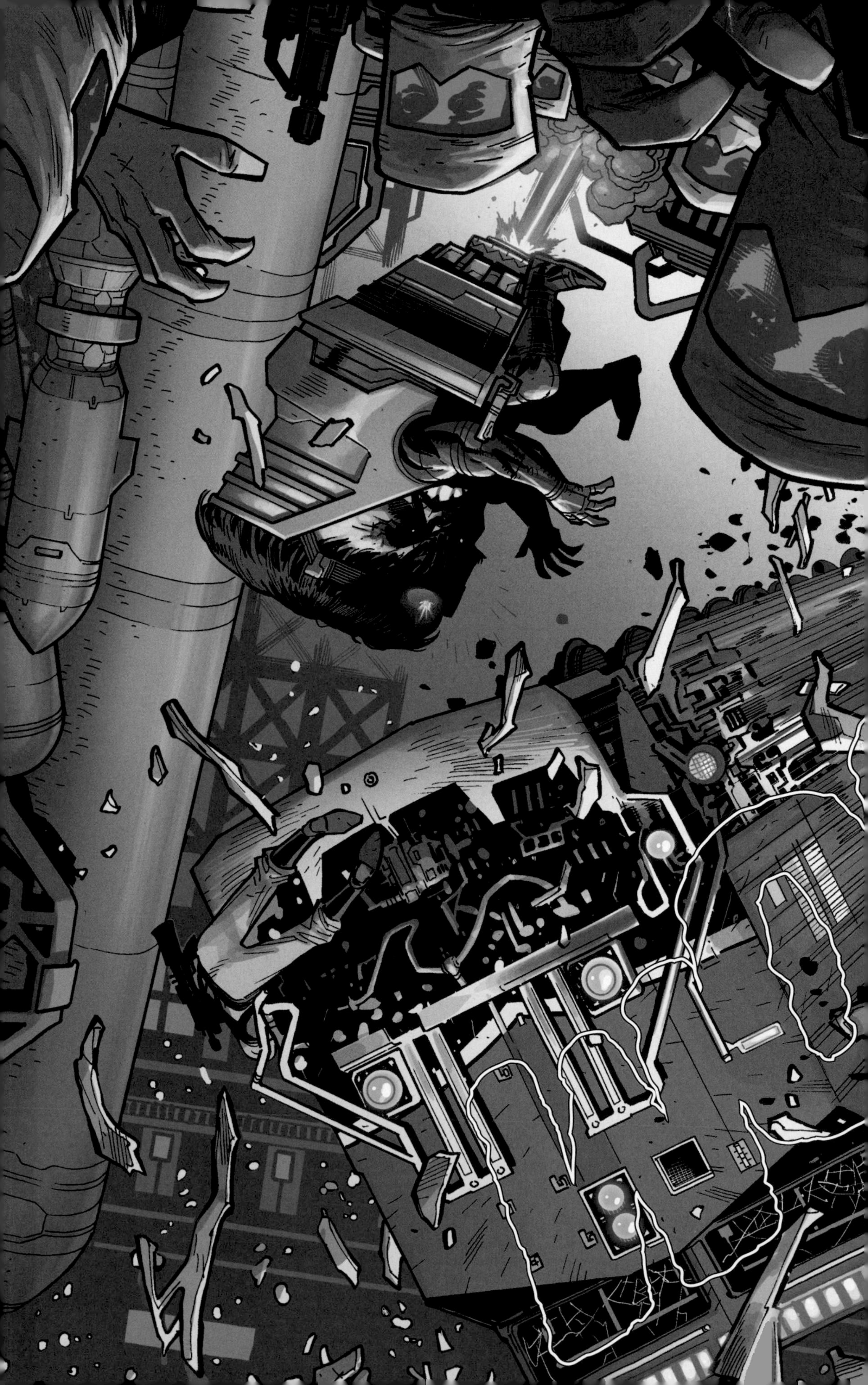

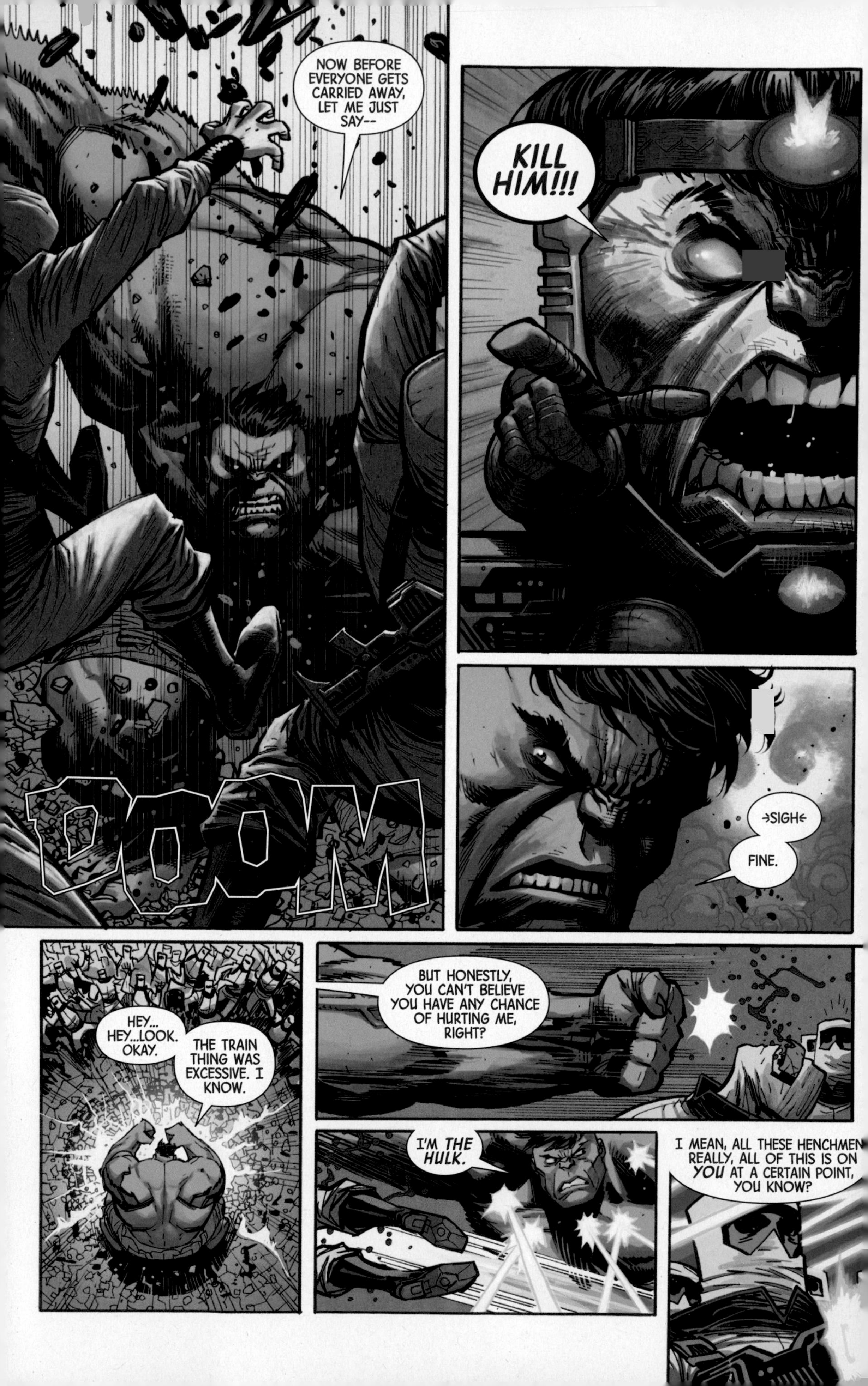
NOW BEFORE EVERYONE GETS CARRIED AWAY, LET ME JUST SAY--
KILL HIM!!!
DOOM
→SIGH←
FINE.
HEY... HEY...LOOK. OKAY.
THE TRAIN THING WAS EXCESSIVE. I KNOW.
BUT HONESTLY, YOU CAN'T BELIEVE YOU HAVE ANY CHANCE OF HURTING ME, RIGHT?
I'M *THE HULK.*
I MEAN, ALL THESE HENCHMEN REALLY, ALL OF THIS IS ON *YOU* AT A CERTAIN POINT, YOU KNOW?

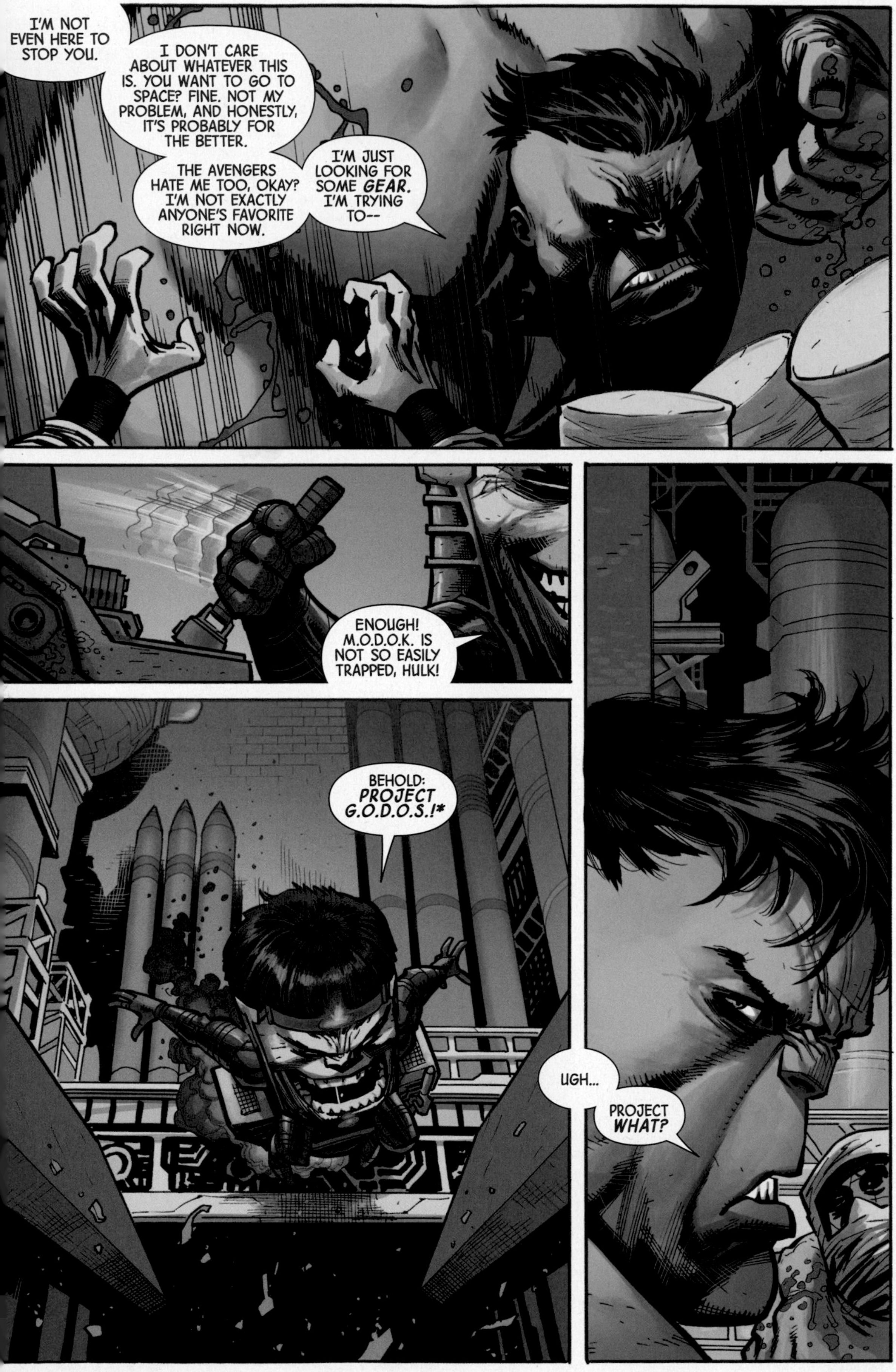
I'M NOT EVEN HERE TO STOP YOU.
I DON'T CARE ABOUT WHATEVER THIS IS. YOU WANT TO GO TO SPACE? FINE. NOT MY PROBLEM, AND HONESTLY, IT'S PROBABLY FOR THE BETTER.
THE AVENGERS HATE ME TOO, OKAY? I'M NOT EXACTLY ANYONE'S FAVORITE RIGHT NOW.
I'M JUST LOOKING FOR SOME **GEAR.** I'M TRYING TO--
ENOUGH! M.O.D.O.K. IS NOT SO EASILY TRAPPED, HULK!
BEHOLD: ***PROJECT G.O.D.O.S.!****
UGH...
PROJECT ***WHAT?***

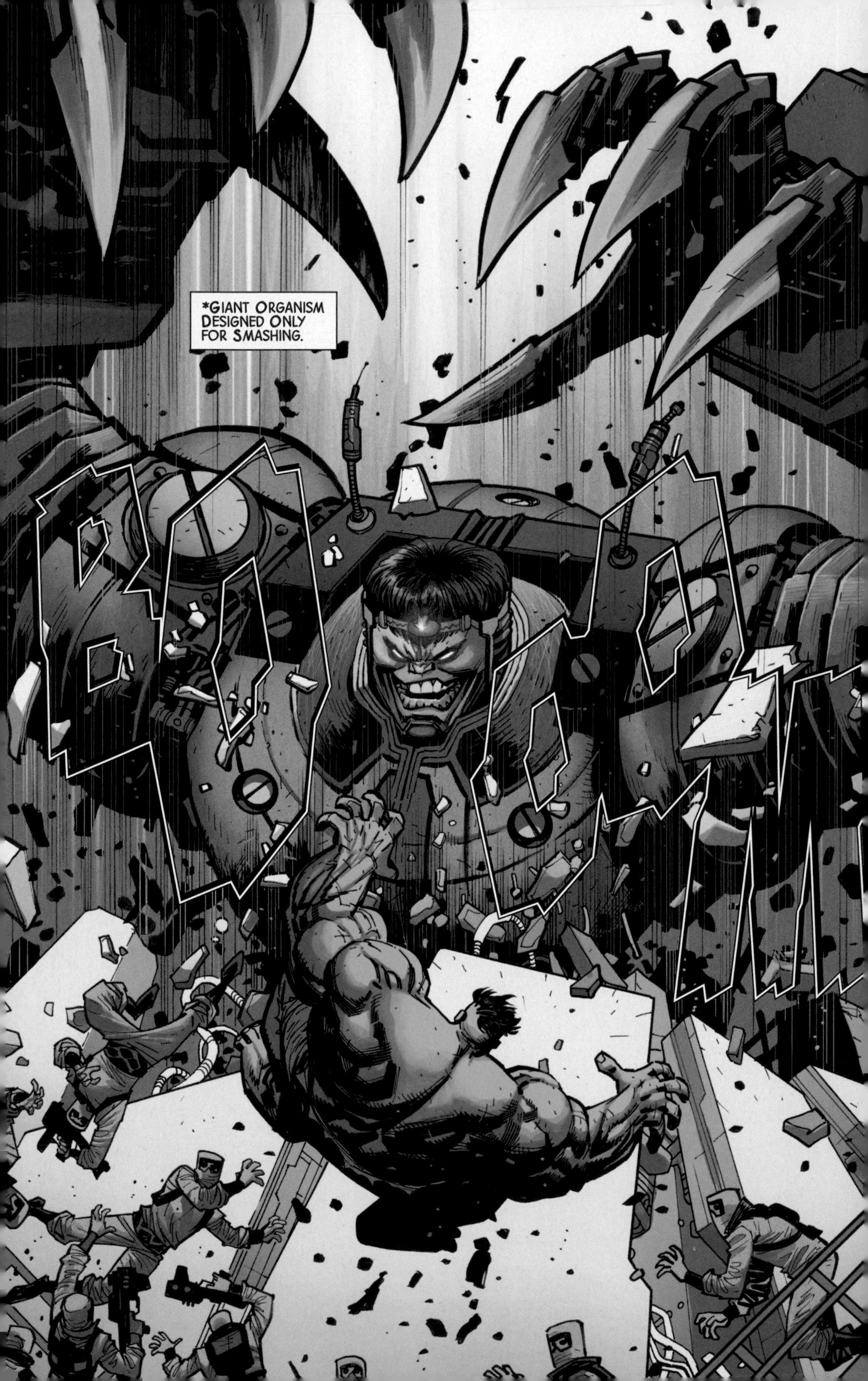
*GIANT ORGANISM DESIGNED ONLY FOR SMASHING.

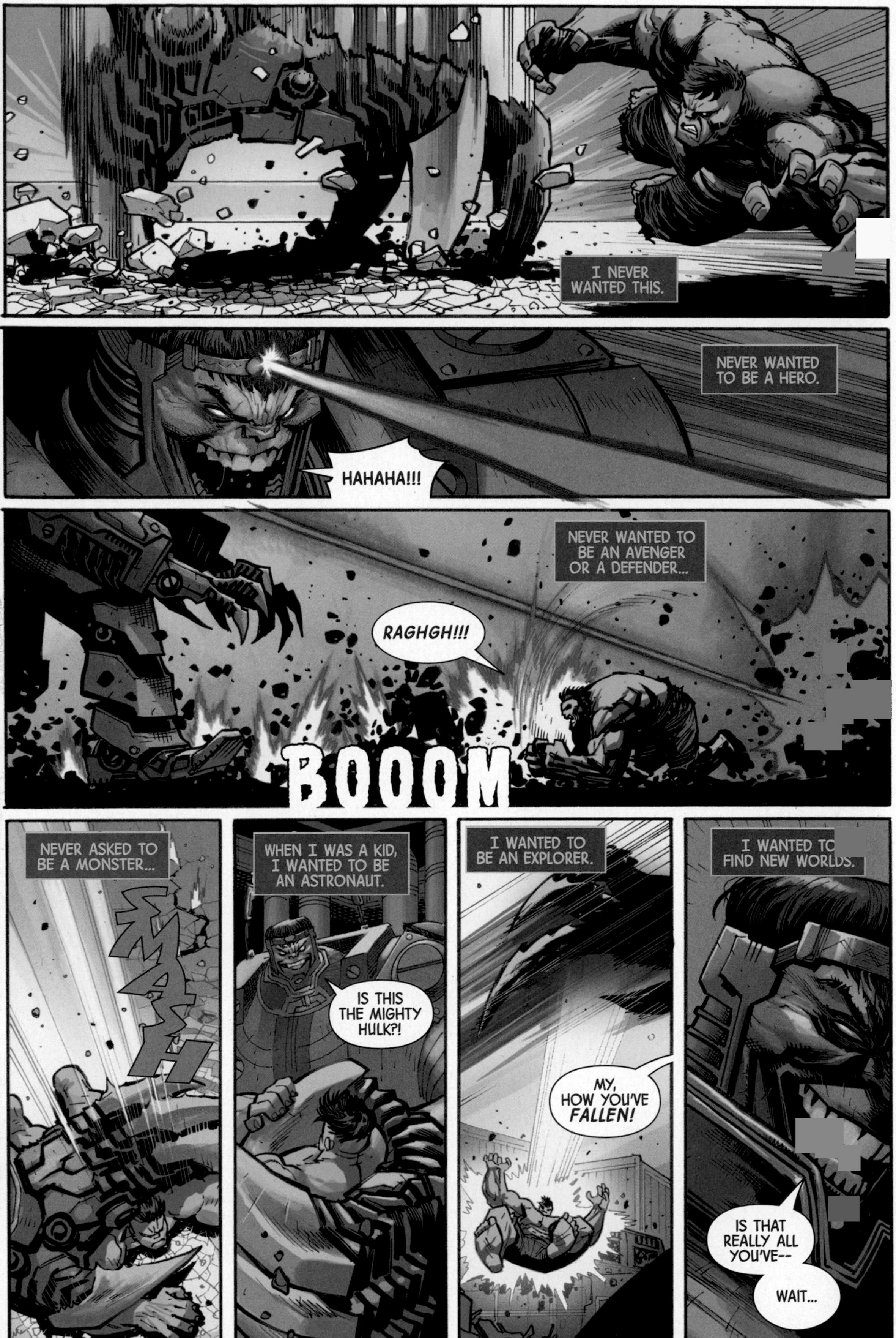
I NEVER WANTED THIS.
NEVER WANTED TO BE A HERO.
HAHAHA!!!
NEVER WANTED TO BE AN AVENGER OR A DEFENDER...
RAGHGH!!!
BOOOM
NEVER ASKED TO BE A MONSTER...
SMASH
WHEN I WAS A KID, I WANTED TO BE AN ASTRONAUT.
IS THIS THE MIGHTY HULK?!
I WANTED TO BE AN EXPLORER.
MY, HOW YOU'VE FALLEN!
I WANTED TO FIND NEW WORLDS.
IS THAT REALLY ALL YOU'VE--
WAIT...

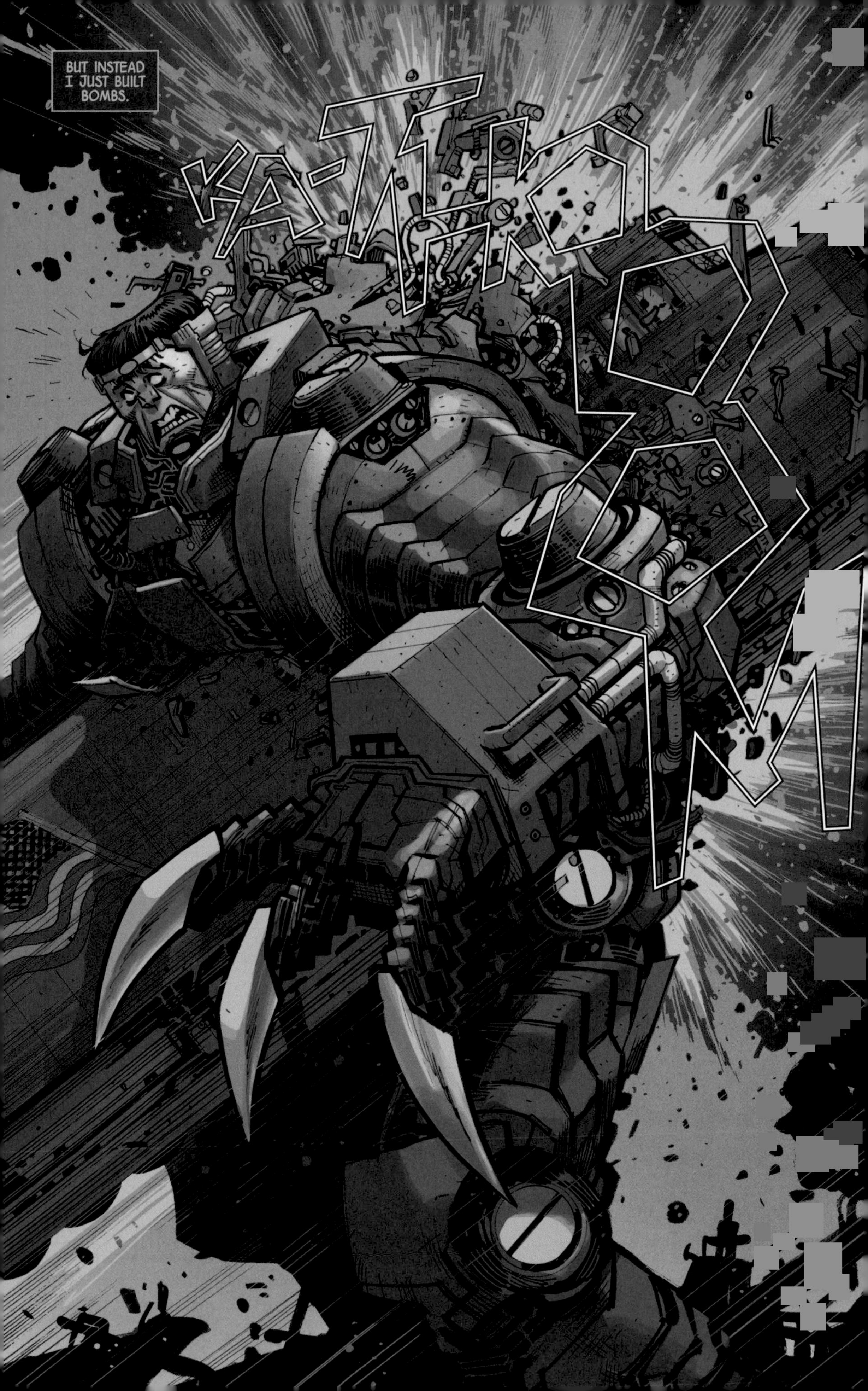
BUT INSTEAD I JUST BUILT BOMBS.
KA-THOOOOM

NOOOiii

I'M GOING TO EXPLORE THE
UNKNOWN IN MY INDESTRUCTIBLE
GREEN SPACESHIP...

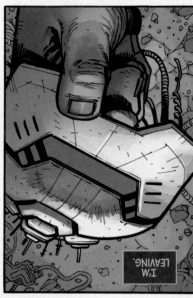

I'M
LEAVING.

NOW IT'S MY TURN...

THIS--THIS IS
ROCKET FUEL!
YOU CAN'T LEAVE
ME HERE!!

DONE MY
TOURS OF DUTY
AS A HERO.

I'VE DONE MY
TIME AS A MONSTER.

BOOM!

NO
MORE.

NEXT:

OPERATION:
SMASHTRONAUT

"...AND I'M NEVER COMING BACK."

#6 VARIANT BY
MARCO MASTRAZZO

#6 VARIANT BY
ALEX MALEEV

ALEX GARNER

JONBOY MEYERS

#6 VARIANT BY
RYAN STEGMAN, JP MAYER &
ROMULO FAJARDO JR.

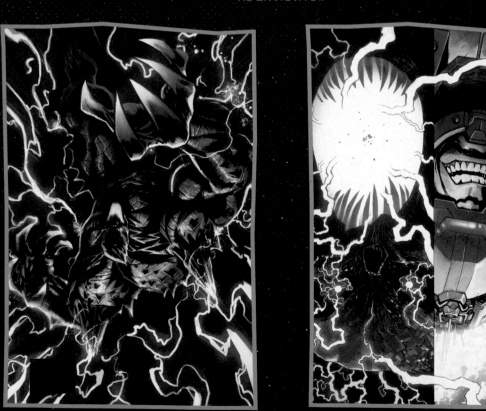

#6 SPOILER VARIANT BY
GEOFF SHAW & ROMULO FAJARDO JR.

#6 VARIANT BY
RYAN OTTLEY & ROMULO FAJARDO JR.